Praise for *Life to the*

At its best, Matthew Wickman's *Life to the Whole Being* achieves the quality of voice it ascribes to its poetic divinity—a "gentle irony" that both winkingly unsettles what one thought one knew and hearteningly ushers one into the richer life that lies beyond the limiting "stakes" that any "creed" places on "the Almighty," to quote Joseph Smith. "Truth cannot begin until my sense of rightness grows confused," Wickman candidly illustrates with heartfelt anecdotes drawn from both his personal life as a friend, husband, father, and practitioner of the Latter-day Saint faith and his professional life as a scholar of literature. One "sense of rightness" that Wickman, in his quest for truth, deliberately confuses in a way that usefully challenges some members of both his faith community and his profession is the commonsensical distinction between "scripture" and "literature" insofar as he unapologetically finds divinity in texts by e.e. cummings, Fyodor Dostoevsky, Louise Erdrich, Gerard Manley Hopkins, Denise Levertov, and R.S. Thomas, among others. In so doing, *Life to the Whole Being* embodies a strong, confessional version of ongoing "post-secularist" work in literary studies and also what many will consider the best of the Latter-day Saint tradition: a "read[iness] to believe all true principles that exist, as they are made manifest from time to time."

—JARED HICKMAN
Associate Professor of English
Johns Hopkins University

Life to the
Whole Being

A
Living Faith
Book

Living Faith books are for readers who cherish the life of the mind and the things of the Spirit. Each title offers an example of faith in search of understanding, the unique voice of a practicing scholar who has cultivated a believing heart.

OTHER LIVING FAITH BOOKS INCLUDE:

Samuel M. Brown, *First Principles and Ordinances: The Fourth Article of Faith in Light of the Temple*

Samuel M. Brown, *Where the Soul Hungers: One Doctor's Journey from Atheism to Faith*

James E. Faulconer, *Thinking Otherwise: Theological Explorations of Joseph Smith's Revelations*

Terryl L. Givens, *The Doors of Faith*

George B. Handley, *The Hope of Nature: Our Care for God's Creation*

George B. Handley, *If Truth Were a Child: Essays*

Ashley Mae Hoiland, *One Hundred Birds Taught Me to Fly: The Art of Seeking God*

Melissa Wei-Tsing Inouye, *Crossings: A Bald Asian American Latter-day Saint Woman Scholar's Ventures through Life, Death, Cancer & Motherhood (Not Necessarily in That Order)*

Charles Shirō Inouye, *Zion Earth Zen Sky*

Patrick Q. Mason, *Planted: Belief and Belonging in an Age of Doubt*

Patrick Q. Mason, J. David Pulsipher, *Proclaim Peace: The Restoration's Answer to an Age of Conflict*

Adam S. Miller, *Letters to a Young Mormon* (2nd ed.)

Steven L. Peck, *Evolving Faith: Wanderings of a Mormon Biologist*

Thomas F. Rogers, *Let Your Hearts and Minds Expand: Reflections on Faith, Reason, Charity, and Beauty*

Life to the Whole Being

The Spiritual Memoir of a Literature Professor

*

Matthew Wickman

This book is published by The Neal A. Maxwell Institute for Religious Scholarship at Brigham Young University in Provo, Utah.

Permissions. No portion of this book may be reproduced by any means or process without the formal written consent of the publisher. Direct all permissions requests to: MIpermissions@byu.edu

♾ The paper used in this publication meets the minimum requirements of the American National Standards for Information Sciences—Permanence of Paper for Printed Library Materials. ANSI Z39.48-19

ISBN: 978-0-8425-0061-6

Library of Congress Control Number: 2021059314
(CIP data on file)

Cover design: Heather Ward
Cover image: "Jesus Walks on Water" by Korovin Konstantin Alexeyevich, used under license from Museum: State Tretyakov Gallery, Moscow.
Book design: Andrew Heiss

Printed in the United States of America

http://maxwellinstitute.byu.edu

For my students, 1 Peter 3:15

For Adam, once lost but a beacon long since

And for Kerry, Hadley, and Elena, always and everything

Contents

CONTENTS

Acknowledgments

Never during my training in graduate school or for most of the first two decades of my career did I imagine writing a spiritual memoir. But now, having completed the unthinkable, never have I written anything that meant more to me. This is mostly because it gave me the opportunity to express, in an extended way, the depth of my gratitude. This is gratitude to God above all, but so many others spring to mind.

Here, and formally, I extend thanks to other authors in the Living Faith series for opening my mind to the existence of a genre like this one for Latter-day Saints. Early encouragement, too, came from my friend and colleague Nick Mason, who arranged a lunch with his savvy and scholarly brother Patrick, one of the early Living Faith authors. Then, a year and a failed attempt or two later, I was moved to try again by separate conversations with two admired friends, George Handley and Morgan Davis.

Morgan paired with Miranda Wilcox to form a dream editorial team of the Living Faith series. Miranda and Morgan did so many things so well: they wisely refused an early draft, pushed my writing in a different direction, offered vital suggestions for revision, expressed belief in the project, found excellent (and exacting) readers for the press, and eventually persuaded the Maxwell Institute board to accept the book.

Along the way, their generous listening and gentle nudges motivated me to keep reaching, keep digging—to risk making myself vulnerable. I could only have taken such risks with trusted friends.

This book was born out of a BYU course I teach titled "Literature and Spiritual Experience." Students from its first four iterations were vital interlocutors for my thinking. I cannot imagine a better group of people, and hence a better university, for shaping a project like this one. While I cannot name every student who contributed in a substantive way to this book, I must mention those who, in the project's late stages, served as a focus group for revised drafts: Sam Jacob, Ashlyn Earl, Erin Lee, Celina French, Emily Nichols, and Ana Hirschi. One student, Moe Graviet, merits special praise. Having heard me speak on literature and spiritual experience at a BYU Humanities Center symposium in 2018, she reached out hoping to serve as a research assistant for work I was doing—any work—on this topic. Moe and I began talking about scholarship on spirituality, she researched and found important sources I should consider, and eventually she became my first and most formative reader. It was Moe who convinced me that a book like this might help her peers who were asking difficult questions about their faith—and who persuaded me, delicately but firmly, that I would need to speak more personally if I hoped to say anything meaningful to them. Without her inspiration and gifts, spiritual as well as scholarly, this book would never have seen the light of day.

So many colleagues and friends have blessed me and influenced this project. Kylie Turley, Jill Rudy, and Mary Eyring impressed me to want to be a better person as well as writer and helped me understand more fully what BYU's educational mission affords. Two former students, Isaac Robertson and Holly Boud, stepped in late to offer invaluable feedback. Participants in a Living Faith discussion group organized by Miranda Wilcox illustrated beautifully how to make a place for the spirit in a life of the mind. Members and friends of the Maxwell Institute offered encouragement and important suggestions in inviting me to present an early version of my work. Through particular observations, extraordinary kindness, and radiant examples of lives well lived, English Department, Humanities Center, and College of Humanities colleagues too many to name (well, okay, one: Brooke Browne—and I could add to this list by the hundreds) have influenced me and therefore this book. Friends from the academic world of literary studies have perpetually opened my mind through their startling intelligence and generosity. Members of my local faith community demonstrate repeatedly what it means to live in spiritual abundance, to say nothing of the stirring examples they provide, again and again, of Christ-like love. And numerous friends from the Society for the Study of Christian Spirituality have helped me see how to make spirituality a matter of study as well as faith.

My deepest gratitude, of course, goes to my family. My parents, Pat and Lance Wickman, have given me life over and over. My siblings, extended family, and in-laws are a source of so much joy. My precious daughters, Hadley and Elena, changed me forever and endlessly for the better when they entered the world. As for Kerry, my wife . . . She is a gift unlike any other, a blessing of peerless magnitude.

Preface

Years ago, while serving a two-year mission for the Church of Jesus Christ of Latter-day Saints, I developed a special admiration for converts. It moved me deeply to see people gain a conviction of truth claims (that God exists, that Jesus Christ is our Redeemer, and that the Church is God's vehicle for assisting us in our eternal progress) and then make sacrifices—often take great leaps of faith—to align their lives with these convictions. Over the years, my vision has expanded to include the experience of friends from other faith traditions who share moving stories about their own conversion and convictions.

These days, I find myself inspired not only by converts who take leaps of faith but by *all* Church members who find ways to remain planted in it. Often, they do so despite facing deep trials of faith: events that rock their foundations, questions they can neither answer nor resolve, and aspects of their religious experience (doctrines, policies, practices, or interactions) that do not inspire healing as much as hurt. In most cases, these are people who see others leaving the Church, often those closest to them: family members, friends, and significant others. They recognize that they too *might* leave the Church and that, in some ways, this might make life easier or less painful. And yet, they stay with the Church for the same reasons that new converts join it: they feel enlightened by God and, on that basis, are moved to act in ways they otherwise would not. They respond to a love deeper than their own.

This book is written especially for them. It is a cousin to a BYU devotional talk I gave on the subject of spiritual thriving, though the book speaks more directly to people who feel the effects of faith crises.[1] That this book exists at all represents my own attempt to take a leap of faith by trying to describe reasons why I remain planted in it. Those reasons, ultimately, are spiritual. As any convert can attest, spiritual experiences draw us closer to God, transforming what and how we see, what and how we know, and who and what we are. Such experiences may come to us in innumerable ways and certainly have to me. Their variety in my own life has inspired and required me to learn how to sit with complexity—to sit even when that also included fidgeting, venting in frustration, or crying out in anguish. But as I have waited on the Lord, abundant blessings have always followed.

The experience of writing this book has been one such blessing. It was a surprisingly long time in coming. I never imagined I would write anything like it, and once the thought took root, I failed repeatedly to bring it to fruition. Mostly, this was because I was sheltering myself in the analytical posture and prose that have become habitual to my work as a scholar. While there is certainly a place for that style of writing, it didn't seem suited to a book rooted primarily in a confession of faith. Then an important thing happened to me in the summer of 2019. I was awarded a fellowship to spend several weeks in Iowa City working on an academic book about literature and spiritual experience. The rigors of that project freed this one to be a little different, to tell a different kind of story. I was also able to put some emotional distance between myself and my calling in a stake presidency in Salt Lake City. I suddenly found myself in two hours of church, not ten (consisting of a mixture of meetings, interviews, and attendance at multiple wards). And instead of sitting across from members in an official ecclesiastical capacity, I found myself in the company of faithful people (from multiple faith traditions) with complex questions about religion and for God. Many professed a faith at once beautiful and broken, prompting deeper reflection over situations I was facing in my own life. I began thinking more pointedly about my own trials of faith—what had gotten me through, which ones were behind me, and the specters that still remained.

During this period of hiatus, I acquired a taste for "real speak," so much so that I sent a too-candid email to a local leader back home, a valued friend and mentor, expressing my concerns about an upcoming stake meeting. This prompted a testy query about the "fermented corn drink" I must be guzzling out there in Iowa. Fueled only by spiritual ferment, I wrote a talk for one of these meetings that reflected this new perspective, a personal history about my own angst-ridden faith. While the talk may have been a little edgy for some in attendance, it seemed to resonate with our twenty- and thirty-somethings and with parents whose twenty- and thirty-something children were facing faith crises. They were my primary audience, much as they are here a critical portion of my readership. I thus seemed to find my voice for this book. My hope is that others will hear in it an echo of their own.

On the Gentle
—Gently Ironic—
Origins of This Book

As I'm calling this book a spiritual memoir, let me introduce it by saying a few words about its personal origins. It began as a course on literature and spiritual experience I developed and now teach at Brigham Young University. But tying the book to the course begs the question of how the course was born, and that's a more complicated matter. It wasn't the product of a single lightning flash of inspiration. Or rather, it was, but that moment itself resulted from long experience and many shorter individual ones over many years. Let me try to communicate something of that moment's gestation by way of five still frames from my own life reel.

January 1986

I'm eighteen and a half, home from college for the weekend, and seated in the office of my bishop. He's white-haired, kind-hearted, soft-spoken—the personification of the Hallmark store he owns. But the velvet glove of his concern is doing little to soften the iron fist of his question: "Matt, are you going to serve a mission?"

For months, I've been suffocating with dread at the thought of this meeting. Now, over the past few days, slow asphyxiation has been replaced by outright choking as I've been chewing over new and strange opportunities too large for my small life to swallow. Indifferent about school, I had pursued a couple whimsical dreams, eventually refusing one ("I think we could use you in Japan; the job would last about six months") and then, just two days before meeting with my bishop, finding myself living another ("I can have you signed to an agent as early as next week"). I try thinking like my parents: *Son, one day you'll come to see these apparent windfalls as mirages* ("in the desert of my abject, underachieving life," I add; I am so tired of my own mediocrity). But from where I sit, the view looks very different. Make that plural—views—for I find myself staring down two equally unimaginable futures: glamorous possibility (*Hollywood*) on one hand and the grim fate gathering behind my bishop's question on the other. Paralyzed by the utter incommensurability between these life paths, I stammer, then fall speechless, then tumble into a virtual pit of lachrymose—tearful—blackness.

I wish I could be alone in my despair, but it suddenly feels so crowded in here. The bishop is staring at me from across the desk, his question hanging in the air (*Matt, are you going to serve a mission?*). My parents, bless them, are smothering me with anxious concern (*What will Matt say? Will he do the right thing?*). My best friend is waiting for me, cheering me on (*Dude, you stand up for yourself in there? You gonna take your chances, embrace your life?*). The girl from high school I've had a mad crush on for two years may not realize it yet, but she's also watching me, or will be, or so I wish (*Matt's doing what? No way!*). There are so many others who also feel present: siblings, grandparents, ward members, youth leaders, neighbors, classmates, peers. "Hell is other people," the French philosopher Jean-Paul Sartre once wrote,[1] and while I won't read this line for a couple years, I already feel its truth as half the world's population seems to have taken up residence in my head. I'm in here too, alas, beating myself up through heaving sobs (*Why are you doing this? You never cry, not even when you wish you could! You're a wannabe actor, an actor at acting, absurdly unable to access your own emotions!*).

But then something happens. From the depths of wherever I am, I do not see as much as feel or perhaps hear a light, a gentle voice, an expression of love, a promise. . . . I instantly sense myself perfectly seen, perfectly understood. . . . My confusion, angst, desire to matter— he loves me in all of it, through it, beyond it. . . . Where do I think these opportunities came from in the first place? He wants for me what I want, if I will just trust him, do it his way. . . . Yes, of course I say yes, how could I not say yes, I don't even care about outcomes, I haven't felt this way in months, in years, ever. . . .

November 1987

I'm twenty and a half and am hitting the three-quarters mark of the two years I will serve as a missionary. I'm in a bookstore in a city in the French Alps, surrounded by tall mountains and, more ethereally, by the shadows of a religious and existential mystery. Its expression is nothing philosophically profound, just an everyday phrase drilling itself into my psyche, a virtual wall of grating sound. "I testify to you that God liv—" *Non, monsieur, ça ne m'intéresse pas.* "There is a purpose to our exis—" *Non, monsieur, ça ne m'intéresse pas.* "God the Father and his son, Jesus Christ, appeared to a young boy named Jos—" *Non, monsieur, ça ne m'intéresse pas. . . . Non, monsieur, ça ne m'intéresse pas. . . . Non, monsieur, ça ne m'intéresse pas. . . .*

My decision to serve a mission had been so traumatizing but ultimately so affirming, and the glow of that decision had lingered so palpably through the months of preparation that followed. I was so full of what felt like spiritual understanding. It seems strange then, incongruous—not part of the promise I felt in that ecstatic moment in the bishop's office—to reflect now on how my mission will end: not with a bang but with a blasé "No, sir, not interested": *Non, monsieur, ça ne m'intéresse pas.*

Scanning the shelf, I come across a name I recognize: Albert Camus. French existentialist philosopher, novelist, playwright. Thumbing through the book, I light on a resonant phrase rooting at the mystery that has been looming over me for months and that I have not been able to name. "*Les hommes meurent et ils ne sont pas heureux*" (Men die, and they aren't happy).

Mind churning, I gaze around the store, less at books than at people. Is Camus speaking to them or to me? In the lingo of my mission, to "die" is to complete your time of service. Missionaries "die," and they aren't . . . Is that true? What happens to radiant joy when it encounters terminal indifference? Or to belief when it morphs into a conviction that nothing will ever change, that what one experiences, day after day, is all there is? Is this what I came on my mission to find? *Non, monsieur, ça ne me* blah, blah, blah.

Where, I wonder, is God in the lives of people who give him no thought? Or at times, in the lives of those who think of him constantly, pleading for direction (which building? door? person?) or, increasingly, for deliverance? Martha, grieving, professed to Jesus her belief that her deceased brother would "rise again in the resurrection at the last day" (John 11:24). A blessed abstraction, the language of everyday testimony. But Mary's belief was more immediate and therefore more rending: "Lord, if thou hadst been here, my brother had not died" (John 11:32). And neither would she, day after mournful day.

For all the dynamism of my conversion experience in the bishop's office, I entered my mission, I now realize, with faith like Martha's. But slowly, that's been changing. With each passing month, I feel a little less capable of religious abstraction. Instead, I feel increasingly raw, like Mary. A new kind of prayer is forming in me, one that will stay with me for decades: Lord, I sense thee both present and absent, caring but distant. Loving but in ways that rarely conform to my expectations. I see, but I do not understand.

4

One way or another, I need that understanding from God about the world around me or perhaps from the world around me about God. I need a more expansive language for my prayers and for the ways I can hear God answer.

Les hommes meurent et ils ne sont pas heureux. It's a melodramatic statement, but I'm a melodramatic twenty-year-old, and that bleak anthem rings true. So, I clutch the book a little more tightly and walk toward the register.

October 2004

The answers come in different ways. They are rarely direct—*yes* or *no*—because the questions I ask tend not to incline that way. Moreover, they are not messages from on high as much as disclosures enabling me to search more deeply within. Neither are they confirmations—the famed burning in the bosom or stupor of thought (D&C 9:8–9)—because I approach the Lord less with my decisions than my broodings. On strange subjects too:

"About those eighteenth-century codes of legal evidence. . . and literary form—the emergence of literature in its modern form as imaginative writing, yes, that's the phrase I want. . . . There's some other connection there, page fourteen, where I begin to make the transition to analyzing that poem. I can almost see it. . . ." Arcane, obscure, seemingly trivial: hardly the stuff of Joseph Smith's famous prayer. The same goes for the answers: sometimes less word than color, less light than image, almost always incremental—line upon gnomic line, always begging revision. A return to my notebooks, a return to my knees.

I'm in my mid- to late-thirties, and for years, my faith has been built on strange spiritual communion like this. After I returned from my mission, I took up the serious study of literature because it seemed like a continuation of my spiritual odyssey. "Counsel with the Lord in all thy doings," the scriptures tell us (Alma 37:37). I would not have guessed it would lead to obtuse conversations like these, my approaching God brooding about my scholarly work and his seeming to respond in fragments—fragments and gentle irony, perhaps the most common answer to the prayers I utter.

On this particular morning in my home office, for example, I open my eyes, gazing blankly at the books and papers littered across my desk and in small piles on the floor. My daughters' tiny feet pound the ceiling as they scamper, giggling, across the kitchen. I need to attend to some task—some writing project or other, some deadline or other. But I haven't been praying today over my work. Instead, I've been uttering that other kind of prayer, the one that confesses—in the same brooding speech—that I am so tired of certain books of scripture, so tired of a certain tenor of ecclesiastical voice, so tired of religious "answers" that do not capture the depth and complexity of human experience.

And what do these prayers yield? No word or color, no light or image, just gentle irony. I emote and feel God gazing on in something like loving, silent amusement. I take it as an indication I'm getting it wrong—again. So, I suppose, this too needs revision.

I say "gentle irony," but actually, my life feels suffused these days with two kinds of irony, two types of disparity between appearance and reality. One is gentle, the other harsh. The harsh variety accentuates, usually with some pain, ruptures between my life's circumstances (so many of which are good) and my feelings about them (which tend to be conflicted and often depressed, as so much of my life carries an aura of disappointment: jobs I should have had, places I should be living, the person I wish I were. . .). Harsh irony plays on the difference between expectation and outcome (how did my youthful dreams and spiritual odyssey devolve into these pedantic concerns in this dingy basement in this small town?). But then there is the other type of irony, the gentle kind I'm feeling right now. Here, there is a feeling of promise, of God's presence amid the disappointments of everyday life. In its gentler mode, heaven's light breaks wordlessly but unmistakably into my fallen circumstances.

More than anything, it's that gentle irony that keeps me in the Church these days. It's a matter of simple courtesy: If the Lord is going to seem to care about the sublime and (usually) ridiculous subjects of my research, then I can care about his Church, even when I feel angry, or hurt, or disillusioned. I feel that way a lot these days, and I have for years. At some point, scripture lost much of its ability to inspire; the insights of Church leaders began to cloy; Church teachings began to seem shallow. But I don't sense these same feelings from God toward the Church, or its leaders, or its precepts. And glancing again at my notebooks, filled as they are with strange ideas and such deep longing—for mystery, meaning, purpose, inspiration—I reflect again that it isn't enough for me simply to give God a piece of my mind. I need to be able to listen and observe, to come and see. To try to understand.

Literature helps me here, for ever since the later stages of my mission, I've been developing a greater sensitivity toward irony—toward ambiguity of phrase and feeling, the distances inscribed into intimacy, the unresolved questions haunting every answer. But religion helps me too, surprisingly enough, after hurting me for so long as one cherished belief after another divulged its all-too-human baggage. My tutor here is the saintly sixty-year-old who called me to serve alongside him in our ward high priests group leadership. He tells me I remind him of one of his sons, a tortured intellectual type. And so, when I occasionally vent my frustrations in his company, he just gazes on with a twinkle of fatherly delight. And then he leads us out to minister, week after week, one home after the other. We talk with the elderly, bless the sick; people warm, visit after visit, to his laughter.

Come and see: this is "pure religion and undefiled" (James 1:27). Its effect on me is cognitive dissonance as it sits awkwardly alongside my uncomprehending frustration. But in my prayers, in moments like these, that gentle irony reminds me I am to sit with both. And I can do this. Life is literary in its way: nuanced, layered. And literature is teaching me to read it a little more deeply, appreciate it a little more fully.

June 2011

I constantly seek inspiration, and I usually get answers—sometimes related to the question I was asking, sometimes not. But with major life milestones, it's different. I do not seek and find; a door opens, and I walk through. I almost feel I have no choice.

That's my epiphany on this gorgeous Sunday afternoon as I saunter down the North Sea coastline. The locals joke that there are two seasons in Aberdeen, Scotland: June and winter. I gaze into endless blue overhead, the ubiquitous gulls hovering in the light breeze. Today is June in every respect—calendar and aura.

But it's always June for me here even when it's cold and dark in January, February. I'm in my mid-forties, and this is our home, sort of. The better half of the year. We still spend the other half in Utah but not for long hopefully. Another year, I remind myself, and then we'll be here permanently. That's the arrangement with the university.

I feel so light here, so happy, divested of so much of the emotional baggage I shoulder back home. I enjoy a purpose here and real professional standing. Two years earlier, when people in my field heard I'd been offered this job, a Big Name had sidled up to me at a conference and expressed surprise: "I've heard of senior scholars getting this kind of joint appointment but never people of lower professional rank." I looked at him as though I were his peer. "It's a gift from God." That's what I wanted to say. Instead, I just smiled and shrugged.

But yes, a gift. That's how I'd received it, as simplistic as that is. I'd been so unhappy for so long about so many things. I'd vested success in my academic life with so much symbolic meaning: my value as a person, my capacity to find happiness, God's presence or at least his willingness to hear me. And so, when I had confessed disappointment with my career—jobs for which I'd been passed over, projects that had lost themselves in the maze of my tortured thinking—so many other things had been implicated. It had all come to a head late one afternoon in a grocery store parking lot in a small town in Utah County as I sat in my car brooding, seething, pleading. Mentors had expected so much of me; I had expected so much of myself. And I felt I was failing. Yet—and this was the insight, the inspiration of the moment—all that suddenly seemed secondary. "I don't care anymore about getting a 'better' job! I just want to contribute! Something meaningful! As a scholar!"

This was an unusual prayer for me: direct, lucid, vulnerable. As soon as it burst from me, I felt something different and strange, an electrical charge, as though my words had pierced the heavens and reached their target. My view of the professional landscape changed instantly; I saw something I'd been missing, a place I could contribute. That night, I shifted the focus of my academic work. Not long after, door after door began opening. And I walked through.

So now, here we are: eternal June in Aberdeen. I sometimes walk across the five-hundred-year-old campus and feel myself floating, giddily, along the edge of a historical and spiritual abyss. There is so much depth to the human condition, so much mystery echoing through it; you really feel it here, in an old country like Scotland. It would be so easy to step over this edge and lose my bearings, my identity, my faith—so easy to shed the weight of impossible beliefs, the burden of religious narratives. But no. I am, shockingly, happy in my faith, happy in the Church (in our Scotland ward certainly), a believer despite all abysses. But unlike at BYU, I feel no compulsion here. There, if I left the Church, I would lose my livelihood. Here, if I wanted to jump into that abyss, to fly downward, I could. I know where the cliff's edge is, and God knows I know where it is. We walk along this ledge together. And for now, I'm happy walking.

Then this morning, in sacrament meeting, a man gave a talk about patriarchal blessings as a guidepost throughout life.[2] It had been years since I'd read mine. So when we returned to our flat, I took the ragged copy out of the back of my scriptures and carefully unfolded it. Reading familiar phrases got me thinking about my journey—how I'd wound up at one place and another: mission, college, marriage, profession. Here, ultimately. That thought prompted me out of the house, to the seashore, and down the coast to ponder the future. For, technically, we still face a choice of where we will be a year from now; we might choose to return full-time to BYU. I need a confirmation of where we should be, which is to say, I desperately want God to understand my happiness the way I do. And when it comes to life milestones, I'm reflecting with some surprise, I do not pray and receive answers: *Go there; do this.* I do not reach a decision and receive confirmation. No, doors open voicelessly, and I walk through.

So, my prayer this afternoon has turned to gratitude: I am so grateful for the doors that opened and led us here. Grateful to be with my beautiful wife and precious daughters, with a job I love in a place I love. I love its history, its culture, and the feeling in the air. I love how being here justifies past struggles (they led us *here*) while allowing me to feel I have something meaningful to contribute into the future. I love this life.

And yet, the feeling won't leave me. Gentle irony again, something I'm failing to understand again.

Please, I have lived through so much emotional winter; please let me stay here. Let it stay June.

December 2014

I'm in my mid- to late-forties and am in my office at school. Back at BYU. This time, I'm in my third year as the founding director of a research center whose likeness I never imagined I'd see in my early years at the university and whose transformative promise *for* the university had been the pretext for my return. Scotland is a small nation, but BYU has always seemed like a small town: filled with good neighbors and happy in its small plot of paradise, although a little suspicious of—anxious about—the outside world. Research centers like the one I now direct, meanwhile, are cosmopolitan hubs: drivers of big thinking and professional bling. Such a center, I thought, might help instill a new culture and make BYU less parochial, make it more like the image projected in Doctrine and Covenants 88: "a house of faith, a house of learning," a house of greater possibility.

It's an aspiration, my version of it, that reeks of arrogance. Better said, a combination of dread and self-loathing. For it isn't the vision of Doctrine and Covenants 88 that I've longed to realize but something much less ambitious, something closer to the generic aspirations of a conventional research university, which functions as the usual home to big thinking and, perhaps ironically, a blessed sense of anonymity. "I'm with them," I want to say—that is, with the coteries of accomplished intellectuals who work at such universities, earn respect from their titles and affiliation, and, in one sense at least, almost seem interchangeable with one another. It isn't that these scholars aren't individuals with their own life stories, gifts, and griefs; no, it's that, individually and collectively, they have a place, they have respect. They belong. Belonging is more difficult when you come from BYU because BYU is not a conventional research university; more starkly, it's a religious university. From BYU, you aren't granted a place in the pantheon of higher learning, you need to earn your way into it and prove you aren't strange—prove, in effect, that you *don't* believe in such superstitions as, say, the prophetic vision of Doctrine and Covenants 88.

I've worked so hard to belong, which means, at one level, to *not* fit in at BYU. Because fitting in at BYU, owning BYU, means choosing vision over belonging, vocation over profession; it means embracing one's religious difference rather than experiencing the blessed, secular sameness of higher education. To work at BYU means claiming the Church, inheriting the legacy of the pioneers, and continuing to build and to sing as one walks and walks and walks and walks. In a sense, relative to the world of universities, it means becoming a missionary all over again—again and again—professing, always, one's different university mission and the vision that inspires it. At some point along the way, I had begun to feel emotionally and spiritually exhausted; I wanted, finally, to come off my mission once and for all, leave that labor to others. I wanted the spiritual rewards of learning, but I wanted to enjoy them anonymously.

Fittingly, the not-so-gentle irony I experienced in returning to BYU and helping organize a "cosmopolitan" research center, intensifying my exposure to new trends and big ideas, has only further diminished the pretensions of my own scholarly work and career. Just a few years ago, just as things began opening up professionally for me, my ideas had begun to seem big almost. Important maybe. Then, returning to BYU and gazing no longer at my own work and field but at the work of many scholars in many fields across many universities, the expanse widened. I thrilled at the view; I'd never thought such brave new things! But the longer I gazed, the more the view grew oppressive. It was so large, and I was so small—so, so much smaller than I had realized. Like Moses, I came to see that I was nothing, which thing I had never supposed (Moses 1:10).

No, actually, I'd always known it.

A cold Scottish wind rises in my soul, blowing swatches of gray across my brow. Let it go, Matt; keep trying at least. Mine's a good enough story I suppose. I arrived at a moment in life when I just wanted to contribute. A door opened, and I walked through—I walked away from BYU. Then another door opened, leading me back. I didn't want to walk through, but I felt beckoned. It's a true story mostly, a simple version of it at least. And many days, I am so grateful—grateful for inspiration and purpose and amazing students and colleagues all around me.

But some days feel a little bleak. Doors open, yes, but others close. And this last time, I turned and stood, facing that door, even after I heard the gentle click of the latch.

I shake myself and try redirecting my attention to the task of the hour—my department's request that I teach a senior seminar. Any subject I wish. But here I am, a couple weeks later: no ideas, no passion, no inspiration. No, I've decided, to something based on the research project I've almost completed. No to something based on another I'm just beginning. They leave me flat. Same with anything trendy, anything "hot."

The emptiness is contagious; it creeps into other corners of my thinking. I feel myself shrinking in an expanding universe. Who am I as a scholar anymore, anyway? As a person? What is my purpose? Do I even still believe in such a thing?

Then something glimmers from the eastern edge of my mind, inspiring an old thought and new questions. I just want to contribute, still. So what if I designed a course around a subject I find inherently meaningful, irrespective of academic disciplines, fields, or trends, or of professional dreams, achievements, or disappointments? What do I value? What *matters* to me?

A response begins taking shape in molten shadow, bearing a vibrancy that feels familiar if also a little uncanny. Images flash before me—images and deep impressions: a bishop's office, a French bookstore, a dim basement, a Scottish coastline; a gentle voice, gentle irony, doors opening and closing gently. Always gently. *Spiritual experience; teach a course on literature and spiritual experience.*

* * *

That gentleness, a particular quality I associate with God's presence—so profound, so patient, yet so persistent—is why I decided to teach a course on literature and spiritual experience. That feeling of connectedness to God is the medium through which I live and move and have my being (Acts 17:28). Without spiritual experience—the feeling of it and desire for it—I never would have pursued a life studying literature, by which I mean the creative expression, usually in poetry and fiction, of what most deeply moves us. For, bereft of spiritual experience, literature means so much less. Informed by it, however, literature responds as almost nothing else can to the variety and richness—the depth, the mystery, the meaning—of our lives. When it registers the pulsations of spiritual things, literature becomes the special instrument of a more divine language.

As the vignettes above illustrate, my story is of a pilgrim more than a guru, of a seeker more than a sage. At no point do I feel I have arrived at ultimate spiritual enlightenment. But at no point have I felt that I, or anyone else, was beneath the Lord's notice or beyond his reach. A spiritual experience is when God's reach results in God's touch, in our discernment of God's presence. Its product is often, though not always, light and peace, conviction and strength; sometimes the view is too big or our understanding too small, leading to feelings of uncertainty, trepidation, even temporary bewilderment. While a formative experience seated in my bishop's office propelled me to serve a two-year Church mission, other experiences have been subtler and occasionally unsettling, even through the persistent gentleness that has always been, for me, a hallmark of the Spirit's presence. These experiences have come in moments of stillness and also loud frustration; they have appeared as epiphanies, whether joyful illuminations or painful self-assessments; they have arrived as feelings, ideas, and life events. Their provenance is always familiar, always divine, but each occasion is unique, always different from the last. Through them, the Lord reaches, redirects, and rescues what is otherwise lost in us. So it has always been with me.

Over time, then, few things have come to seem more important to me than learning how to recognize and respond to the Spirit's inspiration and to read the layers of meaning in my own and others' spiritual experiences. While many of us hope and pray and work for great and noble things—flourishing for societies and the planet—I find that for most people, as for me, spiritual dramas tend to play out on the local turf of our lives, in situations and concerns that are closest to us. And, as I found myself asking a few years ago, since literature is such an extraordinary medium for capturing and instilling the breadth and depth of human experience, such an amazing tool for teaching us how to see and understand—and since I work at a university that empowers us to give serious consideration to spiritual things (a difference from which I once shrank but have come to embrace as a blessed affordance)—why not teach a course on spiritual experience and literature? Or, now, write a book about it?

* * *

Over the past few years, the breadth of spiritual experience and what it means to pursue a spiritual life have come to figure into all my classes at BYU. As I meet individually with students at the beginning of each semester, I ask them what they hope to gain from our class spiritually as well as intellectually. I often find in these preliminary conversations that students associate spiritual topics with, as they see it, controversial issues: the place of LGBTQ+ individuals in the Church, women and the priesthood, how social justice impacts religious belief and practice, and so on. What they hope to gain, in other words, are tools to reconcile tensions they feel in their religious lives. By semester's end, many students' views have changed—not toward these import-ant issues and not in their desire to reconcile religious conflicts but in their understanding of how best to achieve this harmony. This has something to do with our classroom approach, which focuses less on controversial topics per se than on the diversity and authenticity of spiritual experiences. An experience of spiritual things, of the Spirit, I find, helps all of us grapple more assuredly with difficult issues; it enables us to find our footing in the Church as well as in the world.

That classroom precedent is important to this book, for while I will occasionally invoke the difficult issues with which I have wrestled as a Latter-day Saint, I do not try to resolve them here. Rather, I dwell on the nature of my own experiences with the Spirit—on the com-passion I have felt from God in different seasons of life, his patience with me amid troubles of various kinds, and the diverse ways he has reached me and others around me. I attend, that is, to the wonder of spiritual experience and the peace it bestows. Peace that enlightens and heals us even amid conflict.

Let me say a word about the book's title and trajectory. "Life to the whole being" is Parley P. Pratt's summative statement about the gift of the Holy Ghost and the virtually infinite array of its manifes-tations. I discuss that magnificent statement in chapter 1, in which I attempt a conceptual overview of this book's subject. After that, the chapters that follow try to capture a little of what this "life" has meant to me. I take up such topics as spiritual promptings and the effort to follow them (chapter 2), the potential conflict and ultimate harmony between our spiritual and religious lives (chapter 3), God's capacity to speak with us from within the world, including through literature (chapter 4), diverse manifestations of spiritual feeling that widen our appreciation of the emotional range of spiritual experiences (chapter 5), gaps in understanding that the Spirit both resolves and introduces (chapter 6), the anguish of unresolved questions (chapter 7), seeking God as we mourn (chapter 8), divine promises (chapter 9), the effect of wonder in how the Spirit moves us (chapter 10), spiritual transformation (chapter 11), and Christ as the ultimate answer to our spiritual questions—indeed, to spiritual life itself (chapter 12). Impressionistically, the early chapters focus on topics that are foundational to my subject—spirituality, religion, and literature (chapters 1–4). I then explore some of the complexities of a life of faith (chapters 5–8) and conclude with the fruits of a spiritual life: God's blessing, our own gradual transformation, and the promise of greater things to come (chapters 9–12). Throughout, I not only reflect on topics but also rehearse some of my own experiences and journey.

I make no attempt at a complete self-portrait; a memoir isn't the same thing as an autobiography. Far more might and probably should be said, for example, about my childhood home and the role my parents played in instilling in me a foundational sense of spiritual well-being. And were this primarily a book of literary criticism, I might do much more in the area of literary analysis across a much wider range of texts. But with the needs of my students and their peers most vividly in mind and given the complex choices they face, the life sketch and literary examples I share here address my long experience with the perplexities, even crises, of faith—sometimes, though not always, antitheses to feelings of spiritual well-being. In effect, this is a book about my spiritual coming of age.

This means it's also about my relationship with the Church of Jesus Christ of Latter-day Saints, my faith tradition. As readers will see, my relationship with the Church has always been faithful if also occasionally fraught. Neither position excludes the other. I have remained faithful to the Church in large part because I believe—I have sensed, have felt, have witnessed—that God loves it. I have an ongoing experience of that love and, by extension, of the truthfulness of the gospel. And if God loves the Church, I tell myself, then so should I—so *can* I.

Paradoxically, my occasional stumbling block with the Church is caused by that very conviction. God loves the Church, I believe, but he is not reducible to it; he is larger than it, works with it, and blesses it. And because I believe in an experiential relation to God, a dynamic relation to God—he speaks, but sometimes he doesn't; we please him, but sometimes we don't—I also feel most authentic when I am a little unsettled in my religious beliefs and attitudes, when I seek and await further light and knowledge I know I do not yet possess. I feel the same way in listening to others. While nothing inspires me more than simple declarations of faith, such declarations are most meaningful when they are set against life's afflictions, quandaries, and questions and when they thus capture the feeling of an ongoing, unfinished, and deeply personal Restoration. For me, spiritual experience thus usually entails acclimating myself to feelings of reassuring and expansive unrest. I feel truth most vibrantly not in any conviction concerning the absolute quality of what we presently know but in a confidence that God can lead us from grace to grace, line upon line.

That is why I wrote this book, one that seeks to communicate something of the dynamism and diversity of spiritual experiences—their wide range of feelings, impressions, and ideas, their amplitude across mind and heart, their status as both singular events and states of being encompassing the breadth of life. My conviction is that behind all their manifestations is an actual relationship with a real God, a being who is vast, endless, and endlessly expressive as well as deeply kind, extravagantly generous, and the gentlest of listeners. This book hopes to convey something of my experience of that vital reality. It thus professes an imperfect and unfinished but nevertheless living faith.

ONE

A More Formal Introduction

The gift of the Holy Ghost . . . quickens all the intellectual faculties, increases, enlarges, expands and purifies all the natural passions and affections; and adapts them, by the gift of wisdom, to their lawful use. It inspires, develops, cultivates and matures all the fine-toned sympathies, joys, tastes, kindred feelings, and affections of our nature. It inspires virtue, kindness, goodness, tenderness, gentleness, and charity. It develops beauty of person, form and features. It tends to health, vigor, animation, and social feeling. It invigorates all the faculties of the physical and intellectual man. It strengthens, and gives tone to the nerves. In short, it is, as it were, marrow to the bone, joy to the heart, light to the eyes, music to the ears, and life to the whole being.[1]

I love Parley P. Pratt's observation of 1855, a dynamic exposition of how the Holy Ghost acts within and upon us. It describes what it means to have a spiritual experience—better still, what it means to have that experience extended across time in such a way that its influence rests with us, eventually becoming part of our nature. What Pratt's eloquent treatise underscores is that, more than merely serving as a conduit for truth, the Holy Ghost animates every facet of our being: physical, mental, emotional, social, moral, and more. In fact, it animates sub-facets of these categories: not just our physical health but our countenance and sensitivities, not just our mental constitution but our agility and depth of thought. The Spirit's inspiration is thus not limited to providing direction or knowledge but rather becomes a principle of vitality, of life, making it possible for us not only to know but feel, not only to choose but become. Spiritual experience—here, taken to mean experience with the Spirit of God—reveals our most intimate, individual natures as unique creations of God, divine beings "in embryo."[2]

As I explain in the introduction, these thoughts began pressing on me a few years ago as I reflected on the direction of my work as a teacher and scholar. I found myself asking some fairly typical mid-career—and midlife—questions: What do I most value? What do I deem most important? What brings me and others the greatest joy? In short, what do I love? And how can I attend to what I love more fully? Many answers to these questions offered themselves. Relative to my professional life, I am an English professor and, at the time I'm writing this book, the director of a research center. So I love literature and the rush of new and big ideas. I love university life and the friendships it has helped me form with people all over the world. I love so many students—scores of them, hundreds, more—whom I have had the privilege to teach. But one answer kept calling to me with particular insistence, both as something I love and value in itself and as something that binds together all the other things I love. *Spiritual experience. I love spiritual experience.*

To be clear, I do not love spiritual experience instead of other things but rather, and in the spirit of Pratt's vision, as what best enables all aspects of my experience to be most authentic, most themselves, even as it connects my experience to things greater than itself. For all of us, to have an experience with the Spirit is to perceive the world at least partly as God does. This includes discerning connections otherwise hidden from us or feeling more intensely the beauty or meaning of things to which we might otherwise be dulled. It means finding ourselves capable of greater degrees of love and fulfillment, health and hope, self-realization and self-transcendence, and so much more. Redemptive immersion in a world made new through spiritual experience: *this* is what I love.

I derive the framework for my understanding of spiritual experience from the doctrines of the Church of Jesus Christ of Latter-day Saints, of which I am a devoted member. These doctrines teach that spiritual experience is an experience of the Spirit of God. From this foundational principle, I nurture the belief that if we are sensitive to that Spirit, responsive to it, then no matter who we are or where we have been, God can lead us in ways particular to our unique gifts and circumstances, reconciling us through Christ to our Heavenly Parents, in whose presence and likeness we realize our ultimate purpose and destiny. In this way, to have any experience with the Spirit, no matter how small, is to find ourselves on the cusp of something vast. Indeed, it is to experience the plan of salvation in miniature—to sense the presence of God, a purpose to our existence, and the redemptive means whereby we grow to reflect our Creators, our Heavenly Parents, more fully. Paraphrasing the English poet William Blake, spiritual experience allows us to see the world in a grain of sand.[3] Or, to put it in scriptural terms, "That which is of God is light; and he [or she who] receiveth light," who receives the Spirit, "and continueth in God, receiveth more light; and that light groweth brighter and brighter until the perfect day" (D&C 50:24).

This book lends expression to this idea by way of a particular path with which I am familiar, one that passes by way of literature. There are actually four categories in play here: spiritual experience, literature, religion, and memoir. Let me briefly address all four, explaining what I mean by them and how they will relate to each other in the book—how they will form not "a lot of separate things dotted about," in the words of C. S. Lewis, but rather "one single growing thing."[4]

Spiritual Experience

Spiritual experiences are among life's richest, fullest, profoundest, most exquisitely meaningful, most deeply personal, empowering, enlightening, and life-giving phenomena. They blend body and mind, soul and circumstance, connecting what and who we presently are to greater, more expansive versions of ourselves. In this way, spiritual experiences give us direction as we gaze toward the future and also help us make sense and meaning of our pasts. By assisting us in communing through what is best in ourselves with what is good outside ourselves, such experiences guide us to what is sacred, significant, and whole. As such, spiritual experiences foster healing. What is more, they animate our minds, sharpening our powers of discernment, enlivening our perceptions, awakening our memories, heightening our imaginations, and deepening our empathy. They promote thriving at collective as well as individual levels, attuning us more vibrantly to our environments and inspiring us to greater care for creation. These experiences fill us with hope and purpose, they motivate and console, and they direct us to what is truest, best, and most beautiful. They transform our character.

As a general rule, Latter-day Saints value the things of the Spirit and strive to cultivate spiritual lives. My BYU students, for example, have a studied and intuitive grasp of spiritual things. But it also seems fair to say that we as a religious culture could probably be a little more diverse, more discerning, in how we discuss spiritual experience. Great attention is paid to the Holy Ghost as a witness of truth and as a guide to good conduct and good outcomes—to knowing how to act and direct our lives. I have been blessed on multiple occasions by spiritual promptings like these. And, as I write above, my core conviction, buoyed by Church teachings and personal experience, is that if we are responsive to the Spirit, God can work with us no matter who or where we are. But as Pratt remarks, the Spirit does more than direct our actions or whisper "yes" or "no" to things that may be true. It does more than warn or console. It can awaken us, stir us, calm us, conjure memories, stimulate our imaginations, deepen our feelings, steel our nerves, mitigate the effects of illness, sharpen our capacities for critical reflection, channel our creativity, increase our empathy, purify our minds, change our hearts, and so much more. Indeed, a wide array of spiritual gifts is available to us, only some of which are listed in scripture. To oft-documented gifts like prophecy, wisdom, knowledge, tongues, and discernment (see 1 Cor. 12, Moro. 10, and D&C 46), Elder Marvin J. Ashton adds a series of "less-conspicuous gifts":

> The gift of asking; the gift of listening; the gift of hearing and using a still, small voice; the gift of being able to weep; the gift of avoiding contention; the gift of being agreeable; the gift of avoiding vain repetition; the gift of seeking that which is righteous; the gift of not passing judgment; the gift of looking to God for guidance; the gift of being a disciple; the gift of caring for others; the gift of being able to ponder; the gift of offering prayer; the gift of bearing a mighty testimony; and the gift of receiving the Holy Ghost.[5]

That last gift, "receiving the Holy Ghost," may be the most important as it becomes the gateway to experiencing myriad others, as wide-ranging in their expression as the endlessness of the God who imparts them.

This means learning to experience a variety of spiritual manifestations, of spiritual modes of communication, including forms of divine silence as well as speech. And it means becoming comfortable with incomprehension as well as understanding. I will elaborate on this matter in chapters that follow. The principle is this: the more fully we recognize the diverse ways the Spirit communicates, the more fully we open ourselves to the character and being of God. And the richer, therefore, our relationship with God.

Literature

This is a book about spiritual experience and literature. Better said, it's a book about spiritual experience that passes by way of literature. The study of literature has been an important part of my spiritual journey, making the two, for me, a natural pair. What is more, I find it striking how literature reflects many of the qualities Pratt associates with the Holy Ghost. For example, literature stimulates the mind and stirs the heart, fostering greater empathy and thus increasing our capacity to feel and perceive. It opens us to new worlds and other lives, inspiring surprising turns of thought and exquisite—and sometimes anguished—threnodies of emotion. Literature awakens the imagination and ennobles, and sometimes consoles, the soul. As such, it often acts as an inspired medium for spiritual things. In many instances, literature lends form to the meaning and diversity of our spiritual experiences, to their qualities of connectedness, purpose, and ultimate concern. It can sharpen our awareness of the great variety and depth of spiritual feelings, expanding our appreciation and understanding of spiritual things even as it casts them in a new light. For this reason, literature can also act as a springboard for our own spiritual experiences, such that learning to recognize the richness of such experiences in or through literature can make us more receptive to them ourselves.

The term *literature* has a couple different meanings in this book. First, it designates imaginative writing of exceptional quality that crafts particularly thoughtful, creative, and expressive portraits of the world. It thus captures spiritual experience as other forms of language usually cannot. Indeed, literature is one of our most complex forms of expression. It merges the sensuousness of music (in the elegance of beautiful language, most evident in poetry) and the cognitive sophistication of philosophy (not only in fleshing out ideas but in creating entire worlds into which we enter, as we do in novels).[6] While it is all but impossible to communicate the force of spiritual things through language alone—there is no substitute for one's own experience of the

Spirit—literary language at least comes close. It is perhaps our finest vehicle for communicating, even simulating, spiritual experience.

Second, literature represents a special way of experiencing the world, one that often diverges from expected outcomes or lends different color to familiar scenes. Because we associate literature with "fiction" and not "fact," it forms an imagined alternative to what we think we know, born from an impulse to explore new worlds and ways of being. Simply put, literature reminds us that things might be seen and experienced otherwise, and in that respect, it parallels the effects of many spiritual experiences. As I will explain in later chapters, literature became for me the instrument of a spiritual odyssey that began during my time as a missionary. It has helped me navigate the complexities of my own life and expand my view of the world and the place of our humanity in it. I began relating to literature as a spiritual medium less because authors may be inspired in what they write (though this is also true) than because literature is, formally, a revelatory exercise: through it, we see the world afresh. Literature gives voice to what we may perceive, intuit, or hope but cannot (yet) be said fully to know or understand. It is fact in process of formation. As such, literature is a precursor of emergent realities, both in the world and in ourselves: it forges new neural pathways, new capacities to think and feel and be.

In this book, then, I will frequently appeal to literary texts as a way of helping me illustrate incidents or situations that pertain to spiritual experience. More broadly, however, I will also invoke the idea of literature as a spiritual exercise drawing us toward new horizons. Literature, I will suggest, can help us expand our spiritual capacities, nurture our spiritual gifts. Through it, we gain an enhanced perspective on what spiritual experience is and what it is for. It thus accompanies me in the chapters that follow, providing accents to my stories and thoughts, helping frame or elaborate on them, sometimes offering counterpoints, other times serving as chorus.

Religion

Spiritual experiences connect us to ourselves, each other, and the world. Ultimately, they bring us closer to God. Literature is, potentially, a vehicle that can help us better appreciate how and why this is so; it expands our understanding of spiritual experiences and renders us more sensitive to them. These are core ideas of this book. But I would not write a book like this one, a devotional book, were it not for my conviction that spiritual experiences are best fitted to religion and religious practice. Indeed, much as spiritual experience is the soul of the religious life, religion gives necessary structure and form to spiritual experiences.

But asserting a connection between spirituality and religion—the conventional wisdom of many ages—is hardly conventional in our new age. Our current era is often described as spiritual but not religious (or "SBNR"). Distrust for institutional religion pervades Western societies, exacerbated by abuse scandals, the perceived corruption of ecclesiastical leadership, and the association of religious institutions with reactionary political agendas and social causes. More than that, many people increasingly feel a raw dislike for religion: it doesn't suit the urgency and mood of our historical moment. Where spirituality is nimble and feels tailored to each individual, religion seems clunky and conformist; where spirituality inspires us to seek new horizons and equips us to respond to new problems, religion seems to cling to outmoded traditions and legitimate old prejudices; where spiritual practices like prayer or meditation yield immediate peace of mind, religion demands investments of time and resources (often in copious quantities) with little guaranteed return. Even studies that assert the well-being of religious people—greater life expectancy, happier marriages, higher self-esteem, and so on—might be parsed more finely, for the active agent in most of these studies is actually spirituality. Mindfulness and motivation in dietary practices, attentiveness to and care for those around us, techniques of self-actualization and community building—these spiritual habits are the forces of good living, religion often serving merely as their pretext. And so where religion can help us cultivate robust spiritual sensibilities, fine, but in a world of ever-increasing speed and fluidity, one in which crisis and creative possibility are ever-more densely entangled, religion seems less and less equipped to meet our needs. This holds especially true for institutional religion. There's a reason why churches are emptying, and it isn't just the fulfillment of religious narratives concerning legions of evil in the latter days.

Or so goes a common line of thinking. And truthfully, there is little point pretending that such SBNR perspectives lack merit. Indeed, my idea of hell is a world that is religious but not spiritual, and I say this as a devoutly religious person. Ultimately, however, I believe that spirituality and religion belong together even when they do not fit hand-in-glove. The reasons for this belief are layered. Partly, it's born from experience, from witnessing how my own religious experience (of practicing my religion in the context of a religious community) has enriched my spiritual experience (of connection to God and others) in ways nothing else has or could. Several chapters in this book recount such experiences. But this is also a belief born of faith: I believe the doctrinal tenet of my religion that spiritual experience is given to us by the Spirit of God and that the Spirit testifies to the truthfulness of the Church (and, I believe, to the importance of religion more generally).

If my reasoning sounds circular—I believe in religion because my religion teaches me to believe in it—it is and self-consciously so. Religious practice informs belief. In fact, a growing body of research suggests that rituals, intensive life practices, animate not only belief but our very faculties of perception. We are not blank slates; our worlds are conditioned by our beliefs, and our beliefs in turn are conditioned by systems, institutions, and practices. Paradoxically, this makes virtually all thought religious even (and perhaps especially) when it purports to be non- or anti-religious (that is, when it stops recognizing its own implication in faith as a practice—any practice— following from our conditioned perceptions of the world). And so, on that principle, we should be wise in choosing our religions. For, if we do not choose them, they will choose us.

As it happens, my religion is rich in its teachings and practices concerning spiritual experience. Baptism into the Church is the vehicle through which we receive, as a priesthood ordinance, the gift of the Holy Ghost—the most constant and intense way to enjoy an experience of the Spirit. The Church provides a doctrinal framework for understanding what the Spirit is and why it is given to us and thus harnesses spiritual energy not just to good living but a true fullness of life. The Church calls us to serve in ways that require us to seek and then live by spiritual experience. It brings us into the presence of other people whose exemplary behavior inspires us, likewise, to give of ourselves even when such giving is difficult and who provide us with models for becoming more spiritually minded—the very definition of saintliness according to the philosopher William James.[7] Our obedience to religious principles—more specifically, to covenants with God that guide our behavior and shape our thoughts, feelings, and identities—indicates our willingness to follow God even when doing so runs contrary to our own inclinations and to follow God precisely because we feel so moved by the Spirit. The Spirit thus compels what is best in us. And the Spirit, I find, is a gentle contrarian: it resists the dogma of the status quo, refusing to let us rest in the complacency of narrow ideas and shallow understandings, stirring us to expand our minds and deepen our capacity for feeling and action, and causing us, therefore, to revise our relationship with our faith and reexamine our religious practices. Contrary to the famous dictum of Karl Marx's, religion is no opiate of the masses.[8] Rather, it provides an intensive regimen of advanced spiritual living.

Religion is thus the impetus of much spiritual experience and also a key laboratory for the latter's conversion into principles of transformative understanding. As a function of its ritual practices as well as its teachings, of its traditions as well as its communities, religion magnifies our capacity to receive and sustain our proximity to the Spirit. And through the Spirit, God helps us live with religion even when the latter seems harsh or uninhabitable to us, as it has occasionally seemed to me. There is much about religion, still, that is difficult for me. But it is that convergence of spirituality and religion that brings me closer to God. And so, in discussing spiritual experience in this book, I wish to underscore its ultimate harmony with religion. Religion lends spiritual experience form, and spiritual experience infuses religion with life.

Memoir

I love ideas, and I take up ideas at several points in the chapters that follow. But ultimately, this is a book less about ideas than experience—spiritual experience. In fact, I focus on spiritual *experience* rather than spiritua*lity* because I wish to emphasize the experiential aspect of a spiritual life. Spirituality involves a disposition, a cultivation of good habits of mind and body, and an acquisition of virtues that enable us to draw closer to God. In that way, spirituality is about our agency, about how we witness to God that we care about the things of the Spirit. But spiritual experience is not principally about us or our agency; rather, it is about what happens to us, what comes over us. It is about spiritual realities independent of us and about our recognition of those realities, our engagement of them. If spirituality is about our love for God, then spiritual experience is about God's love for us, his care for us, his willingness to impart something of his presence to us.[9]

Memoir in this book registers ways—some few of the ways—that spiritual experience has moved me. But for me, communicating the force of spiritual experience requires something a little different from just rehearsing stories in which I felt the Spirit. In some instances, capturing the tenor of spiritual experience in the context of everyday life means describing the tensions, conflicts, even paradoxes such experiences pose. Some chapters focus less on moments of experience than on prevailing moods during seasons of life—sometimes bright, sometimes dark. Or else they linger over events that were so understated as to almost escape notice. They rehearse situations of new understanding, painful self-assessment, and relative spiritual benight-edness. I take this broad, confessional approach because, as I remark above, the range of spiritual experiences varies widely and because I hope to recreate something of the lived contexts in which my own spiritual experiences have occurred. If I can illustrate these experiences in this way, my hope is that readers will be able to supplement my accounts with their own experiences, their own encounters with the Spirit, great and small.

Behind this approach and the experiences that shape it lies a conviction: If we can attune ourselves to the myriad ways that God is present in our lives and if we live in such a way that we refine ourselves to become more spiritually sensitive, we will feel greater peace and joy; we will connect more meaningfully with others and the world around us; we will experience a deeper sense of promise and security even amid seasons of trial, grief, and confusion; we will find our talents, capacities, and sensibilities augmented, thus melding more fully who we feel we are with who we want to be; and we will enjoy a greater measure of the companionship of God in preparation, we hope, for a more joyful and sustained reunion. In my experience, a spiritual life is not a life apart but a life enriched, a life made whole. The key is to seek the Spirit and then learn to discern and follow it.

TWO

That First Step

It is common for people from multiple religious traditions to seek, examine, and attempt to explain spiritual experiences. Occasionally, scholars turn their own attention to these experiences. When they do, they light on a series of provocative qualities that so many of these experiences seem to share: feelings for a transcendent reality; a zest which adds itself like a gift to life; an assurance of safety and a temper of peace; a preponderance of loving affections; a holistic, integrative approach to life; a concern for what is sacred and meaningful; care for what promotes human thriving; heightened cognitive activity that connects ideas, memories, and emotions; transformative experience with the Spirit of God.[1] The range of description is remarkable and often quite moving: "The spiritual center is the deepest center of the person: the place of surrender to authenticity and love."[2] "Spirituality means following intuitions that can lead to fullness of life."[3] Spirituality is "the divine-human relational process"[4] or "prayer without ceasing . . . prayer spread across the many works and habits of each day."[5]

My academic training is in literature, not theology or religious studies. And I cannot help discerning something evocatively literary about the qualities above that scholars associate with spiritual experience. Spiritual experiences, they note, occur at the limits of what we currently perceive as true, a realm historically associated with the imagination. Dense and layered (at once familiar and yet uncanny, sublime), limit experiences, we might call them, structure our lives and infuse them with meaning. Calling such experiences the deepest center of the person makes the path to spiritual enlightenment a quest narrative; saying that spirituality means following intuitions that can lead to fullness of life makes it into a romance, a story form liberated from the constraints of reductive realism. Literature is a natural vehicle of spiritual experience. But these experiences are not literary in the dismissive way that literature is sometimes invoked, for unlike a cheap novel, spiritual experiences are rarely casually consumed. Instead, they lay claim to us as vital, vibrant, and transformative aspects of who we most truly are, of what in us most profoundly *is* and *is becoming*.

When the thought first came to me to teach a course on literature and spiritual experience, I knew of none of these scholarly sources and had formalized few of these connections. I had what I felt was an inspired idea propped up by little more than my religious training and my intuitions as someone who cares about literature and spiritual experience and had steeped himself in each—separately. This was a good foundation, certainly, but wholly inadequate pedagogically. So where, how, would I begin? I knew of no precedent for a course on literature and spiritual experience, at least none that presented itself in quite that way. (Spiritual experiences suffuse literature in the forms I describe above, but they rarely label themselves spiritual in doing so.) Neither did I know of any theory explaining the relationship between literature and spirituality nor of any methodology for how to explore it. At once thrilled and perplexed, overwhelmed by the blankness of the horizon before me, I diverted myself with other tasks. I still had twelve months until I would be teaching that class. Then eleven months. Then nine. Six.

I needed inspiration—the kind of spiritual experience about which I was slated to teach. And it came in two forms. First, I turned to scripture as a tool for thinking. And second, I felt impressed to take what at the time seemed to be an extraordinary risk: Invited to speak on a panel at a scholarly society's annual meeting, I decided to base my talk on how a particular author portrays spiritual experience. Whatever I knew or did not know about the subject I would be teaching, this would force me to say it. And more than that, it would compel me to profess an investment in spiritual things and thus make apparent to others what I was actually trying to be in my own life.

That this was a distressing thought—that it required inspiration and a leap of faith—is perhaps indicative of the strangeness of my spiritual journey. (Why should authenticity regarding one's religious and spiritual lives require almost comical heroism? Why is it so difficult to appear to be who one is or wants to be?) And it may say something about the hostility of the intellectual environment I inhabit (and more on that below). But the fact that I was even willing to entertain such thoughts and risk, however ridiculously, a degree of authenticity also accentuates the myriad ways the Spirit works with us, entering and redirecting our personal narratives, informing and gently reshaping our identities, helping us live most determinedly and, ultimately, peacefully with what we most desire.

As it happens, my academic life has long been a spiritual workshop, a place where I feel God has helped shape not just my scholarship but my character. This is less a function of what I have studied than how as I have often turned to the Lord for help with intellectual projects and questions that felt too large for me to wrap my mind around on my own. And the help I feel I have received, however modest, has always had a carryover effect, causing me to think differently about my life, including my religion and relationships as much as my academic pursuits. My work has thus always had a kind of quality of metaphor, one area of life opening transformatively onto another: my spiritual life onto my scholarly life, the latter onto my devotional life, and that last onto pulsations and colors of the everyday.

Metaphor is a powerful tool in life as much as literature. Evoking one thing by way of another, as in the phrases "My love is a rose" or "God is love," metaphor helps us visualize otherwise unfamiliar situations or problems; it renders abstract ideas more concrete by connecting them to objects of our experience. More than just comparative, metaphor is transformative: at the very least, it changes how we think about the objects, ideas, or experiences it names. It converts *this* into *that*. But spiritual experience, I find, also changes how we perceive metaphors. Usually, we recognize a metaphor *as* a metaphor. Love is not really a rose, but the figure of speech renders love more sensuous, more vivid. But when we appeal to metaphors to describe spiritual experiences, something happens: the metaphor almost melds with the object it describes. For example, when an experience with the Spirit grafts itself onto other, more mundane aspects of our experience—when, say, friends or members of our faith communities spiritually touch us in performing a kind deed and we say they are acting as the hands of God—the vehicle of the metaphor ("the hands of God") not only passes across its object (our friends), it transforms it: it reveals the wondrous, even miraculous quality of otherwise ordinary people. Our friends, after all, *are* actual children of God, something we may overlook in everyday circumstances. In this case, then, the metaphor is not only descriptive, it is also profoundly true: there is, in fact, something God-like about these friends.

And so it is with other aspects of our experience. If a spiritual experience graces it, it seems changed. Time with friends can also be a spiritual experience, and once we have had such an experience, we think about these friends differently. An experience of learning can also be a spiritual experience, and if it is, we always think a little differently about what we have learned. The same goes for most any experience—time in nature, time working, time singing, time reading, time praying, and so on: if the Spirit touches any of these moments, they become time transformed. Spiritual experience fundamentally changes its vehicles; it converts metaphors from tools for thinking into emblems of a world reborn. In its way, it brings literature, so rich in metaphorical language, to life.

* * *

"And Jesus, walking by the sea of Galilee, saw two brethren, Simon called Peter, and Andrew his brother, casting a net into the sea: for they were fishers. And he saith unto them, Follow me, and I will make you fishers of men. And they straightway left their nets, and followed him" (Matt. 4:18–20). *Fishers of men* is one of the most famous metaphors in scripture. The kind of labor Jesus had in mind had little to do with fishing, of course. But he takes what is familiar to these brothers and turns it, converts it, to other ends (eventually the founding of the church and the saving of souls). *Conversion* is actually a synonym for metaphor, signifying a transformation of one thing into another—a rose into an emblem of love or, here, a fisher into one sent of God, an apostle. And the Gospel narrator depicts Peter and Andrew immediately exhibiting signs of people so converted: "They straightway left their nets, and followed him."

Compare this Gospel metaphor with one in the Book of Mormon when the brother of Jared seeks light for the vessels on which he and his people will voyage across the great waters, presenting before the Lord sixteen small, molten stones:

> O Lord, thou hast said that we must be encompassed about by the floods. Now behold, O Lord, and do not be angry with thy servant because of his weakness before thee . . . [but] look upon me in pity, and turn away thine anger from this people, and suffer not that they shall go forth across this raging deep in darkness; but behold these things which I have molten out of the rock. And I know, O Lord, that thou hast all power, and can do whatsoever thou wilt for the benefit of man; therefore touch these stones, O Lord, with thy finger, and prepare them that they may shine forth in darkness. . . . And it came to pass that when the brother of Jared had said these words, behold, the Lord stretched forth his hand and touched the stones one by one with his finger. And the veil was taken from off the eyes of the brother of Jared, and he saw the finger of the Lord; and it was as the finger of a man,

like unto flesh and blood; and the brother of Jared fell down before the Lord, for he was struck with fear. And the Lord saw that the brother of Jared had fallen to the earth; and the Lord said unto him: Arise, why hast thou fallen? And he saith unto the Lord: I saw the finger of the Lord, and I feared lest he should smite me; for I knew not that the Lord had flesh and blood. (Ether 3:2–4, 6–8)

One of the most striking things in this passage is the brother of Jared's fear when the Lord answers his prayer precisely in the manner he had requested. "Touch these stones, O Lord, with thy finger" leads to "I saw the finger of the Lord, and I feared lest he should smite me; for I knew not that the Lord had flesh and blood." Within the context of the exchange, it becomes clear that the brother of Jared's plea was almost metaphorical in nature: "Touch these stones, O Lord, with thy finger" was a way of saying "illuminate these minerals in some way or other"; touch them, *as it were*. But then the metaphor became literal: The Lord revealed his finger, "and it was as the finger of a man, like unto flesh and blood."

Of the qualities associated with spiritual experience listed at the beginning of this chapter, several apply here. *Feelings for a transcendent reality*—the brother of Jared beholds the Lord. *A zest which adds itself like a gift to life*—he finds himself with a radiant new understanding of God and, therefore, of himself. *Heightened cognitive activity that connects ideas, memories, and emotions*—this experience in prayer builds on others but radically expands the scope of possibility, inspiring a fear that, as the chapter proceeds, will grow into a new degree of spiritual confidence. But the metaphorical play at work in the chapter—better said, the Lord's refusal to allow metaphor to remain metaphor only—seems especially significant. For, in this passage, the *as it were* becomes an *as it is*. This does not render the brother of Jared's experience material rather than spiritual as much as it reveals the transformative force of spiritual things: the Lord will work through a metaphor to make something real, to open the mind of someone with whom he communicates. The same is true of the calling of the fishers in Matthew. In their case, an unimaginable transformation (namely, the founding of Christianity) has already happened by the time Matthew's account reaches its readers, so we take for granted what could only have startled the writers of the Gospels (for who could have foreseen such a global haul of souls?). The story of the brother of Jared, by contrast, divulges the shock of certain kinds of spiritual experiences in real time, even when they take forms we may anticipate. There is something startling about an actual answer to prayer even when we ask for it in faith. Bringing us into contact with something greater than ourselves—something vaster, fuller, more intensely real—such answers change our minds and worlds. We believe, and then we see. And what we see changes us.

In a small way, so it was with me when I contemplated my upcoming class on literature and spiritual experience. What I was asking of God was fairly modest: help me better understand spiritual experience so that I can teach it properly. What I received, however, took me by surprise even though I expected the Lord to answer my prayer. That this answer "looks small unto the understanding of men" (Ether 3:5)—that my story is ultimately about nothing outwardly miraculous—makes it no less real. If anything, the way the Lord took a relatively minor experience and made it an emblem of greater things impressed me all the more. When the metaphor became real, it deepened my conversion. It changed me.

✳ ✳ ✳

A couple months after I decided to teach my course—hence, ten or so until I would actually begin doing so—a friend at another university reached out and invited me to speak on a panel she was organizing for a large academic conference held later that year. I accepted and began casting about for ideas on which to present. As I had recently been through a similar exercise when invited by my department to teach a class, my mind reverted again to connections between spiritual experience and literature. I wondered again whether such a thing was possible and felt a familiar if also unsettling, faith-demanding impulse: *Do it! Take the step!* Tantalized by the prospect of trying something so comparatively provocative, I decided to float the idea past my friend to see whether she would shoot it down. That would put me back in my place.

She did no such thing. She said she loved the idea. And I was both gratified and horrified because someone I valued had validated something I loved, but now I would be compelled to declare and defend that love before a mostly unloving audience.

That last assertion needs some explaining. I love the scholarly world. I read obscure literary criticism as a hobby, fascinated as I am by the shape of beautiful ideas and the force of strong thinking. I count hundreds of scholars as friends and am quietly a fanboy of hundreds of others whom I do not know personally but whose thinking has influenced my own. I give myself liberally to my scholarly work, which means I also bring my religious background with me, and with BYU beside my name, my religious affiliation is broadcast wherever I go. And that's fine. But I'm usually careful about casting my proverbial pearls, suppressing the spiritual accents (the theological paradigms, the prayerful inflections) of my otherwise secular ideas. This is both because I reverence the experience of such inspiration and, alas, because I fear the scorn of my scholarly peers.

Yes, scorn. This is how I perceive the reaction of many secular scholars to the subject of spirituality. Spirituality more than religion—religion per se actually "passes" in many academic circles as it represents bodies of ideas, cultural heritages, and so on. One often cannot help one's religion, certainly not one's religious upbringing. But faith is a different matter: faith, the substance of a spiritual life, signifies belief and belief suggests gullibility and lack of critical engagement, things which are demonized—almost superstitiously as irony has it—in many academic circles.

For this reason, spirituality is especially hard to mask. It tends to evoke either the fragrance of lived religion—of belief in God and afterworlds, carrying with them (for many secular humanists) all the horror of fanaticism and Biblical literalism—or else it conjures the kitschy aura of all things New Age. Scholars of spirituality often label their field "self-implicating," meaning that one only writes about spirituality if one cares about it, invests in it, brings one's whole self to it—*believes* in it.[6] But for that reason, you cannot speak over or around spirituality; you name it, you claim it. A virtual shibboleth in academia, especially among the more ascetically rational, spirituality—a belief in spiritual things—marks you as foreign. (As I joked with an academic friend at another university before speaking on religion and spirituality a year later, "What do I have to lose . . . except, you know, my reputation?" She laughed—in agreement.)

And so, a few months later, when I traveled to the conference, paced nervously in my hotel room prior to my presentation, practiced urbane responses to the incredulous questions I anticipated receiving, enveloped my talk as much I could in the armor of academic jargon, and then stepped before a large room of peers to talk about spirituality, I felt vulnerable as never before—anxious and dizzy and disoriented. It seemed I was walking a plank above an abyss of shame, every pen in the audience a potential sword, every laptop threatening a tweet of infamy. But as I went to the podium, I also felt a calm come over me, a familiar, soothing presence, a distinctively spiritual feeling. My breathing deepened, as did my voice. Time slowed. I gathered myself and stepped into the deep.

The American poet Denise Levertov writes a beautiful poem about the implications of taking such a step and the lingering—spiritual—effects of doing so. Originally titling the poem "Aesthetics of Miracle," Levertov eventually published it as "Poetics of Faith," bringing together the writing of poetry and the experience of religious belief.

'Straight to the point'
    can ricochet,
        unconvincing.
Circumlocution, analogy,
    parable's ambiguities, provide
        context, stepping-stones.

Most of the time.[7]

The poem partly enacts, in these opening lines, a little of the ricochet to which it refers, accumulating examples in a brief, multisyllabic catalog (e.g., analogy, parable), rendering them more vivid through metaphor ("stepping-stones"), and then swerving away almost dismissively, underscored by way of a new stanza and a sentence fragment: "Most of the time." In essence, it's saying, "This is how it's done! You know, sometimes." At this point, ingeniously and in the process of developing its idea, the poem appeals to a more elaborate metaphor: the Biblical episode of Peter walking on water to meet Jesus (see Matt. 14:22–33). And, tellingly, the poem never leaves this metaphor and returns to its original idea; the poet never explains that this figure illustrates the writing of poetry. Instead, the poet keeps our gaze trained on the figure, eventually transforming the poem from being about poetry to being about religious conversion as the poet becomes mesmerized, like Peter, by the image of the approaching Christ:

        as if forgetting
to prepare them, He simply
    walks on water
        toward them, casually—
and impetuous Peter, empowered,
    jumps from the boat and rushes
        on wave-tip to meet Him—
a few steps, anyway—
    (till it occurs to him
        "I can't, this is preposterous"

and Jesus has to grab him,
      tumble his weight
            back over the gunwale).

(ll. 13–25)

The casual retelling of this story requires a little context. Levertov composed the poem as she was undergoing a set of spiritual exercises originally developed by Ignatius of Loyola, the founder of the Jesuits. Consisting in a series of prayers and meditations, these exercises were designed to instill a greater capacity to contemplate the things of God. Levertov was especially drawn to how the exercises encourage imaginative identification with scriptural texts. With the help of spiritual guides, those undertaking the exercises ponder Biblical episodes, striving to visualize themselves within them. From this immersive vantage point, they witness not only the arc of a well-known story but also scores of unmentioned details: air temperature and fragrance, the look and texture of clothing, ambient noise and the murmur of peripheral conversations. Such details bring the stories alive. In the passage I cite above, for example, small additions (the casual nature of Jesus's gait; Peter's exclamation "this is preposterous") supplement the scriptural account.

"'Straight to the point' / can ricochet," and that is what Levertov's poem does once it conjures this episode of Jesus and Peter on the water. While the poem begins with the poet reflecting on the nature of poetic technique—those rules poets acknowledge and learn to ignore—inspiration, it continues, operates differently: it comes to us as "the lightning power / . . . of plain / unheralded miracle!" (ll. 8, 10–11) as it did Peter. This marks a key transition in the poem, one that puts me in mind of the brother of Jared dazzled by the appearance of the Lord's finger. Inspiration is what the poet desires, and inspiration is more than the product of mere craft, of careful technique. Indeed, the "lightning power" that impels Peter to walk on a substance that usually could not sustain him illustrates how inspiration undoes itself as a poetic principle. For inspiration, the poet asserts, is not the result of poetic technique since, by definition, inspiration always arrives unexpectedly. Or, if there is a method that lays the groundwork for inspiration—for Levertov, the spiritual exercises, for example—it cannot guarantee the "miracle" it seeks. The poet labors at her craft only to find that craft alone is limited, for inspiration involves an interaction with the divine, a force we cannot control. Beckoned by inspiration, the poet sinks with mere technique. Paradoxically, therefore, the poet desires to be something more or other than a poet since simply being a poet is not adequate to the miracle needed to produce an inspired poem.

What, then, is a poem but a miracle whose source is not, or not only, the poet herself? This makes a poet less a creator than a receiver of miracles—a recipient of transformative spiritual experiences. Such experiences introduce the unimaginable into the mundane, the otherworldly into the texture of everyday life. *I knew not that the Lord had flesh and blood*: Poets traditionally seek inspiration, but Levertov in "Poetics of Faith" finds herself dazzled by the implications of this facet of the creative process. Accordingly, at poem's end, Levertov never returns from her example of Peter to the initial discussion of poetry writing. Instead, she stays with Peter and the residues of his experience; in effect, the metaphor—to write an inspired poem is to walk on water—commandeers the poem to its own ends:

> Sustaining those light and swift
> steps was more than Peter
> could manage. Still,
> years later,
> his toes and insteps, just before sleep,
> would remember their passage.
>
> (ll. 26–31)

Experiential immediacy—the light steps across the water—gives way to rumination over the indelible impression left by the event. It scarcely seems believable; Peter never saw it coming, but now, "years later" (underscored through its standing as a line unto itself: "years later," "Still"), its significance graces every aspect of his life.

"Poetics of Faith" begins as an abstract discussion about writing, but it concludes as a kind of suspended thought, a floating question, a cosmic vision rolling on large waves across deep water. How does a single event come to define the balance of life? How is it that some metaphors become real? Whatever is "poetic" in poems, Levertov suggests, is secondary, an effect of something else. More important than the poem is the force that inspires it; more transformative than the poetic artifact is a relation it bears to the divine source that makes it possible. This is a poetry of witness, a meditative exercise about the God who transcends poetry or any other product of human craft.

I will make you fishers of men. Christ's metaphor revolutionized the lives of two laborers and eventually billions of other disciples. Likewise, "Poetics of Faith" isn't only about poetics or poetry. It's a metaphor of spirituality—a poem losing its way even as, in a more important sense, it finds itself. Beginning as poem, it is converted to vision.

My talk at the academic conference would have a similar effect on me. In hindsight, it really wasn't a talk as much as a metaphor, a transformative vision, of what and who I wanted to be.

* * *

I spoke during a morning session of the conference. That night, still buzzing with energy, more dazed than fatigued, I lay in the darkness of my hotel room replaying the experience. The audience had been politely quiet when I began speaking, but given the comparative strangeness of the subject matter, people soon grew more attentive. Some stopped taking notes and gazed up in curiosity. At the talk's conclusion, I steeled myself for the question and answer period. And here they came: Question 1. . . 2. . . 3. . . 4. . . . I felt free, unleashed in my responses (I'd already said so much, why stop now?), open to subjects and lines of inquiry we rarely pursue in my professional societies: Why I invoked spiritual experience. . . . Why that subject seems to elude academic conversation. . . . Why it speaks to our moment, our work, ourselves. . . . *Why not?*

Afterward, some people came forward, as they often do, to say a couple words. But the tenor of their remarks was different. Few found my presentation "interesting," which I took as a good sign. Variations on "interesting" are probably the most overused words in literary studies. Usually they signify detached half-appreciation: "I was interested in. . ." means "I hear you, but let me tell you about my own research" or "I will engage your thinking but only so far." My academic talks have generated plenty of "interest" over the years. But this time, what people conveyed instead was "thank you" or "that was cool." One woman said she appreciated my courage.

Later in the day, at a plenary session, I found and sat beside my friend who had organized the panel. She smiled widely, warmly, but we said little to each other; the session was beginning. The scholar introducing the speaker had not heard my talk, and as chance had it, he made a derisive quip about spirituality: "Baudelaire says that anyone wishing to understand Romanticism must also understand spirituality and intimacy." He paused. "I think we can leave spirituality to others." (Chuckle, chuckle: *interesting*.) But my friend gave me a glance and smiled again. And after the talk, she gave me a longer, more thoughtful look and remarked that the speaker, who had addressed the work of the novelist George Eliot, had seemed to misattribute a particular allusion. "I think Eliot was actually referring to 1 Corinthians 13, Paul's discourse on love." It was an unusual observation at an academic conference. More than a bookish correction, it communicated a shared set of values and perhaps even experiences: Christian, believing, *spiritual*.

Now, hours later, replaying that moment in my mind, I stared into the darkness in the direction of the ceiling. The truth is, my talk had been thoroughly mediocre: provocative but underdeveloped, insightful here or there but still, in too many places, insufficiently discerning. Naturally so; I was still learning my subject. That said, something about the talk had moved people; something phosphorescent had expressed itself through my small cluster of opaque ideas.

I had never had an experience quite like this one at an academic conference, and I kept turning it around in my mind. But I was finally growing weary. So, in the fuzz of dimming consciousness, I tried reconstructing its essential parts one last time: my friend presented me with an opportunity, I responded to what I believe was a spiritual prompting, and the Lord sustained me. This should not have come as a surprise. My work has always been a metaphor of my spiritual odyssey. I've learned by now to expect divine help, even if in modest increments that mattered only to me. But I was astonished, nonetheless, at the literality of the situation, at how the metaphor became real. A *spiritual* odyssey indeed: an odyssey this time, literally, about spiritual things.

As Levertov's Peter remarks, it all seems so preposterous. You begin by reviewing a situation the way a fisherman gazes at the sea. Like Peter, however, you may discern something else and, feeling spiritually beckoned, walk toward it across a surface you never imagined could be so durable. You never forget an experience like that, one that breaches the limits of what you thought possible. It changes you, every time; it converts you, again and again.

THREE

On Religion and the Spiritual Life; or, The Elegance of Clunky Things

Let me touch again, as I did in chapter 1, on Parley P. Pratt's reflections on the gift of the Holy Ghost. He calls it a power that "quickens all the intellectual faculties, increases, enlarges, expands and purifies all the natural passions and affections; and adapts them, by the gift of wisdom, to their lawful use." That last phrase, "lawful use," suggests direction; the Holy Ghost turns us to what is right. But it also makes us (our "intellectual faculties" and "natural passions and affections") something more than we would otherwise be. It reveals and helps us cultivate not only our spiritual gifts but our talents. Additionally, the Spirit connects us to others and helps mold us into the kinds of beings to whom others wish to be connected: "It inspires, develops, cultivates and matures all the fine-toned sympathies, joys, tastes, kindred feelings, and affections of our nature. It inspires virtue, kindness, goodness, tenderness, gentleness, and charity. It develops beauty of person, form and features. It tends to health, vigor, animation, and social feeling."[1] Through the influence of the Spirit, we become more mindful, more grateful, more alert to others and the world around us. What is more, by emphasizing the gift rather than simply the fleeting presence of the Holy Ghost, Pratt underscores the effects of the Spirit not only in the moment but as a transformative influence over time.

I was a young man when I first came across Pratt's great description of the gift of the Holy Ghost, and it raised tantalizing questions: What if one were able to realize the promise implicit in that gift? What if one were to build a life, choice upon choice, such that the Spirit remained with us? How would its presence change the tenor of daily existence, its highs and lows? How would it inform our most memorable experiences, the meanings from them we might extract and preserve? And how would it grace the mountain of nameless moments that form the backdrop for our memories, that make up the everyday grist from which we fashion our identities and tell our stories? If we cultivated the gift of the Holy Ghost, would our lives acquire more color, a different sound? If the Spirit were a more constant presence, would our pain feel different somehow? Would it carry a purpose, and a promise, that it otherwise seems to lack? And would our joy have an amplitude, a resonance that would cause it to linger, to echo? Wouldn't the Spirit make things more alive to us and us to them?

* * *

A few years ago, I began asking myself these kinds of questions more earnestly, converting the thought experiment of my twenties into a larger life experiment. To that end, I became more purposeful in cultivating my spiritual life. In addition to reading and learning more about spiritual experiences in general, I tried to better understand how they happen for me. So I began keeping different spiritual journals: one for life events, another for inspiration in prayer, and a third for noting spiritual insights while reading the scriptures. This made spiritual reflection a more regular part of my daily routine. The effects were immediate: becoming more attentive to the Spirit, I felt more peace, a more consistent degree of happiness, and a greater depth of reflection on the people and circumstances around me. New habits formed as I gave more time to projects and routines that invited the Spirit into my life. These days, there are times when, immersed in some activity or other, I simply pause, detach, and bask in the spiritual environment in which I find myself, giving thanks for the joy it brings, the hope— the sense of meaning.

However, the spectrum of spiritual feelings, impressions, and effects is wide, so the answers to my questions from long ago (What if I were more mindful of the Spirit's presence? Would my life carry a greater sense of purpose? Would I feel more alive?) would be a *qualified* yes. I qualify my answers not because the Spirit's presence does not enrich my quality of life experience but because its intensification of my experience makes it more varied. Hence, it provides new perspectives on my questions and struggles without suspending them altogether. Yes, a spiritual life feels richer, fuller; it acquires more depth; it seems more open. But it also sometimes reveals hard truths, disclosing more fully the reasons for my struggles and the nature of my limitations. (For example, an increased desire to alleviate others' suffering attends a heightened awareness of my inadequacy in doing so; greater inspiration in my life pursuits tends to push me further out of my comfort zones; and my growth in patience as a parent coincides with greater grief over the sorrows of my children.) Everyday "worldly" cares—professional, political, etc.—do not fade as much as acquire different shades of meaning, sometimes attached to painful self-reflection regarding the relative inanity of my old opinions or former ambitions. Time speeds up. . . and slows down: life feels fast but also dense, thick with feeling, memory, and association, such that joy and sadness occasionally blur. (I sometimes have trouble distinguishing between feelings of elation and depression, relief and regret.) I connect more fully with others but also, therefore, experience their pain more acutely; I seem to draw closer to God but thus feel more poignantly periods of God's absence, whether in my own life or the lives of others. The promise of healing through Christ thus feels more real—and necessary.

In sum, I now count poignancy, not only joy, among the fruits of the Spirit. But then, of course, there are also stretches of time when I feel spiritually flat, when anxiety crowds out more peaceful and expansive thoughts, when my prayers become empty recitations of things I know I should be feeling more deeply, and when the veil separating me from God feels like a thick block of ice trapping me underwater. My senses dull to the wonder of the world and old patterns of thought and behavior reassert themselves, making me feel claustrophobic within the confines of my life. During these stretches, I become pricklier—more acutely aware of what I dislike in others and disdain in myself. Not coincidentally, I also become more conscious of what aggravates me about the Church, of how it hounds me by demanding my attention, my care, my tithing, my patience, and my time, my time, my time.

I fully acknowledge that the Church is an organizational marvel—a complex weave of ordinances, offices, doctrines, practices, activities, and responsibilities that knit together people from across the globe and sometimes, more miraculously, within a neighborhood or even an individual family. But everyday experience in the Church can obscure this marvel. A paradox informs my religious life in that the only times I truly desire a fuller one, a more energetic one, are when I feel I don't need it—that is, when my spiritual life, which I distinguish from my religious life per se, is strong enough to generate new joys, tastes, and states of mind, including affinities for the comparatively clunky expressions of spirituality one typically finds at church.

Yes, clunky, which is not to deny their many moments of elegance. I recognize that some members experience indecorous aspects of religious experience (e.g., hurtful comments or policies) as painful rather than clunky. I have my own experiences with such pain, as some of these chapters will relate. But in my case, it is clunkiness, not hurtfulness, that is more common. The Church has an exemplary and well-intentioned but mostly lay ministry, and even its few full-time leaders are rarely credentialed theologians. So, especially in the United States, church sermons sometimes feel like folk wisdom for upper-middle-class conservatives. Weekly church lessons are often led by amateur teachers with allergies to ambiguity, constrained as they are to arrive at closure by the top of the hour even when the topics of discussion invite nuance and uncertainty and ask that we sit with them for longer stretches of time. Leaders of local congregations are typically dedicated souls whose day jobs consist of workaday responsibilities rather than either monastic devotion or the kind of professional training that might provide members with more adequate counseling, whether practical, psychological, or theological. Then there are the Church's publicity materials, which tend to reflect the polite, sentimental tastes of its American membership (witness the tinkly, treacly background music to some Church videos). And, of course, there is the legendary industriousness of Church members, the sprawl of meetings and activities and camps and firesides and socials and more, always more, lending an unwelcome nuance to what it means to be *anxiously* engaged.[2]

To be sure, there is an endearing quality to much of what I'm describing—and plenty of exceptions (expert teachers and speakers, gifted leaders, high-end media, and so on). What is more, and such as they are, these are the cultural forms through which so many members mediate the intricacies and nuances of their spiritual lives, and these forms acquire a kind of profundity on that basis. I am frequently moved by the sounds of certain hymns, irrespective of the expertise of the organist or the quality of the voices around me. (My singing voice, I am sure, inspires no one.) For all the anxiety about appearances one finds codified in Church standards of dress and grooming, it seems the Church thrives on a kind of unkemptness, on the obvious imperfections of its members. We are fond of proclaiming that Joseph Smith's lack of education makes the coming forth of the Book of Mormon all the more miraculous and that the Lord loves the simple things of the earth (after all, he called fishermen, not Pharisees, as his apostles). If our talks and testimonies, our leaders and lessons are occasionally clunky, all the better! Or so we profess.

And so, while the inelegance of our religious practice rarely appeals to the aesthetically high-minded English professor in me, the English professor is not the part of me who is the faithful church-goer. The latter is drawn not to cultural elegance but to something completely different about our religious practices and environment, namely their distinctive and unmistakable spirit. This is a spirit that so moves me in phases of life when my own spiritual life is soaring, and it is also what I so desperately need during those moments or seasons when I fall flat. By *spirit*, I mean Spirit, the Holy Ghost, the presence of God expressing divine love through and for his human—all too human—vehicles. When Parley P. Pratt refers to the *gift* of the Holy Ghost, he is yoking the exquisite effects of the Spirit to the ecclesiastical ordinance—the conferral of the third member of the Godhead by the authority of the priesthood—that bestows the promise of the Spirit's companionship upon our baptism. If we make no baptismal covenant—if we consent to no religious adherence—we receive no gift, not the constancy of the Spirit at least: that is Church doctrine.

There is a strictness to this principle but also a kind of poetry to it, uniting the delicacy of heaven with what I am calling the clunkiness of religion. For, at times, the ritual facets of my religion—those awkward sacrament meeting talks, those occasionally uncouth lessons, those callings and assignments nobody wants—seem to be the only constant things that bring the Spirit into my life. As little as I love certain things about my religion, I never cease to be amazed, inspired, by the extraordinary flashes of religiously expressed divinity in seemingly ordinary lives. Perhaps these glimmers take the form of a teacher's insight into a gospel principle or a passage of scripture, or perhaps they manifest themselves in people's willingness as organized groups of women and men (dispatched by Relief Societies and priesthood quorums) to spend long hours helping a neighbor or serving in the community. Most of these spiritual manifestations are the product of the repetitive force of religious observance, which forges these glimmering traces of the divine into durable, Christ-like attributes. I see this process working on and in others and often feel awestruck by the ways it unfolds, this loud hammering of ritual practice yoked to the quiet influence of the Spirit.

It is this prospect, this hope that I too might acquire similar attributes, that redeems the Church's compulsive demands (of attention and care and tithing and patience and time, time, time). These demands, I find, become the Lord's tools for acting on me, and they do so precisely through the clunkiness I otherwise dislike. The awkwardness of religion is crucial, actually, as there is an eloquence of metaphor that speaks through it, a conversion of *this* (plain sermon or fellow congregant) into *that* (instrument and image of the divine). When these conversions occur, I find myself marveling at the sublime juxtaposition of *God* on *earth*, a union associated across Christianity with the singular event of Christ's incarnation, though registered by me, here, as a common quality of religious experience. This is the Spirit at work in human lives one covenant, ordinance, and practice at a time, time after time—the gift of the Holy Ghost bestowed, rhythmically, by way of the Church.

* * *

Louise Erdrich's 2001 novel *The Last Report on the Miracles at Little No Horse* tells of a woman, Agnes DeWitt, who spends most of her life incognito as a (male) Catholic priest on the Anishinaabe reservation. The impetus for her bold masquerade is a spiritual experience she has after being swept away in a flood on the plains. Falling unconscious and facing imminent death, Agnes awakens to find herself in a hut, dry and lying under a sheepskin cover and being fed a venison stew.

> A spoon was held to her lips. She moved toward it, lured like an animal, and she tasted a broth of meat that brought tears to her eyes. Then she saw a man's hands held the spoon and the bowl. She slid her gaze up his strong arms, his shoulders, to his broad and open face.
>
> Kindness was there, sheer kindness, a radiance from within him fell upon her and it was like a pool of warm sunlight.[3]

Once she has eaten, the man lays her back down and then lies beside her, "a very tired man who smelled of resin from the wood he'd chopped, of metal from the tools he'd used, of hay, of sweat" (43). She falls asleep, and when she awakens, she finds herself in an entirely different place, "no comfortable settler's shack, but in an empty shell of a long abandoned hovel with the wind whipping through, swallows' nests in the eaves, no sign of the man, no bowl, no track, no spoon, no sheepskin covering or blanket" (43). At that point, she understands what has happened to her, the miracle by which she has been saved: Christ's person has nurtured her back to life. "Through You, in You, with You. Aren't those beautiful words? For of course she knew her husband long before she met Him, long before He rescued her, long before He fed her broth and held Agnes close to Him all through that quiet night" (43). Converted by this encounter and drawing on a classic mystical trope of becoming the bride of Christ, she pledges her life to her savior. Shortly after, wandering the flood-ravaged lands, she finds the body and written commission of Father Damien and knows what she must do: She disguises herself in his priestly habits and assumes his identity and mission to the Anishinaabe. She becomes Christ's disciple through the medium of the church.

There are obviously several elements at work in Erdrich's novel: mysticism, the fluid nature of gender identity, relationships with and within indigenous cultures, and more. But what draws me to the novel is its protagonist's vocation—Agnes's sense of a call to religious service through a spiritual encounter with Christ. I am especially moved by the novel's portrait of Christ as caregiver, with his rough hands and hair and fragrance of resin and metal and hay and sweat. This is not the majestic, austere image in Revelation of the Messiah astride a white horse, his eyes "a flame of fire" and wearing "many crowns" (Rev. 19:11–12). Neither is it the Christ of the Gospel narratives who expounds parables and principles and inspires theology and creed. Instead, we behold here a simple laborer who shares a life with the downtrodden, attending with special care to brokenness of body and spirit, to whatever it is in Agnes that makes her so ready to seek a fuller life. It is through the rough, weathered exterior of the man's, Christ's, "broad and open face" that the divine manifests itself, heaven taking the form of a venison stew and a magnetic quality of "sheer kindness, a radiance from within . . . [that] was like a pool of warm sunlight."

The aura of this portrait is what I embrace in and about my own religion—roughness revealing an inner radiance. This, I think, is what Pratt wishes to communicate about the effects of the Holy Ghost. Those who enjoy the gifts of the Spirit are in no way superhuman, far from it. But they reflect something of the divine: They find their (modest) intellects quickened, their "natural passions" refined along with their joys and tastes; the Spirit inspires them to virtues they would likely not otherwise possess, not to that degree. While it is true that the *gift* of the Holy Ghost, as Pratt invokes it, is the fruit of a priesthood ordinance, the Church that bestows that ordinance is nothing glorious in itself. It is, rather, a vehicle for something more glorious *than* itself. It is, in effect, the potter's clay. If it were otherwise, if the Church were somehow a majestic end in itself, the radiance of what shines through it would feel less visceral, less real; there would be no dark backdrop against which that pool of warm sunlight, that still life of the Spirit, might appear.

✳ ✳ ✳

I've never seen myself as the church leader type. For most of my life, neither have other people. My father, by contrast, is a consummate church leader, loved and admired by congregations far and wide. With me, it's different. I spent the first couple decades of my adult life as the existentially overwrought dude sitting on or near the back row. I had long hair, then shorter hair but a goatee, then no goatee but a thick moustache that was a little too, well, itself. Then I was clean-shaven but refused to wear a white shirt. Then I wore white shirts but spoke in academic jargon and talked about scripture by way of philosophy. In short, I was obnoxiously, implacably idiosyncratic. Not a good follower, not to most eyes. Therefore, by tried-and-true Church logic, not a leader.

Few of us, it seems, ever feel we fully fit in. However, as I entered middle age, I blended sufficiently into an eclectic ward near downtown Salt Lake City to be called into its bishopric. And one night, dutifully fulfilling one of my new responsibilities, I sat seething through a dreadfully dull leadership meeting organized by the stake presidency.[4] It was a Wednesday in the dark, cold time of year. Like many in the room, I was stressed and overworked and resented being held hostage by presidency counselors dumping information on us that could have, should have, simply taken the form of an email (and preferably one routed to junk mail). Scout camp this and publicity about upcoming firesides that—all well and good in their way. But given my mood, it was a veritable dust bin of ecclesiastical trivia, and there was nothing in it worthy of tearing me away from my family, from my work, or from doing something more constructive and probably better for my soul. At the moment, that would have included jamming a fork into an electrical socket.

Define spiritual experience as you will; on this evening, I was *not* feeling it.

Then the stake president stood and made as thoughtful and impactful a remark as I'd heard in ages in a church meeting. He thanked us for our presence, noting that there was a lot of experienced leadership in the room. (Which was true, I thought, casting a quick glance around me. One of the bishops was a former stake, mission, and temple president; others present were former bishops; several had served in stake presidencies; and so on.) "Of course," he continued, "we all know where the Savior would be if he were here— not with us but down at the Road Home." And he paused and grew a little tearful.

The Road Home was the downtown homeless shelter. The Church had organized a branch near the Road Home and put it in our stake. The stake president was bringing attention to the fact that members of that branch presidency were not in our meeting—they were spared this particular affliction—because they were serving homeless Church members at the shelter, something they did most every evening of every week, blessing the sick and administering welfare. Doing Christian service. *Yes*, I thought, *that is where Christ would be. Not here ticking administrative boxes. He would be at the Road Home.*

A couple years later, that is precisely where I began finding myself—not as a member of that branch presidency and not (but for the grace of God) as a resident of the Road Home itself. Instead, I was now a counselor to our stake president, a calling that took me to the branch occasionally to speak, work with branch leaders, and interview members who desired a temple recommend. One night, I attended a family home evening there and met a member of the branch, a man ten-plus years my senior who sported an ascot cap and carried a complex, expressive gaze fashioned from playfulness and prolonged sorrow. After the brief lesson, he approached me to chat. I found him friendly if a little taciturn, faintly if somewhat defensively ironic: a dignified man down on his luck. And that gaze—it didn't penetrate as much as convey a kind of poetic impulse toward metaphor, a frustrated wish for conversion: of sadness into vulnerability, of loneliness into something like a shared experience of sorrow. It sought community, communion.

When I next saw him, it was in one of the wards in our stake. He'd found a job as an apartment manager and handyman, had a place to live, and was back on his feet if still figuratively limping. He was a good worker and quickly made himself a valued resource in his ward. Time passed: several months. Then one Sunday before Christmas, a year or so after we'd met, I stood in front of his priesthood quorum to sustain him and set him apart as an assistant to the high priests group leader. It was a moving experience to see hands around the room raised as a token of support for this man and then to put my own hands on his head and speak his name. While the occasion demanded that I say a few words by way of blessing, the inspiration I felt was less to speak than to listen, to absorb the Spirit's whisperings: This man was someone the Lord sustained; he was a leader in the Lord's eyes.

He became a friend in the unique way that seems only to happen at church, a brother in shared belief and commitment and love for God if not one in life experience or politics or tastes in music (What were his? Or mine for that matter?). He made it a point, always, to shake my hand before stake conference meetings, that same faintly ironic gaze expressing at once sympathy over the inflated ceremony of such gatherings and also a still deeper affection—something like what Erdrich describes as a softly radiant kindness—beneath that twinkle of unsettledness.

Time passed, again. Then, one Sunday afternoon, freighted with care over the health and hurt and future of a family member, I came across my friend as I was hustling down the church hallway to attend a meeting about which I cared comparatively little.

"How are you?" he asked, momentarily blocking my way.

I stopped moving and melted just a little. "I'm all right. Been better."

He paused and nodded, looking me searchingly in the eye as I stood there quietly. I might have elaborated, I knew; he would happily have listened. But it would have required so much energy of description, so much focused attention on something that caused me such anxiety. Where to begin? And how? And anyway, I had a meeting that was starting in about two minutes.

My friend stood in the silence, still nodding gently. Then he stepped aside. "I'll pray for you," he said, his back now to me as we resumed walking our different paths. (Same place—same church—but such different paths!)

Later in the day, I reflected on that brief exchange. It was less my friend's words than his gaze that stayed with me, that impulse toward metaphor expressing itself through it, this time wishing to convert *my* sadness into vulnerability, *my* loneliness into a shared experience of sorrow. *He's right*, I thought, *I hold things too closely; I should be more open.*

While it came from a different source, I felt a similar gaze on me again that night as I knelt in prayer.

FOUR

God Is a Poet

Why do we need literature? Certainly, there is much to admire in thoughtful, beautifully crafted narratives, poems, and plays, in gripping stories, layered characters, and poignant turns of phrase. But *need* is more intense than admiration, more desperate than mere affection. A graduate school friend and Church member once remarked to me, astutely, that if one surveys all the world's civilizations over the course of known history, one can find plenty of examples of societies that had no concept of private property or insurance industries or professional sports teams or universities or lawyers or finance capitalists or plastic surgeons (and so on and so on). But there is no example, not one, of societies that had no art. Art, apparently, is a universal human need. And that includes verbal art: literature. In that respect, literature is like religion: no society exists without it.

Let me then put my question somewhat differently: Why do religion and literature seem to need each other? Because while they are sometimes held apart in the modern world—I know plenty of religious people who read very little literature and plenty of literary scholars who are atheists—the two are mutually implicating. Imagine Christianity without the Gospel narratives of Christ, dense with such literary features as rising and falling action, protagonists and antagonists, and metaphors and paradoxes; or consider some of the lovely lyrics that grace our hymns. Literature is all through religion. And the reverse is also true. Literature is sometimes said to have usurped the place of religion in the secularizing world of the nineteenth century, to have become the focal point for our collective stories of love and loss, grace and perplexity, hope and redemption.[1] But this only displaces the religious impulse onto literature, such that the very wedge that would divide them becomes the linchpin that unites them more profoundly. If literature becomes a modern religion, then this is only to acknowledge we need them both.

But why? Let me present one thought that takes up the questions I posed in the previous chapter: What if we could live in such a way that the Spirit were always with us? Would our lives carry a new sense of purpose, of promise? Would our joys seem deeper and our sorrows, somehow, lighter? Would we feel more alive? Yes but with qualifiers: that is my experience. As Parley P. Pratt asserts, the presence of the Spirit increases our mental and emotional capacities, deepens our degree of virtue, goodness, and kindness, and even attends to our physical well-being. However, when I live more closely to the Spirit, I also become more aware of my personal failings, more mindful of my natural limitations, more conscious of the ways I curb God's influence in my life. The Spirit opens, or at least reveals, the wounds it also heals.[2] And such wounds find expression in song, in story—in literature.

But there is something else, an additional dimension to that qualified yes. The Spirit enriches how I live, but it also complicates *when* and *where* I live. By bringing more things to my remembrance, it folds the past into the present; by magnifying my spiritual gifts, it makes me a better, more developed version of myself, thus merging the present with the future. It reduces—and expands—life to its essential elements, making the world as I otherwise experience it seem a shadow of itself. When Paul writes of an experience when he found himself transported—"whether in the body, or out of the body, I cannot tell" (2 Cor. 12:3)—he is rehearsing a visionary experience. But really, he might be describing the effects of most *any* spiritual experience, all of which make us feel more alive by condensing and multiplying the effects of space and time. This seems true even of small spiritual experiences, the kind most of us have. For what is an answer to prayer or a feeling of conviction in reading a passage of scripture if not a connection between us and heaven? And, in its way, such connectedness is a literary effect.

I say this not because spiritual experiences are mere products of the imagination but because they bear a complex relation to matters of reality, truth, and meaning. The Spirit makes life more itself, which means it puts life in relation to itself: I am more—or less—myself depending on how spiritually I live. A life *more like itself*—this quality, labeled verisimilitude or trueness to life, emerged historically as an integral effect of literary narrative at the same time that modern scientific methods were being elaborated in the seventeenth and eighteenth centuries. As new ideas of factuality, or of what constitutes fact, entered the world, predicated less on philosophical reason than on experimentation in laboratories, literature evolved into a kind of virtual reality. It modeled itself on discourses of fact—on evidence and objective truth—even as it displaced itself from them. "I was born in the Year 1632, in the City of *York*, of a good Family, tho' not of that Country, my Father being a Foreigner. . . ."[3] So opens Daniel Defoe's 1719 narrative *Robinson Crusoe*, sometimes labeled the first modern novel. Defoe's readers knew that Crusoe was a fictive character, but there was an authenticity to his story, a contemporary relevance to the way he presented himself and sized up the world. Defoe's narrative was vividly lifelike, true to life. It staked a position of proximity relative to these new ways of knowing, "in but not of the world" of fact, of science. This became literature's strategic vantage point. It could mirror life in familiar ways even as it imagined new lives, new worlds into existence. If science gave us facts, literature accorded us meaning; it spoke not only to what is real but to why we care.

In the modern world, literature thus became a special sanctuary of meaning, a spiritual sanctuary. Perhaps it should not be surprising, then, that Pratt's eloquent paeans to the gifts of the Spirit parallel and anticipate claims made about literature. For, in a lesser but related way, literature is said to cultivate similar traits, stimulating the mind and stirring the heart, fostering greater empathy and thus increasing our capacity to feel and perceive. Literature helps us cultivate our sensitivity to spiritual things, opening us to new ways of thinking and feeling. This makes it an inspired medium for spiritual experiences. In some instances, like Denise Levertov's "Poetics of Faith" (see chapter 2) or Louise Erdrich's account of the conversion of "Father" Damien (see chapter 3), literature lends form to the sheer wonder of inspiration. It can sharpen our awareness of the variety and depth of spiritual feelings, expanding our appreciation and understanding of spiritual things. For this reason, literature can also act as a springboard for our own spiritual experiences, such that learning to recognize the richness of such experiences in or through literature can make us more receptive to them in the balance of life.

This brings to mind a verse of scripture often cited by members of the Church: "As all have not faith, seek ye diligently and teach one another words of wisdom; yea, seek ye out of the best books words of wisdom; seek learning, even by study and also by faith" (D&C 88:118). Discussion of this passage often hinges on what these "best books" *are*, but I am most compelled by what these books *do*. Learning from "the best books" is necessary, we read, because "all have not faith"; that is, "the best books" serve as bridges to spiritual lessons we *might* learn in some other way. The implication is that truth is diffused across our experience, with "the best books" capturing and presenting it in richer clusters, making it more apparent and appealing to us. In this respect, these books serve as surrogates for the Holy Ghost, guiding us "into all truth" and showing us "things to come" (John 16:13).

By the same token and as another passage of scripture suggests, literature can help clarify the spiritual experiences we already have. In his epistle to the Romans, Paul writes that "to be spiritually minded is life and peace" (Rom. 8:6). While many people believe this to be true, they also recognize that spiritual experiences can be elusive:

"For we know not what we should pray for as we ought: but the Spirit itself maketh intercession for us with groanings which cannot be uttered" (Rom. 8:26). That is, spiritual experiences enrich our lives, and yet, such experiences are difficult to define, let alone retain, as they sometimes "cannot be uttered" or given form. This is where literature potentially becomes a vital tool. Long imagined as a reservoir of spiritual associations (as William Wordsworth puts it, of "thoughts that do often lie too deep for tears"[4]), literature lends expression to experiences that are of ultimate value, spiritual value, but also seem set apart from the rigors of everyday life and therefore can be hard to understand. Thus, when Christ on the cross utters his plaintive cry of agony—"My God, my God, why hast thou forsaken me?" (Matt. 27:46)—he cites poetry: Psalms 22:1. Through that literary allusion, the Gospel narrative creates a set of associations for what is otherwise unfathomable. Empowering us to reflect on the unthinkable and intensifying our experience, literature makes us more human. And it makes our humanity seem more divine.

* * *

So, returning to the question with which I opened this chapter: Why do we *need* literature? Or, put somewhat differently, why does literature serve a spiritual need (for secularists as well as the deeply religious)? The answer, I believe, has something to do with the gaps we experience as a natural part of life. In their ways, and sometimes by working in conjunction with each other, literature and the Spirit bridge these gaps.

In a vignette I share in the introduction, I describe how my own need for literature emerged when I was a missionary struggling to understand the disparity, the gap, between the greatness of the gospel message and the mass indifference to it I encountered in my everyday experience as a missionary. Clearly, I was a flawed vessel for that message, but clearly, too, there was a complexity to everyday life that did not jive with the image of the gospel I proclaimed. Literature, I thought, might help me understand better, communicate better; at the very least, it might give voice to my angst. My need for literature only intensified when I returned from my mission in early summer 1988 and resumed my college education in the fall at the University of California at Irvine. My favorite class, perhaps the most influential of my life, was a year-long dramatic literature course titled "Drama as a Cultural Imperative." We read play after play, beginning with the ancient Greeks and concluding, eventually, with work from our own late twentieth century. I imbibed the spirit of the course, so much so that during the first term, and in lieu of a final essay, I wrote a short play, driven by my own personal imperatives to express something impossibly vast. From my notes:

> The protagonist is a young person who feels scared, angry, and discontented. Inertia drags him toward failure. But instead of fighting it, he begins to desire it. He feels as if he's living at the edge of a black hole, getting dragged around something that is really nothingness at its core. He wants to experience that nothingness.

It was a strange, poorly conceived piece, plotless and melodramatic. And it was not the only product of its kind. For example, a few months later, I wrote a lyric for a talk I was asked to give at church, a youthful effusion about seeking God in times of disillusionment. Literary scholars sometimes label such work "juvenilia," the immature products of an aspiring writer. I mention them because they capture what I try to describe above, my unformed articulation of raw need—of need for literature.

What is perhaps most curious about these pieces is their timing. I was fresh off a mission, back in school and loving my classes; I had a girlfriend, a car, and was renting a shack on the beach in Orange County. Life was good. But it seemed to me that something essential about it was ending; I felt as though I were falling.

What I was feeling were aftershocks of my mission, a coming-of-age experience that had vaulted me into adulthood by hurtling me, in some ways, into an existential crisis. (I remember the first few days after I returned home, jet-lagged and thus feeling myself in two time zones and also two age zones: twenty-one but out of step with my peers. It took me a while to find my bearings—not just where I was but who.) This was a dilemma of language as much as life. I had not only experienced exotic places but had felt things I could not fully describe or explain—like my love for God, my feeling of his for me and others, and my conviction, born of that love, concerning our divine natures. At the same time, I was beginning to formulate impressions that had accrued on my mission, impressions I did not yet fully understand: "God is not here: not yet, not ever"; "It is terrible to be left so alone." Why these dour words? Where did they come from? They seemed, indeed were, out of step with the love I felt for and from God. They expressed deflated expectation, a sense of defeat and disillusionment. But why?

It was difficult to see it at the time—indeed, I needed literature in the first place because I could not see it—but in effect, these words amounted to impressionistic responses to the gospel message I had been tasked to carry. Nobody had spoken them directly to me: no person I had contacted on the street or on whose door I had knocked. Nevertheless, they encompassed me as a collective voice of unbelief and flat rejection, a less prosaic version of "Non, monsieur, ça ne m'intéresse pas." For most people I talked to, God was not there; they felt themselves to be truly, existentially alone. Almost traumatically, I found myself channeling their experience. In that way, I felt caught between important clusters of words, some I could not adequately articulate (like what it meant, ecstatically, to know that God lived), and others I was only beginning to understand (like what it meant, beguilingly, to experience through others the opposite reality). I thus approached literature, the art of difficult saying and layered understanding, as a spiritual need.

More important than whatever juvenilia I produced, I began reading actual literature. Not just the texts I had discovered, a little naughtily, as a missionary (as reading such books bent the mission rules): work by Camus, Sartre, and Jean Cocteau (I *loved* Jean Cocteau!). Now I was also reading Dostoevsky, the Brontës, and Nietzsche (I *loved* and *hated* Nietzsche!). And in my year-long theater course, Aeschylus, Sophocles, and Euripides. And so much more. I eventually changed my major from drama to English. I lost my teen aspiration to be an actor. And slowly, over years and decades, I began finding the words for my experience, my conversion—for that two-year adventure and crisis that had opened me irreversibly to God and to the things of the Spirit and to an experience of the world. And, therefore, to literature.

* * *

Levertov's poem "Caedmon" eloquently, illustratively explores how spiritual experience and literature open onto each other, inform each other, are practically born from the same impulse. It rehearses the story of the composer of a short but famous seventh-century English hymn. Caedmon was an illiterate cowherd who, one night, had a dream in which an angel visited him and gave him a song about the creation. It turns out that Caedmon had a gift, and after monks at the monastery where Caedmon tended cattle taught him the history of the Christian church, he composed many more songs. Levertov's poem is self-reflexive, meaning that it is a poem about the writing of poetry. Caedmon is the poem's speaker, recounting for us the episode that explains how he acquired his gift—hence, and likewise for Levertov, how we see the poem before us. What is spiritual about the poem is thus, on its surface, the sheer existence of the poem itself, for it is the product of an angelic visitation, of inspiration.

But the poem also accentuates features of spiritual experience more broadly. Take careful note, for example, of the poem's form as well as its content.

All others talked as if
talk were a dance.
Clodhopper I, with clumsy feet
would break the gliding ring.
Early I learned to
hunch myself close by the door:
then when the talk began
I'd wipe my
mouth and wend
unnoticed back to the barn
to be with the warm beasts,
dumb among body sounds
of the simple ones.[5]

Levertov's use of free verse here is distinctive if understated; if heard rather than seen, little marks it as poetry as there are few rhymes and only delicate uses of alliteration among the enjambed lines. With subtle exceptions (e.g., "gliding ring"), this is poetry that sounds like colloquial speech, underscored by small, folksy details (like the use of inelegant words like "Clodhopper"[6]).

From here, however, the poem grows more vibrantly poetic and then, suddenly, even more so, ecstatically so:

I'd see by a twist
of lit rush the motes
of gold moving
from shadow to shadow
slow in the wake
of deep untroubled sighs.
The cows
munched or stirred or were still. I
was at home and lonely,
both in good measure. Until
the sudden angel affrighted me—light effacing

> my feeble beam,
> a forest of torches, feathers of flame, sparks upflying:
> but the cows as before
> were calm, and nothing was burning
>   nothing but I, as that hand of fire
> touched my lips and scorched my tongue
> and pulled my voice
>   into the ring of the dance.
>   (ll. 15–33)

The poem flags itself as poetry with the delicate image of the "lit rush," the candlelight's glow illuminating dust motes against the deep shadows of the stalls. But then, with the appearance of the angel, a different poem breaks out: the lines burst across the page, marked by two dramatic indentations; alliteration breaks into the lines ("a forest of torches, feathers of flame, sparks upflying"), as does Biblical allusion (with the hand of fire touching the poet's lips, evoking a prophetic call [see Isaiah 6]). This is metaphor at more than a linguistic level, with angels mixing with humans, "poetry" and colloquial speech folding into each other, and past (the time of the actual vision) compounding itself with present (in the recreation of that vision in the poem). Relatedly, "the cows as before / were calm"; the spiritual experience is had by the poet alone, meaning that this is more a conversion narrative than a messianic one: it comes to one person, not to all living creatures. Nevertheless, spiritual experience changes us, the poem suggests, with the formal transformations in the poem reflecting that personal dynamism. These changes render Caedmon capable of literature even as it is the poem's literary features—the subtle shifts of language and form—that reveal Caedmon's conversion, his spiritual metamorphosis.

In "Caedmon," Levertov portrays spiritual experience and literature as mutually generative.[7] The former is the origin of the latter—an angelic visitation makes Caedmon capable of poetry—but literature is also what makes spiritual experience communicable. For, minus the "literary" features of the poem, the dynamic uses of language, we would have no way to understand Caedmon's experience, according us less understanding of spiritual experience generally. In effect, and as we witness here, God inspires poetry, but poetry explains the ways of God. Paraphrasing John Milton, poetry justifies the ways of God to humankind.[8] Including illiterate cowherds. And overwrought returned missionaries.

*　*　*

That *we* need literature is an anthropological truism. The realization that *I* need literature was a cumulative epiphany whose full realization only dawned on me once I had returned from my mission and was back in school. But the seeds of that epiphany were laid during my time in France. And one episode in particular stayed with me for years.

I was serving in Riom, an ancient walled town ten miles outside Clermont-Ferrand in the center of France. I had very much imagined my mission as a journey (with a defined beginning and end and a protracted, symbolically potent middle—who, over the course of two years, would God reveal himself to be? And who would he reveal *me* to be?) and had come to a crucial point in the narrative. I had one month left to serve and was reconciling myself to the reality that whatever happened over the last few weeks, there would be nothing substantively different during that time from what I had experienced during the preceding twenty-three months. No new cities or companions or assignments, no dramatic increase in my understanding of French or the scriptures or the gospel. Maybe we would find a potential convert, but we weren't going to convert the nation. No, what I had experienced already in everyday missionary life was just about all there was. I was living the consequences of choices I had made (yes and then no to positions of leadership; no and then yes to reading literary texts in an effort to try to understand "the world" around me) and was distilling the meaning of my mission down to a few basic themes.

And what were these themes? Chiefly, there were two. The first involved the abundance of inspiration: God was all around us, in and through our work. I felt blessed by God's presence every day: directed, filled, and changed. But the second, enigmatically, concerned the tangential relationship between that abundance and material circumstance. Spiritual blessings, I was realizing, did not always translate into measurable outcomes. For how many times—*how many?*—had I felt impressed to talk to a particular individual, knock on doors in a particular neighborhood, or share a particular thought, story, or scripture in a lesson? And how many times had that inspiration failed to produce any tangible result? But it was rarely failed inspiration, not entirely. Because God is a poet. And he had always managed to convert the emptiness of my experience—"*Non, monsieur, ça ne m'intéresse pas*"—into something meaningful, some sign of his love: perhaps something I learned, perhaps an important memory I made. Minus these redemptive qualities, my experience would have been merely disillusioning. With them, it was. . . complicated. Frustrating but lifechanging. Sanctifying, if hard to explain. Poetically true.

But now I had been a missionary for twenty-three months, and it was spring, and the days were growing longer in more ways than one. At the end of one of them, my companion and I were plodding back into the center of town, heading toward our apartment in our six-hundred-year-old building after knocking on doors all day in a new subdivision outside Riom's city walls. We had chatted with kind people over the past several hours; some were people of faith, and many others doubtlessly lived good lives. Predictably, however, we had had no tangible success: no substantive gospel discussions, nobody interested in reading the Book of Mormon or learning about the plan of salvation or hearing the message of the Restoration. Nobody interested in talking about God at all, really. As the day drew to a close, we were weary, and on this day especially, I was flat worn out. Emotionally and spiritually spent. Exhausted by nearly two years of rejection, of irrelevance, of the ridiculous American-in-white-shirt-and-name-badge routine. Nobody took us seriously, and why should they? The rhythms of everyday life in France, or anywhere else, were so powerful, so pulsating, so insistent—who could hear the delicate, counter-rhythmic spiritual meter, the gospel cadence, occasionally lilting above our halting French?

The answer, effectively, was nobody. Not when conveyed by chatty YSAs like us at least.[9] And I didn't blame them: I felt trapped by the absurdity of my missionary identity, constrained by the awkward version of the gospel message we were tasked to peddle with its schematic, sales-pitch-caliber brush-bys of profound concepts and narratives. Christ's atonement in thirty seconds; the First Vision in two sentences: it would take more than a lifetime to fully grasp these things, let alone express them meaningfully. I wasn't searching for a different gospel, but wow, did I ever desire a different way of communicating its message—one that merged more seamlessly with the actual lives of real people, one that spoke in their own language (not French but something more artful and divine: the language of the Spirit). I wanted the tongue of angels (see Alma 29), and I couldn't find it. In the words of Levertov's Caedmon, "Clodhopper I, with clumsy feet."

I brooded often over all this. Brooded, raged. It seemed incongruous with the drama surrounding my decision of whether to serve a mission. I had sacrificed what my youthful, all-too-youthful mind saw as a glamorous opportunity, and I had been hoping to witness some affirmation of that sacrifice while in France, some clear manifestation of why I was there. Instead, day after day, month after month, I confronted the insignificance of my words, the purposelessness of my presence, the emptiness of my imagined sacrifice—and, apparently, the hollowness of my message. The incongruity, the irony, stung. And that pain was spilling over in my letters home, in my reports to the mission president, in my conversations with other missionaries (some of whom—generous listeners—were saintly beyond their years). And on this evening, it was shooting into my mind and heart and field of vision as we trudged back into town, the lurid sun dropping luridly over the lurid, medieval skyline.

But then, as we passed the train station, we saw an older gentleman crossing the street. His appearance was at once singular and utterly emblematic. Short and squat, wearing a shoddy suit and shabby old fedora, he seemed the personification of the old town in the old country, the perfect complement to the old missionary (yours truly) whose spirits were sinking into the old soil saturated with old, old— ancient, unmet—human cares. And as it happened, he was carrying two worn suitcases, no wheels.

My companion and I glanced at each other and veered in the man's direction. We were destined to make a "contact," although, clearly, there would be nothing reportable here in the numbers we charted weekly for our mission president: no gospel discussion, no copy distributed of the Book of Mormon. Certainly, there would be no convert baptism. Naturally—converts were the infinitesimally small exceptions to the general rule, the universal law, of public indifference. But that evening in particular, I was bursting with frustration at the nonsense of such accountability metrics, of their emptiness in a country in which nobody gave a damn. So why should I give one when it came to the normative missionary calculations that so frequently directed our attention? I wanted a different form of expression? How about simple Christian service? We were young, and this gentleman was not; he was carrying suitcases, and we were not.

Much of my mission, of course, was devoted to precisely such acts of service. What set this episode apart for me was not the desire to do a good deed but the backdrop of my thought process in that moment, my frustration at the very auspice of my presence in that place. I had been called to find, teach, and baptize. Allegedly. But there was seemingly nobody to be found, nobody to teach, and nobody to baptize. So I was there for nothing. *Rien* in Riom.[10] Therefore, I could reject my very reason for being. For being a missionary at least.

All this roiled through my mind as we approached the man and offered him a hand. He stopped, turned to face us, broke into a wide grin, and raised both arms. "No, that's okay," he said (in French), "these bags aren't heavy. There's nothing in them!" We all gazed at each other a moment in blank amusement, perhaps at the image of our collective strangeness there on the street corner: two conspicuous young Americans and an old French dandy. Then the man's countenance grew more serious, and something happened inside me. My fevered mind cooled; the world fell still; the sunset behind him morphed into a kind of nimbus, a halo. "You're missionaries, aren't you?" We nodded, a little surprised, as we were the first missionaries—of the Church of Jesus Christ of Latter-day Saints at least—to serve in that old city. He furrowed his brow, and he half-turned and gestured toward the horizon: "You young men have a great work to do. The world is growing darker, more evil. And you're here to help change that. See that you proceed with dignity and honor."

A little more than a month later, I would be standing at the pulpit of my ward building back home in suburban San Diego. In fact, I gave my homecoming talk three times in three wards: our stake had returned missionaries take their talks on the road. And I told the usual stories about people who had inspired me and blessings I had received and baptisms I had witnessed. But I concluded my talk with the story of my encounter with the old man. That experience had moved me with particular force. I did not quite know how to say it yet, but its message was essentially this: God is a poet. And because he is a poet, his word and ways radiate promise. In the name of Jesus Christ, amen.

What had so moved me about our brief and eccentric conversation with that old man? It wasn't what he had said, not exactly. And it was nothing outward and obvious; as Levertov puts it, "the cows as before / were calm." But I was "burning" with vision. In an instant, I saw something more clearly.

The old man had turned back to us and smiled again, thanking us. We shook hands, and he turned and lumbered away. The month that followed, the last of my mission, passed mostly uneventfully. I recall walking around the town talking with people and heading occasionally into the larger nearby city of Clermont-Ferrand to attend church and our weekly mission district meetings. I recall writing a couple more letters home, the usual fare: philosophical, impassioned, maybe a little unhinged. I recall staying up late reading French poems, plays, and novels, dim neon drizzling through our top-floor window. I recall dragging my poor companion into a couple museum exhibits (Riom had received the French designation City of Art and History: *Ville d'Art et d'Histoire*). And one vivid experience I recount in this book's concluding chapter.

But these things blur. Because that old man's words spoke to me so profoundly that it mostly consumes in memory the weeks that followed. "You young men have a great work to do": It was cinematic, really, the old man playing the part of a wizard (a Gandalf or Dumbledore), imparting wisdom that was a little empty and hollow but deeply moving for all that. It struck me as more intimate, more meaningful than any desire he might have expressed to know more about our message. Why? As I've thought about it over the years, I think there were two reasons. First, the vision of a world "growing darker, more evil," with young missionaries riding into town to save the day, fit so perfectly a myth nurtured by teenage fantasy as well as, to a degree, Church doctrine: "Yea, every knee shall bow, and every tongue confess before [Christ]" (Mosiah 27:31). I saw myself, or wanted to see myself, in that myth, that grand story expressing the effects of Christ's imminent, majestic arrival. Just as importantly, on that bright evening, someone else seemed to see me in it.

But second, I felt seen from an utterly unique place of vision. Not from the viewpoint of members in the branches in which I served and not from the perspective of family and friends back home sending letters of encouragement. Bless all of them; I will be eternally grateful for their support. But these words spoken by this old man came from out of the heart of the place I was serving, from out of the depths of France itself. What he said possessed, for me, symbolic significance: it wasn't about that particular moment on that street corner or about the needs of any single individual behind any of the doors on which we had knocked. Rather, he seemed to be speaking about *all* moments and *all* people—a culmination of all things, all impressions from my mission, or (as I imagined it) from any mission. All of us part of the same world, all of us waiting for Something, Someone, greater than ourselves. In that respect, his words felt bigger than any of the myths I cherished, any of the identities to which I clung. To me, they expressed an almost visionary perception of the greatness of God and of a future when all human contingencies and absurdities—when life's pulsating, deafening rhythms in France or anyplace else—would find themselves swept away, carried up, resolved—redeemed—in a grand orchestration of divine history. By implication, such a transcendent history had been slowly unfolding all along even when I couldn't see it through the drudgery of knocking on doors.

It was a vision, a conviction, that had played at the back of my mind my entire mission. And if my sense of divine history was illusory, juvenilia in its own right, it was nevertheless stirring, calling to me in such a distinctive, primordial way. It reminded me that, contrary to appearances, I was not a missionary for the purpose of finding, teaching, and baptizing. No, I recalled (feeling myself transported back to that life-changing moment in the bishop's office more than two years earlier), I was a missionary because it seemed to please God. And whether it led me to converts or to "*Non, monsieur, ça ne m'intéresse pas,*" God's way is truth. And greater things than all this—all the realized and broken dreams, all the fulfilled and dashed expectations, all the wonder and ineffable absurdity of our humanity—awaited all of us.

God's angel, it seemed, had spoken to me from out of the heart of France. And he pulled me, like Caedmon, into a new kind of dance: my future as a serious student of literature was probably born at that moment. Because God animates religion, but God is also a creator, a poet in the broadest, most dynamic sense.[11] And in this instance, or so it seemed, he had employed his infinite creativity to speak not from the Church (from his representatives, his missionaries) to the world but from the world to the Church, to me. He was Lord over all creation, and if I looked closely enough and listened carefully enough—if I learned to read, spiritually, between the lines—then I could catch that divine vision, hear that celestial chorus, from any corner of it. I could speak to it and it to me: a communion of souls united in Christ.

As a missionary, I carried an important message to the world, but the world, personified in that old man, also carried an important message to me. In that moment, I felt, I knew, that the Restoration of the gospel and the coming of Christ were greater than anything I could yet conceive in my narrow religious imagination. And so, I needed to learn more, to see and hear and feel more—to become a better, deeper reader—if I were to discern more of God's beguiling and enchanting and breathtaking—poetic—word.

* * *

I saw that old man once more. It was back at the train station. This time, laden with my own suitcases (and memories and trove of indelible impressions), I was piling onto the train bound for Geneva and the mission home. My time was complete. I found a seat and gazed out the window at my companion. He seemed a little forlorn, a little envious. Just up the platform stood the old man. Same clothes, no suitcases. Neither boarding nor alighting, just standing there. We made eye contact as the train pulled away.

FIVE

Of Campfires
and Canyon Breezes

My scholarly life always felt like a vocation more than a simple professional choice. The practical details of that life—How far did I need
to pursue my education? Where? By what rules, spoken and unspoken, does the profession operate?—only dawned on me little by little
and usually later than they should have. Eventually, those details
threatened to become all-consuming, leading to what I described in
the introduction as the strange prayers I would utter about obscure
subjects—subjects important, I'm sure, only to me and, it seemed, a
most long-suffering, gentle, and kind God. A spiritual memoir like this
one, addressing my sense of vocation more directly, thus represents
a return to my origins.

These origins, however, are complex. In the beginning, especially
in the months and years that followed my mission, my unformulated,
unrealized life path felt unconscious and almost compulsive—a raw
expression of spiritual needs I struggled and often failed to understand.
It was in the early throes of that chapter of life that a decisive event
occurred. It was a small thing, but I recall it vividly. It was 1988, and
I was in the bookstore of the University of California at Irvine, back

in school after two-plus years as a missionary in France. I was standing in the philosophy section holding a copy of Friedrich Nietzsche's *Thus Spoke Zarathustra*. One of my professors, a dynamic teacher and an atheist—he performed the one and made sure we understood the other—loved the story of the decline of religious belief. Nietzsche was his favorite author and *Zarathustra* his favorite book. And here it was in my hands: the summit of human understanding, or so my professor made it seem. I opened the book and read a paragraph or two, then dropped it back on the shelf. The tone was outrageously blasphemous, the subject matter strange: a set of extended, anti-Christian parables. But Nietzsche's style was magnetic; I couldn't walk away. The book held me transfixed: Eve before the tree of knowledge, the serpent hissing in the background. So I picked the book back up, opened to a new page, read some more, then put it back down. And so it went for a long time: thirty minutes probably, maybe forty-five.

I eventually walked away, and as I did, I experienced a familiar spiritual feeling. Members of the Church sometimes describe it as warm and fuzzy, but it's more nuanced than that. It involves a peculiar kind of heat, like a campfire. For me, at least, the warmth of this fire feels intimate, personal, and yet seems born from someplace outside myself. It is moral and reflective—and therefore cognitive—as much as emotional. Usually prompted by present circumstances, this warmth also often carries with it layers of past associations (this occasion reminds me of another, which reminds me of another. . .), such that it almost seems to condense time, rendering individual life moments virtually eternal. The feeling is at once personal and universal, centering and ecstatic, *here* and *everywhere*; you lose yourself in it even as you seem to find yourself through it. By the time I was twenty-one and standing in the UCI bookstore, I had come to associate this feeling with God's Spirit and had learned to do so while living in a crucible far from home. That is what my mission experience had felt like to me: a crucible, a refiner's fire.

Walking away from that book was one of the last times the returned missionary prevailed over the budding scholar. And the victory, if that is what it was, was short-lived: I returned a few days later and purchased it. The feeling that next time was still spiritual but different—not warmth and light exactly but not confusion or a "stupor of thought" either. It was more like a breeze wafting in from a distant canyon, tingling the skin and carrying an enchanting fragrance of dark earth and deep pine. It did not convey divine approval as much as something like a gentle smile and perhaps a slight shrug as if to say, "So, this is how it is to be. Well, all right."

Leaving the bookstore that second time, my backpack heavier by one book, the world seemed to grow much larger. And my place in it felt much less defined.

* * *

The world is charged with the grandeur of God.
   It will flame out, like shining from shook foil;
   It gathers to a greatness, like the ooze of oil
Crushed. Why do men then now not reck his rod?
Generations have trod, have trod, have trod;
   And all is seared with trade; bleared, smeared with toil;
   And wears man's smudge and shares man's smell: the soil
Is bare now, nor can foot feel, being shod.

And, for all this, nature is never spent;
   There lives the dearest freshness deep down things;
And though the last lights off the black West went
   Oh, morning, at the brown brink eastwards, springs—
Because the Holy Ghost over the bent
   World broods with warm breast and with ah! bright wings.[1]

Gerard Manley Hopkins's 1877 sonnet "God's Grandeur" is a tour de force of religious poetry. Its first eight lines set forth a general condition that divine glory suffuses the world, though most of humankind, bludgeoned by compulsions toward subsistence ("Generations have trod, have trod, have trod"), cannot sense it. Recapitulating the classical structure of a sonnet, the concluding six lines then pose a solution to this problem. And it is a spiritual solution: ". . . the Holy Ghost over the bent / World broods with warm breast and with ah! bright wings." The poem attests to the Spirit's presence both propositionally as a straightforward assertion and also pyrotechnically through a range of galvanizing linguistic effects: alliteration (or repetitive sound: "It gathers to a greatness"; "all is seared . . . bleared, smeared"), homonyms (words having two or more definitions: "The world is *charged* with the grandeur of God," meaning filled with a current or else commanded; "And, for all this, nature is never *spent*," meaning exhausted or else consumed, depleted), metaphors ("the bent / World"), energetic similes ("*like* shining from shook foil"; "*like* the ooze of oil"), metrical variation (each line modulating its stressed syllables to accentuate particular words and images), and enjambment (absence of end-line punctuation, as in the figure of "the ooze of oil / Crushed"—an emblem of Christ sweating blood in Gethsemane). Such rhetorical devices enliven the poem, enabling it to signify in multiple registers, almost multiple dimensions. The poem itself is as "charged," as dense with meaning, as the world over which "the Holy Ghost . . . / broods" watchfully, carefully, "and with ah! bright wings."

It would be a few years before I would discover Hopkins's poem. When I did, I loved it; I shared the poet's vision of a world overfull with a sense of the divine. At twenty-one, however, I was essentially flipping the poem's order: where "God's Grandeur" moves from problem to solution, I was taking leave from the solution—the gospel I had preached as a missionary, the reputed answer to our biggest questions—to a deeper examination of a world "charged" but also "seared . . . bleared, smeared . . . [and] smudge[d]," a world beset with problems and largely insensitive to the presence of God. This was, comparatively, the world of Nietzsche's Zarathustra. *Thus Spoke Zarathustra* lends elaborate expression to Nietzsche's famous assertion that "God is dead." God was not dead for me, not ever. But certain conceptions I held of God needed to die. This realization had been dawning on me for some time. I had a deep conviction of the kindness of God, the goodness of God but felt impressed that I also needed to become more comfortable with the greatness of God, the vastness of God. I had grown accustomed to approaching God seeking answers; now I needed to attend to the abiding mystery, the darkened corners, in the answers I received. I loved the light of the gospel, but I needed to learn how to dwell in divine shadow.

By "divine shadow," I mean defining aspects of our experience that can help us better appreciate who God is but that defy reduction to familiar representations of God's blessing. For example, the covenant to "mourn with those that mourn" (Mosiah 18:9) acquires different meaning after one has sought God in the depths of one's own abiding grief. (Such grief may make us better able to "comfort those that stand in need of comfort" and even "stand as witnesses of God" in powerful ways. But as many people learn, the cost for acquiring such capacities can be staggering.) Likewise, spiritual questions that routinely direct the lives of believers—Is this good? Is it right? Is it true?—carry a more haunting sound amid the echo of other questions that evoke more somber life circumstances: How could this happen? What does it all mean? Why hast thou forsaken me?

These questions, my own and others', had been forming in me for some time. And in some ways, I had it easy compared with many who face serious questions today. When I resumed my life as a college student after my mission, there was no internet teeming with information that assaulted my faith. We were still many years away from social media, so I was not bombarded with tales of how people had felt liberated leaving the Church. I have usually found these tales to be more complex and less triumphant than they often appear, but the loudspeaker effect of social media would have made it harder to parse their implications (including their hidden conflicts), and it would have made my own struggles to stay in the Church more painful. I would have felt even more lonely and misunderstood, more unappreciated or at least underappreciated by those outside as well as inside the Church.

As it was, the questions that began forming at the edges of my mind possessed an existential gravity that was the negative corollary of the dazzling wonder of inspiration. Our most difficult, most painful questions also bespeak the divine, but they are often born not of light but shadow. They are probably best categorized under the heading of theodicy, the probing of reasons for the existence of suffering and evil. During my twenties, I began feeling hit especially hard when friends (or friends of friends) grieved, or when I learned that classmates or members of my religious community were former victims of abuse and were dealing with its long-term consequences (including destructive habits), or when I considered the social and emotional (let alone physical) effects of disability, or when faithful members of my ward sought blessings of healing but appeared bereft of divine assistance. I felt stung by prospects of friends and acquaintances who were lonely, or felt betrayed, or who shouldered the daily burden of clinical depression with no relief in sight.

Perhaps all this suffering was a series of divinely orchestrated trials designed to sanctify the valiant. Just as likely, it was simply random, a function of our habitat in a world conducive to our subsistence if not our comfort. I would often reflect on the day, a year or two earlier, when a branch mission leader had arranged for a local radio station to interview my mission companion and me. The station was near the center of town, Christmas was almost upon us, and as we drove away after the interview, I gazed out over holiday shoppers and made a brief calculation. What if the mission president brought all two hundred missionaries scattered through central and southeastern France into this smallish city? What if our mission reached its baptismal goal for the year (something like two hundred convert baptisms) and all the new members lived in this one city? In place of a branch, the city would have a thriving ward. But that ward would still represent a small minority of the local citizens, an even tinier portion of the inhabitants of the region, and an infinitesimal fraction of the people in my huge mission area. What then did key doctrines of the restored gospel (the plan of salvation, Christ's sacrifice, ordinances and covenants, principles of good living) mean relative to the mass of humanity? If God was God of the whole earth and if the Restoration was central to his plan, why did the things that supposedly matter most count (literally, *count*) for so little—a few needles scattered randomly among an endless field of haystacks?

These were the kinds of questions born by canyon breezes, a silent God gazing on through the darkness. Responses I felt to these questions seemed to be variations on Christ's injunction to "come and see" with the further instruction, "but you may need to hold your gaze a long time—for years, maybe a lifetime. Perhaps longer." Motivated by my mission experience in a largely post-Christian nation—and now, as a college student, by my education in ways the secular world believed God to be dead—I wanted to understand not what it meant to know truths that others didn't (the religious equivalent of a secret—which church is true?) but rather what it means to find God in a world where he also, effectively, is no longer there—where his spirit "broods," as in Hopkins's poem, but is barely recognized as such. Like the men on the road to Emmaus, I wanted to feel my heart burn within me even as I mourned. Or like Mary Magdalene outside the tomb, I wanted to encounter the living Christ in a world where it only seemed possible to believe in gardeners.

I wanted to understand how God could so love the world, this world, that he gave his only begotten son. I wanted to experience something like redemption. And for that, I needed to feel the canyon breeze as well as the campfire.

* * *

During that next phase of life, whose traces still linger with me, my living faith entwined itself around an abiding sense of faith crisis. But by "crisis," I do not mean an assault on my faith as much as a series of transformations of it, new perspectives that added dimensions to it, deepened it, draped shadows from it. Literature emerged as a vital mediator (and sometimes a metaphor) of this relationship, one obtaining less between faith and doubt than between seeing and understanding, the former usually outstripping the latter. While I fought *Zarathustra* all the way through, scrawling notes of protest in the margins, I tacitly assented to one of Nietzsche's core tenets that literature is a unique and important vehicle for seeing. For literature is composed of words, but it is also a remarkable instrument of silence and shadow, of what is new and unfamiliar. It cultivates *poetic* faith, temporarily suspending our anxieties of not knowing. Trafficking in fabricated plots, characters who never lived, and phrases too achingly precise to apply to any contexts other than the poems in which we find them, literature is at once hyper-attuned to everyday life and seemingly indifferent to it. It affords new vistas and new feelings more readily than conventional wisdom or moral platitudes. Literature can be *like* life, but it also renders life in newly vibrant forms, dislodging us from our preconceptions by showing us that things might and perhaps always will be more various and complex than we had thought. Situations—creations—multiply endlessly. Literature is thus life otherwise; it makes us attentive to what is not present as much as to what is, to what still might be as much as to what has been.

At a certain point in Western history, this kind of regenerative activity began to seem the necessary counterpoint to the mess Western thought and civilization had made of things. Nietzsche, a philosopher, cast his magnum opus in literary form ("When Zarathustra was thirty years old he left his home and the lake of his home and went into the mountains": the book's opening sentence[2]) partly because he wished to convey his ideas in a livelier way and partly because literature represented a departure from a universe of dead thinking. *Zarathustra*, Nietzsche's parable about a world made new when God expired, struck me as the perverse cousin of the restorative vision proclaimed by Joseph Smith.

In its way, the Restoration of the gospel is a profoundly literary event, one that punctures the horizon of secular expectation and renders our lives more complex by reminding us that they defy conventional experience. God lives; we are here by choice; the atonement of Jesus Christ makes possible the full realization of our potential as children of Heavenly Parents: In the spirit of literature, the truths of the Restoration too present life otherwise. And yet, or for that very reason—because the Restoration is ever new, because there is still so much more to be revealed, because we only ever know a fraction of all that is true—it compels us to live not only with what we understand but also with all that we do not. It conveys God's shadows as well as his light. To participate more fully in it, we thus need to learn to see, hear, think, and feel more deeply; to sit a little less anxiously with what we cannot know or with what we will only come to know over time; to wait in stillness as the principles by which we live acquire greater depth. In short, we must cultivate richer spiritual sensibilities.

Such sensibilities come in myriad forms as there is a virtually infinite array of spiritual gifts. Some attune us to God's silence as well as his speech. These gifts in particular—of patience, endurance, compassion, and the desire to learn, to *see*—can help us recognize how the Restoration sits between two poles, one representing the clarity of God's instruction and the other his silent gaze as we scramble to put into practice the principles he knows we barely understand. If we can develop these sensibilities, these spiritual gifts—if we can grow comfortable with God's speech and with his silent, gentle gaze—then we may be shaken, but we will not be devastated, incapacitated, when we learn of unsettling chapters in Church history, or when loved ones leave the Church, or when our prayers seem to go unanswered. For silence and shadow, we will know, are also vital modes of divine communication, a reminder that understanding happens slowly on an eternal timescale. It will remind us that when we encounter silence as an answer to prayer, we may be finally asking questions big enough or facing situations complex enough to merit from God the respect of a sigh, a nod of empathy, a renewed promise of grace. This alone can reassure us that, with his help, we can handle this—that we've got this.

* * *

Lord, I can handle this; I've got this. Brazenly, and perhaps a little deludedly, that was my attitude when I began reading *Thus Spoke Zarathustra*, embarking on a spiritual journey that would lead less through the well-lit neighborhoods of Sunday School answers than along dark, starry roads on the back side of mountainous existential questions. How can we know whether the Book of Mormon is true? How are we blessed when we heed the counsel of Church leaders? How may we best serve those who stand in need? These were questions, posed in Church lessons, that informed my religious life, and I kept them close by me. But the questions that captured my imagination, that truly called to me, were more like these: What are the long-term consequences of suffering? What does it mean to live in, to endure, God's silence? What happens when you outlive old truths?

Like Joseph Smith, albeit to a lesser degree, I believed the Lord could answer all my questions. And as I look back over the scrawl in my copy of *Zarathustra*, I'm taken with how naïve I was, how little I understood, but also with how I seemed to grasp at least some of what was most important. The book opens with the title character ascending into the mountains, spending ten years there, then finding he longs once more for company. As he descends into a forest, he encounters an old man, a saint, who recognizes Zarathustra as a disruptive force. Ten years earlier, the saint reminds Zarathustra, "You carried your ashes to the mountains; would you now carry your fire into the valleys? Do you not fear to be punished as an arsonist?" When Zarathustra replies that he is leaving his sanctuary because he loves humankind, the saint replies, "Man is for me too imperfect a thing. Love of man would kill me." Instead, and from his sequestered state, the saint makes and sings songs. "And when I make songs I laugh, cry, and hum: thus I praise God." The two then separate good-naturedly. "But when Zarathustra was alone he spoke thus to his heart: 'Could it be possible? The old saint in the forest has not heard anything of this, that *God is dead!*'"[3]

Nietzsche's point is easy to see: religious thinking, personified by the saint, has grown old and hoary; it no longer speaks to what is most pressing in our experience and, in fact, is fundamentally misguided in some of its core assumptions about life and the world. But my returned missionary self was outraged: "A hollow conception of God,"

I etched in the margin. And across the top of that page, "Zarathustra has no depth; he merely presents the obvious plan of an already existent emptiness."

The notes are naïve but canny. "Zarathustra has no depth": I did not yet know it, but late in his career, Nietzsche would outline an influential philosophy of surfaces, eschewing depth in favor of appearance. And the "already existent emptiness"—that is one of the premises that made Nietzsche so focal to later existentialist philosophers like Jean-Paul Sartre: In the absence of inherent meaning, confronting emptiness all around us in an expanding universe, we must create what is (or counts as) true and good. "A hollow conception of God": yes, and that is why I was drawn to the book in the first place as it articulated the flip side of what most beguiled me. For me, God's shadow was a sign of depth, his silence a form of speech, but for many, I knew, divine shadow and silence represented absence—nobody and nothing there.

These views of Nietzsche's seemed profoundly wrong to me. But what I perceived as a lapse in his thought nevertheless gave powerful expression to a prevailing idea, to a general mood—to the strange echo of silence breezing darkly from out of the depths of the canyon.

SIX

On Gaps and Defamiliarization... but Mostly Gaps

On the corner of Cherry Street and Vine,
the dump truck operator notices my son
and me watching from the sidewalk,
invites us to climb in the cab for a ride.
My four-year-old helps push the levers
up and down, observing how the shovel
digs up dirt and rocks, metal teeth grinding
the hard red earth, widening and deepening the hole.
My daughter passed when she was about your son's age,
the man says, suddenly. *Leukemia. A fighter.*
They have the same light brown hair.
Then he changes the subject, points out the pedals,
how one pedal makes the truck move forward,
and the other makes it stop.[1]

Anya Krugovoy Silver seems never to have wanted to write her poem "Pedals." At fourteen lines and with a thematic break, or volta, between the first eight lines and the concluding six (when the truck operator mentions his daughter), the poem resembles a sonnet. But by refusing the classical rhyme schemes associated with the sonnet—for that matter, by employing several enjambed lines in the octet—the poem almost effaces itself: the language is conversational, prosaic, metrically irregular, rarely overtly "poetic." What is more, the poem outwardly occupies itself with such banal subjects as the everyday care of an energetic young child and unremarkable information about a truck's mechanical system. The poem courts boredom.

But, of course, these intentionally bland features offset the startling disclosure that the truck operator's young daughter died of leukemia and that his gesture of kindness to an excited boy doubles as an act of mourning. The italicized lines fracture the poem—and render it meaningful. On that point, the collection of poems in which "Pedals" appears, *Second Bloom*, is preoccupied with the poet's own terminal cancer diagnosis. Knowing that the poet died the year following her volume's publication and that we are reading a mother's anxieties about her son as she herself faces the grave, we suddenly find the poem dense with import. The tensions in its form—its self-erasures and abrupt changes of tone—are brought home all the more powerfully by the modesty of the poem's presentation, its conversational (and, hence, deeply ironic) style. Death chillingly inflects everyday experience even as that experience comes to seem almost sublimely blessed, graced with childlike wonder and the kindness of strangers, as a function of its mortal fragility.

"Pedals" is powerful because of the existential gaps that tear through its fabric of everyday life. So much in the poem goes unsaid or seems downright unspeakable: the grief of the truck operator, the anguish of the poet, the imminent (though still unconscious) mourning of the son. But these tacit reflections on matters of ultimate value that haunt Silver's poem also render it spiritual: the poem has a life beyond its outward preoccupation with levers and digging and pedals. And that spiritual life expresses itself through the deep reflection on the radiance of existence expressed through the frenetic but heartrendingly mortal energy of young children (alive today, though not always). In this poem, to become as a little child is to lose oneself in the joys of the everyday *and* to have those joys abruptly taken away. It is to confront in perhaps the most poignant way possible the gap between experience and meaning, between the intensity of life and its sudden extinction. That gap represents something of a breaking point in the poem. Silver's poem is gloriously broken—glorious *because* it is broken, its spiritual significance at once constituted and shattered by the implication that all things and all people die, even those who seem, and should be, most alive.

To some extent, all literature comes from brokenness, from the breakdown in systems of expectation and meaning, from complexity introduced into simplicity. It is born from the complexity, the beguiling uniqueness, even of simple things: love, loss, hope. Without brokenness and the gaps it opens, we would have no need for literature, no need for any story or image showing how life may be, or always is, otherwise. But neither would there be any spiritual experience, any imperative to "lay aside the things of this world, and seek for the things of a better" (D&C 25:10). Spiritual experience is literary in part because it comes from and then sometimes causes our brokenness. It reminds us that we too may always be, or already are, otherwise.

* * *

Consider the relationship between two manifestations of spiritual experience—of experiences with the Spirit—in Latter-day Saint lore. Each is part of a larger life story. Episode 1: "I am going like a lamb to the slaughter; but I am calm as a summer's morning" (D&C 135:4). Episode 2:

> Years ago I read in a Church magazine the story of a girl who was living away from home and going to college. She was behind in her classes, her social life was not what she had hoped for, and she was generally unhappy. Finally

one day she fell to her knees and cried out, "What can I do to improve my life?" The Holy Ghost whispered, "Get up and clean your room."[2]

The first episode, recounted by John Taylor, are Joseph Smith's words as he departed Nauvoo to deliver himself to the law in Carthage, Illinois, where he would be imprisoned and then shot and killed. The second is a story told by Larry R. Lawrence in the October 2015 general conference about a college student who received a surprising answer to prayer. In the first instance, Joseph's peaceful disposition is taken as a sign of his prophetic mantle, the Spirit implicitly playing the role of a sustaining influence, the Comforter.[3] The second case, folksy and mundane, presents the Holy Ghost in the role of guide in directing one's life, often in ways we do not expect. The first story is sublime, the second a little ridiculous (and self-consciously so: it drew a laugh from the congregation at general conference). Together, they reflect different kinds of spiritual experiences and the wide range of moods (tragic and comic, exalted and prosaic) that accompany them.

To some extent, this range informs any spiritual experience, each being composed of what is great and small, divine and human. In bringing heaven to earth, spiritual experiences also introduce a measure of chaos into paradise inasmuch as we, flawed mortals, suddenly become part of the record of heaven. This is a subtext of the biblical story of Moses's encounter with God through the burning bush as God draws Moses's gaze by a supernatural apparition but then finds it more difficult to turn Moses's mind. "And Moses said unto God, Who am I, that I should go unto Pharaoh, and that I should bring forth the children of Israel out of Egypt?" (Ex. 3:11). A burning bush that is not consumed is a miracle Moses can see, while his capacity to liberate an oppressed nation is one he cannot. And the former does not transfer easily to the latter. The Exodus narrative thus juxtaposes divine power and human ambivalence: "I AM" meets "I, Moses, am not."

This space of communion and dissent, a kind of divine comedy, is evocatively literary. Literature is born from the complexities of our

experience, from sublime (and occasionally divine, inspired) encounters that expand the horizons of the possible, and from instances of
weakness and accident that divulge humans in their frank and fallen
mortality. In like manner, spiritual experiences are themselves tellingly
complex. They exceed or rather expand the limits of our capacities,
making what we might have thought impossible suddenly seem possible or rendering actual what we had never envisioned. And yet, in
another way, they reveal our limitations precisely in the process of
appearing to surpass them, thus accentuating our mortality at the
moment they connect us to heaven. The effect is exalting but also a
little estranging, uncanny. In literary terms, defamiliarizing.

Defamiliarization describes literature's power to make us pause
and reconsider things we thought we already knew, causing us to see
the world afresh. In the words of T. S. Eliot, in a defamiliarized milieu
we "arrive where we started / And know the place for the first time."[4]
This knowing again, almost feeling born again—a virtual experience
of redemption—is inherently spiritual. It's revitalizing but also a little
unsettling as it reveals gaps in our present understanding. The theologian Rowan Williams believes that such experience lifts our minds
to God. He remarks that there is an important distinction between
description, which relates "what we say and what we perceive," the
world of everyday facts, and literary *representation*, which engages
objects of description for the purpose of opening them to examination. To represent something is "to embody, translate, make present or
re-form what is perceived."[5] And because our perceptions change over
time—throughout our lives and across generations—representation is
a medium for revealing new truths, for reminding us of what we had
not previously recognized, and hence of the ways we dwelled (and
continue to dwell) in comparative darkness. "To live and speak from
a place of non-anxiety" regarding this perpetually unfolding condition
of life "is one plausible account of 'faith.'"[6]

A life of faith thus involves recognizing, straddling, and sometimes leaping across gaps that riddle our existence. In most cases,

we accrue small islands of understanding surrounded by oceans of unknown details and unimagined possibilities. The feelings of fullness we associate with spiritual experience create virtual bridges across these expanses, although they do not usually close them altogether. On the contrary, they reveal them.

On that score, Latter-day Saint doctrine preaches the importance of building a relationship with God—it understands God as a being we may come to know—while recognizing that the process of divine disclosure is virtually endless as the horizon of what we do not yet know about God continually recedes. Our experience of God thus perpetually breaches the limits of what we know; the gaps grow along with our understanding. This is why most answers to prayer rarely occur only once; they stay with us in memory and grow with us. We revisit them in reflecting not only on what was communicated but how it was transmitted, how we felt at the time, what subsequently transpired, what we learned from the experience, how it changed us, and so on. To marvel at such experiences, to recognize that they expand (beyond) our understanding at the moment of initial reception, is to grow in faith. It is to employ what Williams calls representation as a spiritual practice.

Spiritual representation, like literary representation, thus reminds us that there is something perpetually more to encounter, something previously unappreciated or unseen—something newly if not yet fully defamiliarized—in what we deem most important. This is true even of experiences that bring us feelings of peace, for they compel us to become something or someone more than we presently are. Nobody leaves an experience of God unchanged, however mundane or even ridiculous that experience may seem. (To Moses, God spoke through a burning bush; to the college student in Elder Lawrence's story, he spoke through a messy room.) In effect, then, behind every doctrinal treatise are volumes of poetry and novels waiting to be written, countless situations to be more richly represented, innumerable gaps to fill; behind every religious conviction is a spiritual experience that will challenge and expand it. In this respect, at least, spiritual experiences are less about what we know than the direction in which they point us. As bridges to the unknown, they extend beyond the understanding and virtues we are coming to acquire. Such experiences are, in effect, literary exercises pushing us to the limits of the worlds we know and inhabit.

Of course, this is also what makes spiritual experiences difficult: there is a rigor to the ways they push us. They rarely present us with an image of the world exactly as we desire it. Instead, they mark the limits of what we know and who we are and then compel us beyond these limits, revealing gaps in our understanding and prompting us to attend again to things we thought we already knew. Most spiritual experiences are precursors to full understanding, much as frequent or extended experiences of the Spirit are preliminary, preparatory, to entering into the full presence of God.

∗ ∗ ∗

Spiritual experience presents a paradox for religion and vice versa. Religion provides the doctrinal framework for the understanding of spiritual experience (for what it is and why it is given to us), but spiritual experience perpetually surpasses the limits of our religious understanding, revealing new things about the religious principles in which we believe. In this way, spiritual experience is "bigger" than religion, for it recasts religion as a living organism in process of perpetual change. But minus its religious foundation and the doctrinal orientation it provides, minus a grasp of the plan of salvation, spiritual experience appears vague, becoming a set of inexplicably intensified sensations, feelings of heightened but fleeting connectedness to something greater than ourselves. For this reason, there is no spiritual experience that does not involve, that does not introduce, at least a small measure of faith crisis. I do not mean that such experiences fill us with doubt, for spiritual experience can be thrillingly, powerfully self- and life-affirming. However, because it is also transformative, it vaults ahead of the religious understanding on which it nevertheless relies. And yet, and by the same token, these exuberant "crises" also help us understand our religion more completely and thus live it more fully.

These, then, are the inevitable if somewhat paradoxical questions that follow: How does religion make it possible for us to maximize the value of spiritual experiences? And yet, what does religion *not* bring to our understanding of spiritual experience? Better said, how do spiritual experiences reveal gaps in the religious understanding on which they depend?

It was the gradual emergence of these questions that prompted me to begin studying literature in the first place. Literature, for me, became a way to negotiate the difference between beautiful gospel concepts and the complexity, the depth, of human and spiritual experience. This is not to deny the poetic quality of religious doctrines about spiritual things. For, make no mistake, Latter-day Saint doctrines pertaining to spiritual experience are beautiful: clear, compelling, and powerful. "All things unto me are spiritual," the Lord declares (D&C 29:34). Hence, a spiritual experience is any that involves spirit, that "conscious intelligent individual entity that had an existence previous to mortality."[7] This would pertain to an experience of any living thing, all things having a spiritual existence prior to their earthly creation (see Moses 3:5). Technically, gospel understanding endlessly proliferates the sources of our engagement of spiritual things.

More typically, though, our church discussions of spiritual experience are not this expansive. References to it tend to focus less on the spiritual *being* of things and more on the Spirit as a motivator of right actions and a revelator of what we are to *do*. Spiritual seekers are cast less in the image of contemplatives than action heroes. As we read in the Doctrine and Covenants:

> Put your trust in that Spirit which leadeth to do good—
> yea, to do justly, to walk humbly, to judge righteously;
> and this is my Spirit. Verily, verily, I say unto you, I will
> impart unto you of my Spirit, which shall enlighten your

mind, which shall fill your soul with joy; And then shall
ye know, or by this shall you know, all things whatsoever you desire of me, which are pertaining unto things
of righteousness, in faith believing in me that you shall
receive. (D&C 11:12–14)

"Do[ing]," "walk[ing]," "judg[ing]"—spiritual direction involves acting, even (or especially) in situations that are still a little foreign to
us. Trusting in the Spirit, or in an initial prompting, will lead to a
fuller understanding: "And then shall [we] know," at least to a new
degree. Then the process continues, a cosmic labyrinth of countless
small steps. Elder Richard G. Scott describes spiritual illumination
as "a power, beyond [our] own capability, that a loving Heavenly
Father wants [us] to use consistently for [our] peace and happiness."
Accordingly, "spirituality yields two fruits. The first is inspiration to
know what to do. The second is power, or the capacity to do it. These
two capacities come together."[8] Spirituality thus converts experience
into knowledge and knowledge into power; born as an impression, it
fuels tangible realities. Spiritual experience brings goodness to pass.

This is an idea with wide currency in Church teachings, and it
takes both clever and exalting forms. Consider again Elder Lawrence's
story of the life-changing, if outwardly absurd, message from beyond
the veil: "Get up and clean your room." The central idea behind this
droll story is wholly earnest: "The journey of discipleship is not an
easy one. It has been called a 'course of steady improvement.' As we
travel along that strait and narrow path, the Spirit continually challenges us to be better and to climb higher. The Holy Ghost makes
an ideal traveling companion. If we are humble and teachable, He
will take us by the hand and lead us home."[9] The Spirit reaches us
wherever we are, no matter the situation; it will speak to us in and
through our circumstances, ridiculous (room cleaning) and sublime. Marion G. Romney, a former counselor in the Church's First
Presidency, expresses this same idea on a grand scale: Spiritual "guidance is a reality and is available to every person, and . . . if followed it

would lead to a solution of all our problems—individual, national, and international."[10] Why is this? Because, explains Douglas D. Holmes, the presence of the Holy Ghost is a unique blessing, "the greatest gift a mortal can enjoy"—indeed, greater than such grandiose but transitory spiritual manifestations as "the administration of angels," the witnessing of "many miracles," and the vision of "wonders in the earth."[11] While these events dramatize the reality of God, the persistent presence of the Holy Ghost, even in the mundane contexts of everyday life, helps us negotiate life's complexities. It accords us a measure of understanding, a brightness of hope, and an array of spiritual gifts. Together, they assist us in transforming our circumstances and, through them, our character.

I have always believed such things. What is more, I have lived many of them: I have felt enlightened by the Spirit, I have sought and received spiritual direction, I have found spiritual power to achieve things beyond my own capacity, and I have experienced gradual (and sometimes dramatic) transformations by the Spirit. Becoming more sensitive to spiritual things, I have felt myself drawing closer to God.

But back to the gaps. They always seem to remain. Life is filled with them. And while some represent lapses on my part, on our part— mistakes we make, distractions that lure us, times we pull away from the Spirit—others are not of our own making. They may be heaven- sent (trials we call them), or they may seem random and estranging (like when bad things happen for no apparent reason or when new paradigms rock our foundations). Or, and this is what I suggest above, gaps may be caused by some of our most powerful spiritual experiences themselves. These latter may be the most difficult to reconcile. For, if the first—our trials—confronts us with challenges (seeming Goliaths to our David) and if the second—new paradigms—spawns difficult questions, then the third—the crises opened and not simply answered by spiritual experiences—represents a peculiar form of divine silence, of truth being spoken and our not grasping it. To cite one example close to home, I think of the cognitive dissonance experienced by some devout parents of gay children. They face the challenge—often the inspired injunction revealed through prayer and plenty of hard experience—to turn on a dime from expressing love by teaching "correct principles" regarding chastity and marriage to expressing that love even more earnestly as stress fractures appear in those same principles under the weight of their children's actual lives. Each of these imperatives can be true simultaneously; there is no necessary contradiction between them. But the gap that opens there—to love and then to love with new understanding, to see a child's life first in one way and then another—can place a heavy burden on faith.

This is where questions of spiritual *doing* convert back into questions of spiritual *being*: What is the nature of the God who answers prayers, but whose truths always exceed the answers he provides? How is the goodness promised through the Spirit brought to pass even in the face of affliction? Who are we even to receive such inspiration? And what are we inevitably missing? To paraphrase the title of Elder Lawrence's talk, what lack we yet?

Incomplete enlightenment—the very spiritual experiences that illuminate us also reveal gaps, the limits of our understanding: "And if men come unto me I will show unto them their weakness" (Ether 12:27). How do we live with these gaps? How do we make these "weak things become strong," as this verse in Ether concludes? These are spiritual questions. And, like literature, spiritual events are often at their most impactful not in imparting wisdom but in measuring the distance between our expectations and our actual experience of the things of God. They are at their most poignant not in revealing the world as we want it or think we already know it but in casting outward across life's open expanses. Some spiritual experiences only happen when we outlive, outgrow, our beautiful concepts. These experiences help us discover truth again, defamiliarized.

* * *

O sweet spontaneous
earth how often have
the
doting

     fingers of
prurient philosophers pinched
and
poked

thee
, has the naughty thumb
of science prodded
thy

     beauty   . how
often have religions taken
thee upon their scraggy knees
squeezing and

buffeting thee that thou mightest conceive
gods
     (but
true

to the incomparable
couch of death thy
rhythmic
lover
     thou answerest

them only with

     spring)[12]

The American poet E. E. Cummings composed this untitled poem
(usually named after its opening line, "O sweet spontaneous") in
the 1920s. Written in the form of a prayer, replete with an object of
apostrophic address—"O sweet spontaneous / earth"—the poem

comprises a meditation on the imbalanced, even slightly abusive, relationship between life and meaning. While the former is a source of exquisite abundance and an endless wellspring of inspiration, the latter—meaning—consists of a series of aggressive, even violent, extractions. Philosophy, science, and religion have "pinched / and / poked ... prodded ... squeez[ed] and / buffet[ed]" the earth in order to produce "gods": truths, secrets, idols—imagined keys to unlock life's mysteries. But earth doesn't speak the language of human projection, communicating instead through the fecundity of "spring," the fertility of new life and thus new mystery. But as this only perpetuates the enigma that philosophy, science, and religion strive vainly to solve, life's silent profusions whet the appetite for new gods. There is thus an ironic, even impish innocence to earth, an endless provocation to the human impulse toward wonder that provides no recourse for satisfying that impulse. Humans, then, live at odds with nature, forever seeking to graft meaning, purpose, onto a branch that cannot support the weight of our need. To live is to want to understand, but to seek understanding is to look past the wordless bounties of living.

Poetry, here, occupies a parallel position to the theo-poetic (or god-making) disciplines of philosophy, science, and religion in that it also responds to earth and its abundance. But poetry's approach is different: it does not try to solve life's mystery as much as highlight it, honor it—even worship it. (The poet's invocation of earth takes the form of traditional prayer with the language of "thee" and "thou.") Where other disciplines seek understanding, poetry celebrates what eludes it. And it does so formally and syntactically as well as thematically. Numerous stanza breaks accentuate lines that, individually and collectively, offer no answers, only paradoxical riddles, or koans: "thou answerest // them only with // spring." The poet also plays with spaces inside the lines, beginning one with a comma and interspersing another with an extended blank in front of the period. This is a poetry of gaps. And so, where other disciplines put themselves at odds with nature, poetry will try to emulate it, creating and living with the voids we encounter in our drive to know. For the poet, we live once we cease trying to master nature—once we cease trying to extract meaning about God, life, earth—and instead accommodate ourselves to its mysteries, including its "rhythmic / lover": death. To be, to survive, we must let go.

Spiritual disciplines often describe this as being present, encouraging such states of mind through exercises focusing on the breath: in. . . out. . . in. . . . The poem's own rhythms reproduce something of this flow, its mostly unpunctuated lines creating a cadence of flattened concentration: "O sweet spontaneous / earth how often have / the/ doting // fingers. . ." Given the poem's subject matter and prayerful form, such syncopated phrasing amounts to a mystical speaking into wisdom but wisdom of a particular kind: unknowing. This is thus an apophatic poem, that is, one that evokes what is "unknowable and ungraspable yet at the same time existentially foundational."[13] A classic fourteenth-century work of mystical theology refers to this apophatic quality of spiritual experience as a "cloud of unknowing." If we wish to know God, it asserts, we must not presume to know too much: "In the beginning it is usual to feel nothing but a kind of darkness about your mind, or as it were, a cloud of unknowing. . . . Learn to be at home in this darkness. . . . For if, in this life, you hope to feel and see God as he is in himself it must be within this darkness and this cloud."[14] The point is not that we are incapable of communing with God but that God is so far beyond human understanding that to impute characteristics to God, to claim to know God and God's mysteries, is to project onto God our own (limited) paradigms, our own concepts and needs. It is, in the words of Cummings's poem, to pinch and poke and prod and thus act like "prurient" philosophers, "naughty" scientists, and "scraggy" religionists. But "thought cannot comprehend God. And so," the mystic concludes, "I prefer to abandon all I know, choosing rather to love him whom I cannot know. . . . By love he may be touched and embraced, never by thought" (46).

This, I suppose, is the occasionally maddening genius of the Latter-day Saint emphasis on spiritual action—on action first and foremost with understanding (perhaps, though incompletely) to follow. Such an approach induces gaps in our understanding, and how could it not? As a Catholic friend observes of her own tradition, "The more seriously a disciple seeks to know the Spirit and to attend to its promptings, the more the apophatic dimension becomes the predominant experience." Here, "one has a conviction of knowing truth and being moved at a depth never experienced before, yet without knowing in the usual cognitive and intellectual sense."[15] So, in the words of Elder Lawrence, rehearsing a litany of folksy, everyday, action-oriented spiritual impressions: "Get up and clean your room. . . . Don't raise your voice. . . . Take time to ponder before you pray. . . . And be patient while driving; don't exceed the speed limit. (I'm still working on that last one.)"[16]

* * *

When I was seventeen, my father was called to serve as stake president. The visiting General Authority who called him was Elder Boyd K. Packer of the Quorum of the Twelve Apostles.[17] After stake conference and before heading to the airport, Elder Packer came by our home to talk with my parents. As he was leaving, they summoned me from my room to meet an apostle of the Lord. Though none too enthused about being thrust into the center of attention, I dutifully descended to the front door. I instantly found Elder Packer very warm, very friendly. His topic of conversation, not so much.

"You're a senior in high school, is that right?"

I nodded. I could feel him sizing me up.

He told me he had something of a "prophecy" to make in my case. "It will not be easy for you, but you will choose to serve a mission. And you will look back on that decision as one of the most important of your life."

I nodded again, words dropping out of my mouth without communicating anything substantive. But I was not pleased. The fact is that I planned to serve a mission—I viewed it as more or less inevitable—though I usually tried to keep the prospect out of mind.

It exemplified others' expectations of me, and I found the bare fact of those expectations depressing. The following year, things pretty much unfolded as Elder Packer had foreseen: the decision proved far more brutal than I could ever have imagined (as enticing reasons not to go presented themselves with painful allure); largely through the grace of God, inspiring me in the moment, I made the difficult choice to serve; and I eventually viewed that decision as one of the most important of my life.

But there are gaps. Wow, are there gaps.

My mission experience opened my mind in ways nothing else could. But for that reason, it complicated everything. I gained a deep conviction of the gospel message I carried but a deeper conviction of the reality of a God who was vaster than that message (or at least my understanding of it). I developed a bright appreciation of the Church as a special vehicle for God to direct his children but a more vibrant belief in a God who reached people whom the Church would leave cold (certainly with me as its messenger). I came to see how God intervenes in everyday human lives and thus influences history, but I also became painfully aware of the myriad ways we bear the consequences of our decisions—and sometimes face them relatively alone. And yet, I had also learned that my feelings of loneliness did not preclude God from influencing my life at depths I could not fathom.

So much of this was beyond my narrow capacities of mind and perception. In so many ways, I lamented, God passed by me unnoticed.

Hence, I came to know that the Church was "true—but." But the world was huge, and God was greater still. So many things were true, many of them inarticulate and seemingly beyond the reach of my personal religious imaginary. Yes, I privileged Church doctrines concerning our collective human origin, purpose, and destiny. The difficulty—the gaps—emerged in reconciling that privilege with perspectives I was reading from across the spectrum of cultures and the depth of history. The challenge was to hold together, in one thought, the framework of my religious understanding with the God who was opening, and blowing, my mind.

And so, I began trying to learn about the ways of God and God's creation, in scripture and elsewhere, "by study and also by faith" (D&C 88:118). (Doctrine and Covenants, meet Albert Camus!) And each of these directives opened gaps in the other. This made me feel intensely grateful. . . and somewhat anxious. Blessed. . . and burdened. Liberated. . . and a little disoriented.

Years later, when I happened to be home between the completion of my master's degree and the beginning of my PhD, Elder Packer came into town on Church business and stayed a night with us. Once again, I found him very warm, very friendly. But once again, I found the topic of conversation difficult.

"Matt, I understand you're studying literature."

I nodded.

"Who is your favorite poet?"

As they had years before, empty words fell from my mouth. This time, whatever I may have said, I was reflecting that I'd never considered that question. Literature, for me, had nothing to do with favorites. It was all about gaps—opening them, bridging them, learning to live with them. This conviction was one of the great takeaways from my mission: God exists, and (so) there are gaps. Though I doubt this conclusion was what Elder Packer originally had in mind, I was thinking to myself that the coexistence of these beliefs was, for me, one fulfillment and outcome of his prophecy ten years earlier, one prominent reason why my mission experience had been one of the most important of my life.

Noting my difficulty in answering his question, he professed a preference for William Wordsworth and John Keats. I stammered and stuttered and came out with E. E. Cummings. A poet not of wisdom or beauty but of vast, blank spaces—a poet of unknowing. Elder Packer nodded but seemed unimpressed, or perhaps he was just a little tired. It was growing late.

So, the next morning, I took a poetry anthology to my mom's small photocopy machine and copied a Cummings poem for him. I don't recall which one. What I remember is feeling irked by an expletive on the anthology's opposite page and carefully placing a blank strip of paper across part of the page to cover it up. I wanted to present a cleaner image. But as I handed Elder Packer the copy, my eye was not on the poem but on the blank spot, the gap I'd created. I was wondering, a little anxiously, whether this man who had been so kind to me, this servant of God, would notice it was there.

SEVEN

Holy Saturdays

I had come off the stand and was chatting with people filing out of the chapel when I ran into my friend Melinda. Warm and intelligent, successful in her career, valued in her ward—a beloved friend, neighbor, daughter, sister, and aunt—she also wears scars from emotional wounds and feels the ache of old spiritual questions. Recently, she had begun grieving the loss of her father.

I love talking with Melinda. More than her lively intelligence, it is her faith that moves me—tough and tested, open about its pain and uncertainties, and alert to inspiration and the myriad ways it shapes her habits and hopes. Relationships are precious to Melinda, so she rarely wastes time with empty conversation: ask her a question, you get a thoughtful reply. In response to my query, then, about how she was getting along in the wake of her father's death, she began describing some of the emotional and spiritual toll of recent events. As it happens, she had just returned from a visit to a sibling who was dealing with a life-threatening illness. Wiping at the corners of her eyes, she confessed to feeling that she seemed to be moving randomly through life, that as those closest to her were either dying or facing the prospect of death, she was ever more conscious of her relative rootlessness: no husband or children, nothing at home anchoring her to the life she had built, and no clear legacy extending generationally beyond her once she is gone.

As I listened, complex feelings began forming; points and counterpoints rattled through my head. *No, I silently protested, Melinda's legacy is all around her in the many lives she touches, not least those of her nieces and nephews.* But then, *Yes, I conceded, what she's saying carries a ring of authenticity.* As I brooded on why that was, a second set of impressions began coalescing. *There is always such a good spirit about Melinda, perhaps because she feels some things so deeply, faces them so candidly. Christ seems to bear her up.* The thought to which this impression was tethered, however, was sobering: *Please, may we all prove so fortunate. Because we're all floating randomly through the universe. Nothing we know or love is permanent, at least not exactly in the way we know or love it. She speaks for all of us.*

The effect of this internal dialogue was all too familiar if also a little unsettling, triggering—the Spirit's rainbow arc of peaceful reassurance shimmering above a dark gray sea of mortal dread.

✳ ✳ ✳

The last time I ever went trick or treating, I was fourteen and in ninth grade. I don't remember my costume or "costume"; dressing up wasn't the point, candy was. My friend's parents drove us to the neighborhood where they used to live; the area was less rural, and the houses were closer together, making for more doors per hour and a maximum sugar haul. They dropped us off at a small shopping center, telling us they'd meet us there at such-and-such a time. And off we went, dashing up and down streets, getting a few strange looks (we were tall and gangly and no longer "cute"; no one seemed delighted to see us when they opened their doors) but also, happily, heavy bags.

At some point, we decided we'd had enough and began meandering slowly back toward the village center meeting place. Down the street, a gang of four boys was walking in our direction. As they got closer, I could see they were a little older, a little bigger, all dressed like death rockers, all mean-looking. They weren't trick or treating; they were on the prowl. And as they approached and sized us up, they began snickering. It's easy to see why: we were no longer little boys but were not yet "men" like them (at least, as I imagined they saw themselves); we must have looked ridiculous. Still, their mockery stung our fragile adolescent egos, and once they were about half a block behind us, my friend, John, turned and yelled at them. It was a nonsense word, a coinage about tackling invented by one of the guys on our freshman football team, someone so much better and stronger and cooler than we were. In our mouths, it was a kind of primal if pathetic assertion of dignity.

I'd been slinking down the street in shame and hadn't looked behind us when John sounded his barbaric yawp.[1] I did note that he seemed jittery when he turned back around but whatever: we were at the corner where the quiet neighborhood opened onto the multi-lane avenue, and as luck would have it, his parents were just driving past. They saw us and pulled over, saving us the extra half-mile trek to our meeting place. We climbed into the back seat of their car, and when I glanced out the window, I was startled to see the gang of death rockers standing on the corner and glaring, panting, right where we had just been. When John yelled, they must have come running back for us; had his parents not driven by right at that moment, these older teens would have beaten the living tar out of us.

I've thought about that incident numerous times over the years. It's a classic story of deliverance, of divine intervention in the teen-age mode. What were the odds his parents pulled up right at that moment? A thousand to one? Ten thousand? More? They did not know where we were nor we them; cell phones did not exist, and we were earlier than we'd planned to be. Had his parents not been driving in the far right lane, they couldn't have pulled over, or if they'd come by thirty seconds later or pulled up a couple hundred feet up the street, we'd have been bloody pulps by the time we made it to the car. Time, place, circumstance—all was absolutely, almost unthinkably, miraculously impeccable.

But as I've reflected on that story, I've considered how frequently such miracles do *not* occur. People are not delivered; I am not delivered. We have the life beaten out of us by illness, unkindness, injustice, poverty, lack of opportunity, discrimination, disability, anxiety, depression, abuse, trauma, rejection, unfair obligations, unmet expectations, unwelcome desires, poor timing, addictive tendencies, character flaws, and so much more. Divine assistance arrives too late, if at all.

If John's parents had not shown up? Or all the times later in my life when, facing some daunting situation or other, no miracle saved me? When I was left to fend for myself? I've scuffled in those circumstances—we all do, I suppose. And sometimes we make it out okay. Just as often, though, we end up bloody, bruised, dazed—taking a beating and then wandering randomly, like Melinda described, not really knowing where we are but quite certain that whatever it was we came here for, it wasn't for this.

✳ ✳ ✳

Where are we? And why? These are questions frequently posed by the twentieth-century Welsh poet R. S. Thomas. Some critics refer to Thomas as the poet of Holy Saturday, the day between Christ's crucifixion and the resurrection. This is when Christ "went and preached unto the spirits in prison" (1 Pet. 3:19), connoting in some Christian traditions elaborate theologies regarding Christ's union with the dead. More simply, Holy Saturday attests to "the reality of worldly suffering," to hopes dashed and not yet resolved through the glories of the resurrection. It is thus "the decisive day within the Christian narrative that confronts the believer with the full power of worldly suffering and its apparent victory over the powers of Good." In the Holy Saturday moments of our lives, we find ourselves wrestling "with divine silence and absence."[2] Divine silence can be deeply perplexing, and Holy Saturday evocatively captures its implications. Holy Saturday experiences are complex constructs of hope amid bereavement or delicate feelings of unextinguished promise amid bleak realities of pain, absence, and loss. Such experiences complicate our faith, but they do not extinguish it entirely. Sometimes, even, there can be about them a kind of thrill, almost an ecstasy—because Holy Saturday is for believers, for those who hold to their convictions despite so many reasons to lose faith.

Thomas's poem "Kneeling" is about one such instance of betweenness, of toggling between competing feelings of mortal absence and divine presence. It is told from the perspective of a clergyman accustomed to seeking inspiration and finding he is not quite equal to it:

> Moments of great calm,
> Kneeling before an altar
> Of wood in a stone church
> In summer, waiting for the God
> To speak; the air a staircase
> For silence; the sun's light
> Ringing me, as though I acted
> A great role. And the audiences
> Still; all that close throng
> Of spirits waiting, as I,
> For the message.
>   Prompt me, God;
> But not yet. When I speak,
> Though it be you who speak
> Through me, something is lost.
> The meaning is in the waiting.[3]

The location, a church, is one of inspiration, as is the impending activity—a sermon or prayer. But what impresses the speaker is something different about the setting, something that is not tangible as much as inflected by the memory of past spiritual experiences: "the air a staircase / For silence"; "the sun's light / Ringing me"; "all that close throng / Of spirits." These objects of attention are not really objects at all, not in the material sense; impressionistic in nature, they bear traces of moments in a church or in the process of delivering a sermon or prayer that previously moved the poet. And what he desires, what he awaits, is "the message," which is to say, to be moved once again by some force of inspiration. For without that spiritual infusion, "something is lost. / The meaning is in the waiting."

That concluding line, highlighted in the poem by being the only one that forms a complete sentence, captures the poem's mood and idea. "The meaning is in the waiting," and so this is a poem about anticipation that some new impression, some new message, will come to the poet once again, as it has before. He has been changed, converted; and so, open to God, he awaits the Spirit that animates him, that animates all things: air, light, matter, speech.

These positive associations give the poem a happy, expectant feel. But behind this optimism are more sobering thoughts, Holy Saturday thoughts. For, as the poet confesses, "When I speak, / Though it be you who speak / Through me, something is lost": his transcriptions of the divine word distort it, obscure it, producing the wrong kind of silence—gaps in the sacred message. Is he even worthy, then, to receive what he awaits? If he does, how will he do it justice? So, his waiting involves trepidation. And perhaps, too, a small measure of dread. For, to be graced by inspiration is to risk being opened to God, changed by God in ways we cannot control. But then again, what if the inspiration he awaits, that we await, does not arrive? Or what if it does, but it still seems beyond us, such that its meaning becomes uncertain? How would we tell the difference between inspiration beyond our capacities and inspiration that never came at all? What if we were changed not by what touched us but by what failed us or we it? What if we were open but were simply left waiting? What if that waiting were all the "meaning" we ever had?

Melinda's description of random, rootless drifting through life— that is an experience of Holy Saturday. And all those times I have not been rescued by some miracle of deliverance—times when I've prayed but have been beaten up by life—those too are Holy Saturday experiences. All those friends, family members, and acquaintances who have found themselves struggling through crises great and small without answers or remedy, who wait on God without explanation or consolation—Holy Saturday disciples, all.

* * *

The scene is still imprinted so vividly on my memory, perhaps in part because it was so visually striking, at once beautiful and strange. It was well after midnight, and my friend Robert and I were walking along the long, wide beach outside the rundown shack I was renting with someone I'd met in our singles ward. I was twenty-one and in the middle of the school year I would spend at UC Irvine before transferring to BYU. Nobody else was on the beach and for good reason: not only was it deep at night, it was winter, a strong wind was blowing off the ocean, and storm clouds were moving in, alternately obscuring and framing a full moon. The play of light and shadow was haunting—the moonlit sands a faint neon blue, the ocean black and hissing.

Earlier in the evening, Robert and I had driven seventy-five miles south to San Diego to meet up with my girlfriend and one of her friends from the Latter-day Saint institute at UCSD.[4] It was a good time: good company, good conversation. But for me, the ulterior motive of having Robert along was to solicit his help as a therapist to diagnose my ailing relationship. And now, walking along the glowing, windswept beach, we were analyzing it. Robert was a wonderful if still amateur therapist—attentive and insightful, reassuring and provocative. A decade later, it turns out, he would formalize that gift in becoming a licensed, clinical psychologist specializing in couples counseling.

Gradually, however, the conversation began drifting to something Robert had brought up on the double date, seemingly out of the blue—how, before he had joined the Church at eighteen, he'd sexually experimented with men and women and how that experience had convinced him that homosexuality was counterfeit love, a devilish tool to turn hearts away from the things of God. It had caused a stir, Robert blurting it out forcefully from the back seat. He said it probably sounded harsh, but he knew, he'd been there. But now, as we walked and sat on the blue sands, he began softening that judgment.

No, he said, he had no more interest in dating men, but some of those former relationships were so alluring still in his memory; they had opened channels of feeling he did not wish to close, channels through which he felt more connected to himself and to God. These gentler words struck me as strange but true, so at odds with Robert's unsolicited confession and diatribe earlier that evening but so in keeping with the sensitivity that characterized him, a sensitivity reflected in the deep night's aura of moon and cloud, shadow and glow. We would return to the topic frequently over the next several months.

I would think about those early conversations three years later when we were both living in Utah and Robert was engaged to an amazing woman. He was so happy at first, then increasingly anxious, then agonized and falling apart. He began speaking angry words against the Church, then broke off the engagement, then burst out of the closet. Eventually, he married a male partner.

Other friends lived similar stories. One night, a new BYU roommate, Kent, a sensitive and intelligent soul who soon became my dearest friend, told me he needed to talk, that I seemed to be a good listener. We went to a buzzing Provo restaurant, and over ambient chatter, he told me he was gay and planned to leave the Church after graduation, if not before. Kent sometimes expressed rage at God, not over his sexuality but over the fate that had befallen his father, who had died of cancer while Kent had been serving his mission. His father was already gravely ill before Kent left for his mission, and some of his last memories of his father were of hearing him scream out in the night from pain. When his father died, Kent's mission president persuaded him to stay out on his mission and not attend the funeral, said that's what his father would want. Kent felt devastated in the aftermath of that decision and worse as time went by. These days, those memories fueled intense anger. I watched that anger flicker at moments on this night, during this conversation. But anyway, he said, casually returning to the main subject, he was curious: How much had Robert told me about his sexual experience with men?

A couple years later, when I was earning my master's degree in New York City, a guy moved into our ward and became a peripheral part of our social network. He was shy but friendly, dependable: I called him one evening to assist me when a ward member requested a priesthood blessing. On a couple later occasions, we caught dinner or movies. His manner was a little odd, detached but endearing; he emitted a kind of gentle longing, a fraternal melancholy—the personification of a lonely, self-effacing smile. After he moved, I learned he'd been in support groups trying to redirect his desires from men to women, still a common practice in the early 1990s.

These and other friendships opened my mind to what it means to come of age when some of our defining life experiences do not fit the orthodox religious mold, when the incomprehension of Holy Saturday extends indefinitely into the future, when God seems not to be where we expect him. I very much felt God's presence in or around the lives of these gay friends. I would often reflect on that late-night walk with Robert—on how my angsty need to talk about my relationship with my girlfriend almost caused me to miss the plaintive tone in his description of former boyfriends. That tone was so different from the stridency of his anti-gay zeal earlier in the evening. With the passage of time and the more I thought about that contrast, the more I believed that God had supported the young convert in his chaste resolutions—conversion is good, attempting a leap of faith is good—even as, later, he had abided with the gay man in his conflicted sadness and gradual process of self-understanding. I saw it as a gesture of healing and reassurance of love.

Discerning God's presence there in that later moment, though, was complicated. For, in my religious culture, especially during that era, it was easy to hear ecclesiastical echoes of the diatribe Robert had launched on our double date but harder to catch the pastoral response to the other side of his story, to those tones of longing sounding faintly on our walk along the beach. To that extent, it seemed at church that I was hearing so much more about what was *right* than what was *true*, especially in the late 1980s and early 1990s. For truth, I was coming to believe, is about more than clarity of doctrine. It's also about the particularity and intensity of our experience, about all those silent internal pressures and unforeseeable circumstances that shape our minds, our hearts, our spirits. Truth, it seems, is about discerning God's presence in unimaginable, seemingly random situations. It's about feeling the trace of God's Spirit in the lives of others—and, through it, coming to love others—even or especially when their experiences unsettle our sense of rightness. Rightness is loud and has all the answers; truth speaks quietly, a virtual whisper across the wind and waves.

* * *

Literature involves plenty of beautiful thinking and saying. But at its core, especially in the modern world, literature is often about a peculiar kind of experience: it's about all those places in God's universe that fall outside the scope of simple rightness, all those lives that don't fit their circumstances, their era, their own social and cosmic imaginaries. Literature is a space for pondering things we had not anticipated and do not know how to reconcile. Like Holy Saturday, literature brings figures of redemption, renewal, into conversation with the pain of randomness. For the failure to fit—the sense of being random—is not, or not only, about enduring. We often envision redemption as a perfection of present circumstances: bodies made whole, loved ones reunited, life's best moments extended into eternity. But for those who don't fit, redemption is not the answer, at least not imagined that way. For even if it arrived, it would not involve us—not as we imagine ourselves.

Us, not them—relatively few people face the same conflict as my gay Latter-day Saint friends, but virtually everyone accumulates experiences that spill over the rim of their religious understanding and splash into life's darkened corners. For my stalwart mother, for example, who faced the death of a young child with graceful heroism, to be reunited with her son would be ecstatically wonderful, but it alone would not erase the traumatic—and sanctifying—effects of all those years of grief. Or again, I think of a moving talk I once heard a woman give about how she had left the Church in large part because of stinging life disappointments. When she returned, she said, it wasn't because she found answers or fulfillment, she simply missed the company of Church members, the casual inspiration of everyday life. The disappointments endured, unresolved and unanswered.

These parts of ourselves demand more than what the scriptures call restoration, in which corruption or fallenness is raised to incorruption or perfection (see Alma 41). They demand more, even, than to find enlightenment as to why things were as they were: why we suffered as we did. For our biggest questions don't lend themselves to cheap "a-ha!" epiphanies in which all is suddenly resolved. Many such questions may not seek explanations as much as remedy, like storm-torn vessels begging harbor. They need, we need, the kind of healing found in the extended presence of Christ. As part of that healing, we long to be heard, to lay our experiences before him. We want him to feel the wounds in *our* hands and feet, in *our* sides.

So it is that literature is born. A certain kind of literature anyway. Giving voice to such longing is the apparent vocation, the invocation, of the poet Christian Wiman. Having lived with the pain and disorientation of cancer (its disruption of the lives he was building as a husband, father, and poet), Wiman is familiar with what I am describing by way of a formative conversation with a friend on a beach late at night—that is, he has lived through experiences that are profoundly real, that are true, but that don't fit our conceptions of how things are supposed to be. He understands a life that doesn't "fit." Wiman takes inspiration here and finds his reason for (religious) being from Christ:

> I am a Christian because of that moment on the cross when Jesus, drinking the very dregs of human bitterness, cries out, *My God, my God, why hast thou forsaken me?* . . . I am a Christian because I understand that moment of Christ's passion to have meaning in my own life, and what it means is that the absolutely solitary and singular nature of extreme human pain is an illusion. . . . Christ's

suffering shatters the iron walls around individual human
suffering[.] Christ's compassion makes extreme human
compassion—to the point of death, even—possible.[5]

Wiman appeals to a God of visceral feeling, a God less of transcendence
than presence in our fallen circumstances—a God of experience who
is real, who is *there*. As Wiman writes elsewhere, "You don't turn to
God in a crisis because you are afraid, at least not primarily. You turn
to God because, for once, all that background chatter in your brain, all
that pandemonium of blab, ceases, and you can *hear*—and what some of
us hear in those instances is a still, small voice."[6] To help us hear, even
see God and God us—to bring us, collectively, life in the Spirit—is, for
Wiman, the function of poetry.

His poem "Music Maybe" gives expression to this process whereby
our sorrow is radicalized, becoming fuel for a richer life in the divine
presence:

> Too many elegies elevating sadness
> to a kind of sad religion:
>
> one wants in the end just once to befriend
> one's own loneliness,
>
> to make the ache of inwardness—
>
> something,
>   music maybe,
>
> or even just believing in it,
> and summer,
>
> and the long room alone
> where the child
>
> chances on a bee
> banging against the glass
>
> like an attack of happiness.[7]

Here, sadness sees (or wishes) itself converted into "an attack of happiness." But what also finds itself converted is religion, the "sad religion" of elegy becoming "something" else—"music maybe." This is what we see in the last part of the poem where the child "chances on a bee / banging against the glass," and we recognize in that image the jubilant energy of life, of summer personified in the small body of a buzzing dervish. The "*attack* of happiness" is not necessarily happy, certainly not for the disoriented bee, whose vitality is almost painful, "banging" as it does against a substance thicker and vaster and more durable than itself. But such intensity of feeling, even if tragic, is no longer "sadness"; it radiates life. And life is never more itself than when it renders us dizzy as we ricochet from one stage or experience to another—here, in the poem, from elegy to ecstasy; from "religion" to a kind of divine infusion of spiritual energy. Poetry is that infusion: it not only *represents* life, it *presents* it, generates new attachments and realizations through its catalytic language. It exudes a keen, almost painful joy, a kind of soul-splitting exultation.

The spirited work, or play, of Wiman's poem exemplifies one of his credos: "The task is not to 'believe' in a life beyond this one; the task is to perceive it. . . . No one ever believed in God before perceiving God."[8] God first, creed second; experience first, doctrinal explanation later. This is the order life demands; this is what I began discerning on that late-night walk on the beach with a good friend. Robert's religious convictions concerning the rightness and wrongness of sexuality sounded harsh, but they were, in their way, beautiful—the product of prayer and fasting and faith, of a bold experiment in conversion. They were born of love (for God) if also hatred (of self). To that extent, they were also at least a little confused, as he began attesting years later in anger (now declaring love for self if also still hatred, this time for the Church). Hatred and anger, even when expressed as a reflexive reaction to suffering, may inhabit corners of right and wrong, but they rarely inform truth. Truth we only find in a higher key: "He that loveth not knoweth not God; for God is love" (1 John 4:8).

Wonderful metaphor, "God is love"—a poem unto itself. I worry sometimes that we distort it when we invoke it too casually, project our experience onto it too freely. The challenge, in Wiman's words, is not to "believe" in divine love but to perceive it. It's a task made more difficult by God's refusal to conform to our sense of rightness—to answer our prayers as we expect or give us what we need when we believe it most essential. God, it seems, loves us for who we are even as he moves us to continue to grow, to change; and change sometimes happens through the painful shedding of the selves we were and the views we held. Meanwhile, we fight for preservation, for fulfillment as we imagine it. And so, we try to intuit God's poetry in the apparent randomness of our circumstances or in the blows we suffer when there is no miraculous deliverance on life's street corners. We seek to discern God's love in the absence of what we typically call divine intervention.

* * *

At some point in my twenties, I grew tired of rightness but also felt that truth as God understood it was beyond me. And so, with friends like Robert, I became angry. And I was angry and therefore confused for a long time. I was angry on behalf of gay friends who felt they had no place in the Church; angry on behalf of *all* friends whose dreams of partnership and marriage and family were repeatedly disappointed and eventually extinguished (at least "in this life": a phrase I despised when used as consolation). I was angry on behalf of people whose lives were blighted by illness or accident, angry on behalf of those who felt shunned or who suffered injustice (and at those who per- petuated it even if unwittingly). I was angry on behalf of religious believers whose joy was dampened by chiding secularists and on behalf of secularists whose patience was taxed by believers' denials of cold reality. But I was not only angry "on behalf of," I was angry in my own circumstances—angry at my religion because of things I was learning as a student and then, later, at the disillusionment I felt in the profession of higher education (so much arrogance toward religion, so little understanding of it). I was angry at the hurt that had accumulated from years of being single and then, later, at the burden I felt carrying traditional familial responsibilities (e.g., to "provide," so patriarchal). I was angry at issues I did not understand (like some of the messy details of Church history) or, later, felt I understood only too well (like the reflex habits of religious thinking and the delusions and prejudices it shelters). I was angry at those who spurned my faith tradition ("*Non, monsieur, ça ne m'intéresse pas*") and then, later, at those who embraced it too enthusiastically, too naively. I was angry at the narrow bandwidth of religious "truth" or at its confusion of truth with rightness: the discourse I was hearing at church seemed so good at mimicking Robert's shallow screed on the double date but so poor at engaging the fuller version of his narrative, the one he shared later that night on the moonlit beach.

There were so many people around me, it seemed, who were so angry, and there are probably more now than there were then. How do we deal with that anger? How did I? Some people mitigate the toxic effects of their anger by sublimating it into political causes, and sometimes they level those causes against the Church. Taking up against the Church has never been my reflex—I have tended to hear God speak with me through the Church, not against it—though I certainly have my causes and nurse my hopes. But even when these causes and hopes, mine or others', strike me as wobbly, I can usually detect in them the flayed truth of personal suffering. And that always gives me pause.

If I gradually became more comfortable with not fitting, with the random drift of circumstances, this may be because I found myself taken with what I describe above as the poetry of faith—its poetry more than its politics: less the noisy construction of a godlier kingdom and the effort to make things fit than the graceful whisperings of God's Spirit through kingdoms that were already here. It was in listening more deeply that I experienced, in Wiman's words, those "attack[s] of happiness" that compelled my attention and revealed the divine presence across the gaps of my existence. Indeed, I found sometimes that God converted these gaps into metaphors, transporting me from one state into another: sadness into joy, dogma into something like a sacred encounter. When things that didn't fit suddenly didn't need to; when they suddenly, strangely were deeply okay as they were; when I felt alone and defeated and then, out of nowhere, God seemed present and things felt ecstatically good and whole—that is what moved me.

It still does. In recent years, for example, I've experienced it through my younger daughter. When she was little, she would occasionally ask for priesthood blessings when she was ill. On one dramatic occasion, I returned home at night from a church meeting to find her writhing from severe stomach pain and begging for a blessing to heal her. I called a ward member, we administered to her, and my wife and I sat with her until she fell asleep. A couple hours later, she trotted into our bedroom and announced that she was feeling completely fine—a miracle in the life of a young child and, for our little family, an important story for a season. As the years passed, however, her (now chronic) illnesses grew more complex, the writhing more diverse and extended. Priesthood blessings alone were no longer sufficient—a painful metaphor, it seemed, of a child growing beyond my reach of influence. She began drifting and so did I as a parent; letting go, accepting suffering—not struggling to heal—became the order of the day. Letting things be became a theme across multiple areas of life: work, church, friendships, and more. But the answers to my prayers, I found, also grew in richness and intensity. The more I began reeling from life's blows, the more I would occasionally find myself overwhelmed by a sense of God's presence in the most random times and places, like the morning when I sat in despondency and began a prayer with the words "Well, I'm still here" and felt overcome with divine love or the evening when a powerful answer to prayer came to me as I walked down a long city block, the winter wind scraping tears of joy and gratitude across my cheeks.

It's the randomness of these experiences, actually, that means so much to me. It's in the randomness that I feel most acutely "attack[s] of happiness," all the more compelling because they occur outside any framework of expectation, threading themselves through my existence despite the tatters in the life I keep weaving so unskillfully. The randomness matters because the divine visitations it invites do not fit, but they happen anyway. They are pure grace. And so, no, I do not know how to reassure Melinda in her sense of rootlessness, but I do feel Christ bearing her up. No, I do not know how best to make sense of the story Robert shared with me late that night on the beach (Why was he drawn away from those formative experiences and toward the Church? And why did he eventually recede back into them like the ebbing of the tide?), but I do feel the truth of his pain. No, I do not know exactly how to console any who have sought divine deliverance only to feel themselves abandoned and beaten by the bullies of everyday circumstance. I myself have experienced the miracle of such deliverance, and yet I have often felt God's love and presence more profoundly, more lastingly, when life has pummeled me to the earth.

I am grateful, deeply, for the doctrines, rituals, and benchmarks of my religion: they lend my life form. God works through them, again and again. But I believe he works outside them, too—or, perhaps better said, he reveals a religion that is larger than the set of meanings I routinely infer from it, a religion in which codes of conduct and frameworks of belief also yield something more than mere codes and frameworks. At their edges, and after the stridency of "the wind . . . the earthquake . . . [and] the fire" they can engender, I sometimes discern something different: "a still small voice" (1 Kgs. 19:11–12). I suppose I'm one for whom truth begins once my sense of rightness expends itself—in some cases, once it's beaten out of me. I then find myself standing a little more humbly alongside others in an attitude of prayer, pleading that God will see us on our Holy Saturdays, dazed but still waiting. Waiting on the Lord.

EIGHT

A Time to Mourn

One morning in late winter 2005, I glanced into the mudroom where our dog usually slept and found him wheezing and unconscious. An old dog, he was taking his last breaths. I called out to my wife, Kerry, who had owned this dog (and its litter mate, who had died the previous year) since before I knew her, and she came running. So did our daughters, ages five and three. Their gazes rotated from us to the dog and back; mine passed, anxiously, from the dog to Kerry to our children. I picked up my younger daughter and held her as the deathbed scene reached its crescendo. When our cherished pet took his last breath, my wife and older daughter fell to the floor beside him, weeping. My younger daughter, meanwhile, buried her face in my shoulder, wearing a scowl but making no sound, shedding no tear. I took her down the basement stairs to my office and rested her in my lap in the big chair at my desk. We sat in silence. After a couple minutes, a sob burst from her, then another, and another. I hugged her as she bawled and bawled.

Not quite ten years earlier, before I met Kerry, I had returned one morning to my New York City hotel room to find the phone's message light blinking. It was my father; it was urgent, he said. When I reached him, he told me a member of my Los Angeles singles ward had called our family home to share the news that my good friend Tonja had been killed in a small plane crash. I hung up the phone and sat in silence for a few minutes. Then I went out to see friends, which was the purpose of my brief side trip to New York on the heels of an academic conference. I told these friends—some, old NYU classmates; others, old ward members—about the death of this other friend whom they did not know. They asked if I was all right; I said sure, this was life, life was nasty. Awful things happen. One friend, more perceptive, kept circling back to the subject over the next couple of days. It was good to talk, I told her, but yes, I was all right. Yes, I was sure.

I returned to Los Angeles late in the week. Early on Sunday, I drove by Tonja's home and sat parked out front for a while, pondering. After sacrament meeting, several of us flocked to console each other. The bishop pulled a few into his office to discuss plans for the memorial service. He noted that I was her best friend in the ward, so he wanted me to speak. Who else should we ask? We'd need some music, and perhaps the family could help us prepare a slideshow.

As he went over logistics, I began to shake. The friend on my left put her hand on my back; the one to my right locked arms with me. I tried to concentrate on taking easy, deep breaths. I was moving into a new apartment that week, and for another day, that task kept me occupied, helped me breathe. But that evening, Monday, I decided to drive down to the family home for a couple days to collect my thoughts and write my talk. As I cruised south through soft neon, thinking on what I might say at Tonja's service, a sob burst from me. Then another, and another. As Los Angeles gave way to Orange County and Orange County to San Diego, I bawled and bawled.

✳ ✳ ✳

Like my daughter when she was little, it takes me time to wrap my mind around death. Actually, even when I'm finally able to find emotional release, I don't think I ever truly wrap my mind around it. I say this as someone who, for most of his life, has called death an intimate companion. Intimate but deeply strange.

Death and I became acquainted on a warm summer's day when I was seven. I got home in the late afternoon to find my parents' closest friends sitting with them in our living room. They were smiling as I walked in, though the room was silent. I looked from one face to another, especially at my mom's best friend. Her eyes were glistening.

My dad spoke up. "Hey, son, do you want to go play catch?"

I retrieved my baseball glove and ball from my room, went to our backyard, and took my place at a corner of the lawn. But instead of walking to the opposite corner, my dad sat on a short ledge and beckoned me over. The air seemed heavy and very still.

"Your brother died earlier today."

Adam, who was five, had been gone from home for about a week. He'd fallen sick, like I had, but he hadn't been getting better. So, they'd taken him to the hospital. I'd been there once to see him, though more than the familiar sight of my brother, it was the strangeness of the place and him in it that had left the deepest impression.

What does one do in these situations? You console the parents, that's what you do: so I reasoned in the moment. That's what all those friends were doing in our living room. You hold a moment of silence, then you try to take their minds off it. So, I sat still for several seconds staring at the grass, at the house. At the grass.

"Do you still want to play catch?" When I finally spoke, my voice was quiet, though it seemed deafening.

His was soft but firm. "No, I don't think so." And we sat in silence. After a while, he got up and walked back inside. He may have expected me to follow, or maybe he wanted to give me space to grieve. Either way, I stayed seated on the ledge.

It seemed so, so still, that heavy, gray Los Angeles air. I couldn't hear any insects, any birds, no cats or dogs. No life whatsoever. It was just me. When I went inside, I tried to avoid all the friends in the living room.

I never cried over Adam's death, not that I remember. I had insomnia over the next year, which was awful. (My bedroom was suddenly so large, so empty, so dark.) My performance in second grade was erratic, supposedly. I got into more fights on the playground. But no tears, not until I was eleven and my cat Tiger went missing for two days. My mom gave me the news, as gently as she was able, when I got home from school. The neighbors had found him underneath their porch, their small dog yapping and yapping in Tiger's face. He couldn't move, he was so ill. He had leukemia, she said; the vet had had to put him down, she said. I sobbed and sobbed and sobbed.

*   *   *

"Mr. Ramsay, stumbling along a passage one dark morning, stretched his arms out, but Mrs. Ramsay having died rather suddenly the night before, his arms, though stretched out, remained empty."[1] The sentence is one of the most shocking in literature as Virginia Woolf kills off the protagonist of her 1927 novel *To the Lighthouse* only halfway in. This not only alters our expectations for the second half of the novel, it modifies how we reflect on the first half. The entire story becomes elegiac: Mrs. Ramsay was alive, the still point at the narrative's center. And then, suddenly, she was gone.

Once we weigh this circumstance, it seems that even the first half of the novel was foreshadowing and mourning Mrs. Ramsay's imminent absence. We now understand, for example, why Woolf seems to linger on Mrs. Ramsay's aging appearance, deftly attaching her beauty, that radiant but fading aura of personhood, to other concerns: "When she looked in the glass and saw her hair grey, her cheek sunk, at fifty, she thought, possibly she might have managed things better—her husband; money; his books. But for her own part she would never for a single second regret her decision, evade difficulties, or slur over duties. She was now formidable to behold" (6). Or, to cite another instance, "with stars in her eyes and veils in her hair, with cyclamen and wild violets—what nonsense was he [Mr. Tansley, the failed philosopher] thinking? She was fifty at least; she had eight children. Stepping through fields of flowers and taking to her breast buds that had broken and lambs that had fallen; with the stars in her eyes and the wind in her hair—He took her bag" (14). At one point, the narrator poses a question that Mrs. Ramsay's death one hundred pages later will render haunting: "Was it nothing but looks, people said? What was there behind it—her beauty and splendour?" (28).

The novel's implicit answer to that question is *life*. Mrs. Ramsay is the vital emblem of life, and her aging only renders that life more complex, at once present (in trace and memory) and absent. In this way, *To the Lighthouse* is not only a meditation on love and loss. It is also, fittingly, an intensely spiritual novel about the elusive qualities that enrich life. In the words of one critic, "life" for Woolf represents a "field of energies in which the data of the senses dance mote-like in the fitful rays of the imagination."[2] The question that so preoccupied Woolf, and to which she devoted herself in her fiction, concerned these "energies" that engage our senses, awaken our minds, and attach us passionately to the world. What is "life," this wonderful and mysterious *spiritual* force that differentiates us from inert matter? Recall some of spirituality's features: zest; intensity; a feeling for what is sacred and meaningful; a care for all that promotes thriving; heightened cognition that connects ideas, memories, and emotions. All these features represent life—"*life*"—at its fullest; indeed, one scholarly definition of spirituality is "fullness of life."[3]

This, then, appears to be why Woolf creates such an elegiac novel. Only the specter of death can fully accentuate, in negative, what is so precious about life; only the death of those we love can cause us to linger over what it was that attached us so deeply to them and to everything around them in the first place. Even Mrs. Ramsay engages in such reflection. During a large dinner, she gazes over the table at family and friends and ponders the splendor of it all:

> Everything seemed possible. Everything seemed right. Just now . . . she had reached security; she hovered like a hawk suspended; like a flag floated in an element of joy which filled every nerve of her body fully and sweetly, not noisily, solemnly rather, for it arose, she thought, looking at them all eating there, from husband and children and friends; all of which rising in this profound stillness . . . seemed now for no special reason to stay there like a

smoke, like a fume rising upwards, holding them safe together. Nothing need be said; nothing could be said. There it was, all round them. It partook, she felt . . . of eternity. (104–05)

A sense of boundless possibility ("Everything seemed possible"), of "joy which filled every nerve . . . fully and sweetly," and of "profound stillness," a feeling of the sacred, "holding them safe together," in Woolf's inimitably circuitous prose. It's a profoundly spiritual moment in a novel filled with them. And the agent for all this spiritual intensity in *To the Lighthouse* is not religion but death—or, in other words, that hinge where "life" opens onto "eternity."

* * *

I met Tonja at her baptism. She was a member of our large LA ward, or so she thought. She'd been away from the Church for many years and had recently returned. But they could find no record of membership, not at Church headquarters and not in the ward in her small hometown in the mountains of northern California. She remembered being baptized as a young girl, she said, but if she needed to be baptized again, okay, she could do that. They asked her who she wanted to speak at her baptismal service, and she said the Sunday School teacher. Our friendship developed from there.

I loved many things about Tonja. She was pretty and smart and creative and ambitious and a little edgy, carrying the aura and residual habits of someone unburdened by religious mores. It felt freeing to be around her. I was such a betwixt-and-between character in those days, straddling youth and maturity, school days and professional life (being in the first year of my PhD program at UCLA), and belief and cynicism (at once battling and courting religious disillusionment). And straddling relationships always—not that I would move from one to another, but each one seemed to cut across categories, particularly friendship and romance. There was the girlfriend (or was it the best-friend-who-was-a-girl?) I had been so close to in the year and a half after my mission; there was the woman to whom I wrote love letters when I was in college but who viewed me more as her smitten poet-in-prose than as a prospective fiancé; there was the fashion mogul in New York whose Village penthouse dramatized, in its chic difference from my humble grad student quarters, the unlikelihood of a connection that was nevertheless vibrant and genuine. Heck, there was even Robert, one of my best friends who, after he came out of the closet, would introduce me as the man who would be his husband if I were gay. And so on, and so on: I was perpetually in between, never simply one thing or the other.

And so it was with Tonja too: we were instant friends and almost but not quite more than that. We would talk dreams, frustrations, futures, and our other relationships—a kind of dating game taking the outward form of mutual solace. Her sheer presence meant so much to me as she possessed a magic that close friends and more-than-friends from that betwixt-and-between stage of life always seem to have—a power to conjure a sense of possibility, even of promise, through the tiniest hint of suggestion. For example, she was a budding film producer in a small production company, and one day, she asked me, searchingly, why I was getting a PhD in literature. "You should write screenplays instead. There's a lot of money in it." I had once fantasized about working in the film industry, so Tonja's words reawakened old dreams. For years afterward, I canonized her remark as virtually prophetic, nurturing the thought of fleeing academia for a life in movies. It became a north star shining above the dimness, and occasional grimness, of my academic life.

There was then, for me, an aura about Tonja, about our friendship. Adding to it, I found myself immortalizing small moments with her the instant they occurred, like the time we were talking as she brushed her hair, an old song on the radio suffusing her room with melancholy. Or the time I made her blush by whispering something mischievous in the foyer outside our chapel. These tiny capsules of memory arresting the flow of time haunted me even as they were happening. And so, while her death made no sense, it almost seemed as if I'd been preparing unconsciously for her loss. As I had, seemingly, for every meaningful relationship since I was a boy. I'd learned that good things, the best things, can disappear with devastating suddenness.

But *her* death, no, it made no sense. She was gifted and enterprising and, at twenty-five, through no fault of her own, she spent her last moments in a welter of metal and flame. When she died, my betwixt-and-between life, all the delicate bridges I'd built between categories, collapsed as well. The years, it turns out, had rendered them brittle. So I found myself experiencing something a little different from sheer grief: I felt myself falling. I did not doubt that God existed, but I now knew I did not understand a God who permitted such things to happen—a God who took vitality and promise and twisted it into complexity, into (something like) literature, into (something like) elegy. I did not wish to live in a novel like Woolf's *To the Lighthouse*; I could no longer take life's layered ambiguities, those situations, however "beautiful," that refused the dimensions of solid and easy rightness. For weeks after Tonja's death and despite the fact that classes were starting back up at UCLA, I could not bear to read, to focus my mind on anything. I sat in my apartment gazing blankly at white walls. At night, I would drive along Sunset Boulevard, heading east into slummy Hollywood and then west all the way to the gaping Pacific, staring beyond the city into the dark sky, not so much praying as gazing in God's direction, incredulous. I could feel myself bleeding out through the windshield. My life was losing all shape, all identity. I was "without form, and void" (Gen. 1:2).

* * *

Mrs. Ramsay, too, was given to self-emptying gazes across vast spaces. One evening, she finds herself awake in the deep of night, peering across the bay at the lighthouse beam "coming regularly across the waves first two quick strokes and then one long steady stroke" (61). Her mind begins drifting outward, toward it. The sensation is soothing.

> For now she need not think about anybody. She could
> be herself, by herself. And that was what now she often
> felt the need of—to think; well, not even to think. To be
> silent; to be alone. All the being and the doing, expan-
> sive, glittering, vocal, evaporated; and one shrunk, with a
> sense of solemnity, to being oneself, a wedge-shaped core
> of darkness, something invisible to others. (62)

It's a strange self-image, this "wedge-shaped core of darkness," for it
isn't much of a "self" at all. We build selves through our attachments,
our experiences, our relationships and projects and dreams. But here,
in this episode, Mrs. Ramsay finds herself taking all those associations
of selfhood apart. As she does, she reflects that beneath appearances,
there is something primally shared about life, something "dark" and
"spreading" and "unfathomably deep; but now and again we rise to
the surface," we assume our everyday identities, "and that is what you
see us by" (62). In her case, wife, mother, aging beauty.

But evenings like these, gazing across the bay and toward the
lighthouse, connecting with something primal, reveal the illusory
quality of the outward identities, the structuring features of our lives:

> Losing personality, one lost the fret, the hurry, the stir;
> and there rose to her lips always some exclamation of
> triumph over life when things came together in this
> peace, this rest, this eternity. . . . Often she found herself
> sitting and looking, sitting and looking, with her work
> in her hands until she became the thing she looked at—
> that light, for example. And it would lift up on it some
> little phrase or other which had been lying in her mind
> like that—"Children don't forget, children don't forget"—
> which she would repeat and begin adding to it, It will
> end, it will end, she said. It will come, it will come, when
> suddenly she added, We are in the hands of the Lord.
>
> But instantly she was annoyed with herself for saying
> that. Who had said it? Not she; she had been trapped into
> saying something she did not mean. (63)

This is a provocative, and telling, turn of events. Mrs. Ramsay suddenly finds herself channeling a popular current of thought during the early part of the twentieth century. Many writers, Woolf included, sought imaginatively to fashion a new world untethered to traditions of all kinds, including religion. Religion, like those outward features of Mrs. Ramsay's identity, had something artificial and compulsive about it, something that did not open people to transcendence as much as mire them in ideas in which they no longer believed. Hence, one critic remarks that "there is a gap between [Mrs. Ramsay's] secular 'belief'" in the absence of God "and the continuing inner authority of emotions, along with the interpretations of the world embedded in them, that have been bound historically to religious language."[4] Mrs. Ramsay's appeal to God is thus a sign of her entrapment in untruth ("she had been trapped into saying something she did not mean") but also a reflex of what draws her, draws us, to things of value. For her, God (as object and symbol of religion) is what is wrong with our present existence even as God (as vehicle of spiritual purpose) is what makes life—or "*life*"—so meaningful in the first place. This is where the novel's preoccupation with spiritual experience becomes especially compelling because it helps us understand how Mrs. Ramsay is, here, drawn toward spirituality both in the form of religion ("We are in the hands of the Lord") and in the open-ended allure of transcendence (in feeling carried out of herself and across the bay). The episode asserts her connection to something greater than herself. As a result, a sense of the divine remains with Mrs. Ramsay even though she no longer claims religious belief per se.

This feeling of loss of self and tradition, and of loss of explicable if not vital connection to God, describes my state of mind in the wake of Tonja's death. "We are in the hands of the Lord": such a sentence could only have sounded obscene to me at the time, though I could not escape the conviction of God's involvement in anything concerning Tonja, including the horrible accident that had taken her away. On that score, there was a sense I had of God's abiding presence in my sorrow, of his silence alongside my mourning, almost a form of solidarity. No explanation for Tonja's death could have seemed adequate, religious or otherwise, but this sense of shared grief felt different. I found myself offering prayers of anguish—and of gratitude for the ability even to offer such prayers. For this divine silence, this note of collective sorrow, was strangely healing. It recomposed, if not my sense of self and purpose, certain foundational experiences. Gazing back some twenty years across a bay of time to my backyard on that summer afternoon when I learned my brother was dead, I now discerned God's presence there as a lighthouse beam piercing the dense fog of my hurt and incomprehension. That light had always, somehow, stayed with me and was with me still. It did not answer my questions; it did not make everything okay. But I knew I was not alone, then or now, in that heavy, gray Los Angeles air.

* * *

Tonja's memorial service was planned for Friday. That Monday, I moved boxes and some furniture into my new apartment. A woman in the ward whom I did not know, Kim, called and arranged to meet me there. She was assigned to create the program for the service, and she had the idea to make a collage on its cover. I had some of Tonja's paintings, poems, books; Kim wanted to borrow them, make an image of them. So she came by after work to pick them up. Light was dimming in my apartment as the electricity would not turn on until the next day. Nevertheless, she stayed and listened to me pour out my grief as dusk passed into evening. After she left, I drove home to San Diego, bawling and vowing to Tonja, wherever she was, that I would try to say something to help people at the service understand her better. To help them, all of us, memorialize her.

I prepared my talk over the next couple of days, alternating between sorrow and fits of rage. My dad happened to come into my room during one of those latter moods. Unable to restrain myself, I began venting—partly at God, mostly at the Church. It was so, so inadequate at lending meaning to events like these, I said; its doctrine was so lacking in depth, in detail. "Where does the Church say Tonja is now?!" I screamed. "The 'spirit world.' 'Paradise.' But what does that mean?! How meaningless is that?! Imagine if I get up to speak on Friday and say to everybody, 'Do you know who Tonja was? I'll tell you. She was... an American.' What the hell would that mean?! It wouldn't mean anything! So now we say 'Tonja is in the spirit world; she's in paradise': it's like saying 'She's an American!'"

My father had been a church leader practically my entire life: bishop, stake president, regional representative. At the time, he was a newly called General Authority. That probably made my venting more pointed. For I was his son, and I had been born, any of us had been born, for what? To die, ultimately. All religious explanation seemed so flimsy, so flat in trying to account for life's richness, let alone the feeling of its extinction in our loved ones and eventually ourselves. And my dad and all the ecclesiastical authority he personified could say nothing to make that reality any less excruciating, any less cruel.

I waited for him to speak, practically defying him to dish out some trite religious drivel. But instead, he just sat still on the edge of my bed, looking me earnestly in the eye. He began to tear up. "I'm so sorry, son. I'm so, so sorry." Something in me broke, and I began sobbing, the way one might have expected of a seven-year-old boy in our backyard some twenty years earlier.

The memorial service was held later that week. I gave my talk, experienced a day or two of catharsis, then settled into my own wedge-shaped core of darkness. I began taking my nighttime drives through Los Angeles, staring at and beyond the city, at and beyond the sky. The school term started, not that I cared. I felt the same indifference for church—for the talks and lessons at least—though I took some solace there in the presence of friends.

Speaking of which, Kim, who created the program for Tonja's memorial service, had said something to me during our dusky conversation that struck me as particularly absurd if also unusually generous. She said she knew it sounded awkward, but as I was talking, she was thinking that I should meet her sister. This sister had had several friends die, and Kim thought we'd have a lot to say to each other. She lived in northern California but occasionally came down this way for work. Would I be interested in getting together?

Death is so dehumanizing to those who are left behind—suggesting, as it does, the emptiness of everyday life, of work-sleep-work-sleep and the dreams we forge in compensation—that I found Kim's gesture moving. It was the worst imaginable moment to be set up on what amounted to a blind date, but for that reason, it seemed to lean into the absurdity of all existence. It was defiantly hopeful, and that defiance spoke to me.

So, a few weeks later, Kim knocked on my door, and we began making our way to her car. She apologized for tagging along. No problem, I said; if her sister preferred a group conversation to a conventional date, that was fine. It was kind of them to be willing to talk at all.

I climbed into the back seat, and Kim got behind the wheel. "Matt, this is Kerry." When the woman in the passenger seat turned and smiled, something in me broke again. But this time, it felt like happiness.

NINE

Promises Kept,
Promises Pending;
or, Dear Kerry...

God keeps his promises: one of the great themes of scripture. "I do set my bow in the cloud, and it shall be for a token of a covenant between me and the earth," he vows to Noah after the flood (Gen. 9:13); "I will make of thee a great nation," he pledges to Abraham (Gen. 12:2); "there hath not failed one word of all [God's] good promise, which he promised by the hand of Moses his servant," exclaims King Solomon (1 Kgs. 8:56); "I send the promise of my Father upon you," Christ assures his disciples (Luke 24:49), later received by them as "the promise of the Holy Ghost" (Acts 2:33); "I will fulfill my promises," God declares regarding the house of Israel (2 Ne. 10:17); "I, the Lord, am bound when ye do what I say; but when ye do not what I say, ye have no promise," he warns the Latter-day Saints (D&C 82:10); "Fear not, little flock; for it is your Father's good pleasure to give you the kingdom," Christ promises to all who love him (Luke 12:32).

God's promises figure centrally in the religious imagination of Latter-day Saints, who make a series of covenants with God: baptism, confirmation, priesthood ordination (for men), and temple covenants (in which priesthood rites and promises are received and shared by both men and women). A former General Young Women's president of the Church described her covenants as "an expression of [her] faith" which help her "focus on the big picture, not just the immediate."[1] Another leader, Barbara Thompson (formerly of the General Relief Society presidency), declares that "making and keeping sacred covenants enables us to have the Holy Spirit with us.... Keeping covenants [brings] true joy and peace," perhaps because they lift us above the vicissitudes, confusion, and disappointments of the everyday.[2] A covenant is a promise that binds the present to a more glorious future.

Those everyday disappointments weigh heavily though. They've made me more reflective about my own covenants. I've made them, the big ones I mention above and also hundreds, probably thousands of smaller ones: "I'll try harder"; "I'll be better"; "I won't leave." And while I believe that the Lord knows better than to always hold us to our word ("Just get me out of this situation, and I promise I'll never do anything stupid like this again": a recurring prayer as a teen), he always keeps his word to us. However, especially when I was in my twenties and entering my years of faith crisis, I was frequently moved to wonder about the form that word would take. Did God understand his promises to me the way I did? Or what if he kept his promises much later than I was expecting? If God deferred fulfilling a covenant until some distant moment, would "I" still be present to recognize it? Would I, as I then knew myself and as one who believed he *needed* at least some promises fulfilled, witness God acting on my behalf? Or would the realization of promises only come to some future being, some future iteration of myself?

$$* \quad * \quad *$$

Dear Kerry,   *from Christmas 1996*
     ... Do you know the memory I most treasure from the twenty-four hours leading up to and including our wedding [last March]? It isn't the

ceremony in the temple but rather the previous day we spent together getting the marriage license, going to lunch in the so-so Mexican restaurant, walking through Pic 'N' Save, and hanging out in my brothers' apartment—basically, doing nothing and enjoying the nothingness. Then and now, it was less the ceremonial pronouncement that moved me than your presence in the midst of mundane things. Then and now, I loved less your role in the collective eternity that was to be than your poetry in the private eternity that already was. . . .

✳ ✳ ✳

I returned from my mission in early June 1988. I was twenty-one. Sometime in August, it must have been, I found myself at a church dance, the scene as depressing as ever. (I have no good memories, not one, of church dances. And I've been to a few.) Just like the bad old days, I was back in the gymnasium of our ward building, the lights were dimmed, nobody was on the dance floor, and few people were lining the walls. Everybody who was anybody in my peer group was elsewhere. Feeling alone and like a total loser—basically, feeling myself transported back to my high school years—I was asking myself why I had bothered showing up and when, and how, I could get out of there. And then, suddenly, from a door across the gym, a woman entered, led by her friend, and began walking to the middle of the floor. I was instantly, ecstatically beside myself. "That's her!" I exclaimed half out loud to nobody in particular. "That's her! She's different than I remember her, but it's her!" I rushed to intercept her, barely feeling myself move. She was startled to see me—it had been a long time—but she gazed at me expectantly, and a little bashfully, waiting for me to speak. I was overcome with joy, though I found myself tongue-tied. I never expected this day actually to happen even though I knew, somehow, that it must.

Then I woke up. Of course, I woke up. However vivid, the dream was too good—and too melodramatic, too teen-movieish—to be true. Nevertheless, like Lehi's strange dream about a tree, mine had instantly persuasive force. It felt like a divine message, one I could not fail to understand. But as time passed—and by "time," I mean the next several years—the dream detached itself from any prospect of fulfillment. It seemed less real than surreal: psychologically and even spiritually true but not outwardly so. It was nothing of this world.

In another sense, of course, it was thoroughly enmeshed in this world. "That's her!" That's Jan: a girl on whom I'd had an enormous crush in high school. I remember the day, hour, occasion, and place when I first saw her. (It was a high school assembly, faces streaming into the gym. Suddenly, there was one I had never seen before—a petal on a wet, black bough[3]—holding me transfixed.) I have loads of stories—some deeply embarrassing, some a little endearing—about how I maneuvered to introduce myself to her, how I asked her out, how I said awkward things to her trying to be cool or express my feelings . . . We had next to nothing in common, but I found her intoxicating. To my young heart, she personified romantic attraction. And so, when I had this dream, when I saw, again, this different-Jan-than-Jan (this person who wasn't her but looked like her, uncannily evoked her: "She's different than I remember her, but it's her!") and when I once again felt charged by these energies of soul, I knew, or thought I knew, how it would feel when—if—I met the person I would eventually marry. And that was problematic because, at the time, I was dating my best friend, an extraordinary woman, and our relationship was growing serious.

✳ ✳ ✳

In October 1989, a little more than a year after my dream, I transferred to BYU. That first year-plus after my mission had been rich in learning and friendship. However, as the months wore on, the canyon breeze (as I describe it in chapter 5) began blowing more crisply. By the time I left for Utah, that breeze had become a stiff spiritual and emotional headwind. So, it seemed symbolic and fitting that on my first morning in Provo, Catherine—my best friend and girlfriend—called to break up. Ever since my dream the previous summer, I'd had a foreboding this would happen and believed it was probably for the best. But I suddenly felt very alone, winds of doubt and disillusionment whipping all around me.

That loneliness would deepen over the months that followed. It wasn't for lack of good friends. Some of it, I'm sure, was a product of the kind of low-grade depression and anxiety that are common among college students. But common as it may have been, it felt cosmic. I was particularly haunted by the last conversation I'd had with Catherine. She'd grown tired of the stagnation that, for the previous year, had come to define our relationship and had decided in a burst of inspiration to transfer to BYU. Arriving six weeks before me, she had flown back home to San Diego for a long weekend, and the two of us had driven back to Utah. The mood in the car was heavy, dense with a spirit of defeated expectation. But we were accustomed to such things, I thought (or the defeated returned missionary in me thought); our friendship had seemingly evolved through them. And as we entered Provo in the quiet of night, I was grateful for this relationship with someone so good and with whom I had shared so much history. She was a promise of sunshine and blue sky, of better days behind and ahead. Portentous dreams and old high school fantasies notwithstanding, could I imagine a better life partner? Wasn't it time I grew up and embraced my life, my future?

Then, early the next morning, the phone rang. "Matt, I can't see you anymore. Not now, not for a while." Catherine had met someone during the six weeks we'd been apart, someone seemingly free of my emotional and spiritual burdens. Understandably, she found the contrast liberating. "I need to give this a chance, Matt, and I can't if you're around. So, I don't want you calling me, I don't want you writing. Please don't stop by." Part of me, the best friend, was thrilled for her, thrilled at her, even there in the moment, over the phone. I knew how difficult this must be for her, knew how closely she and I were knit, knew some doubts she already harbored about this new person in her life. But I also knew what, in her own life, she was running from—and what, with her determined spirit, she was running toward—and I believed in her and her future.

Of course, the rest of me was instantly bewildered, disoriented. Ever since I was a boy, I had understood, only too intimately, the fragility of all things, all relationships; everyone and everything, I knew, were mortal, capable of dying. Had I somehow lost sight of this with my best friend? What had caused such forgetting? How could I have been so careless?

Catherine's voice streamed from the phone; white, empty sunlight spilled through a window. My gaze fell on desiccated leaves crumbling on a dingy landing. Within a week, it would be snowing.

✳ ✳ ✳

Dear Kerry   *from Christmas 2003*

     ... I missed you last week, with you and the girls being far from me. [Note: We spent Christmas that year with Kerry's parents. She flew out early with our daughters as I was wrapping up my semester.] *I chuckled privately that it was almost a week of phone conversations before we had the occasion (mostly because of little people tugging on you from your end of the line) to discuss anything other than "business": the girls this, the house that, the pets the other. Responsibilities and distractions are the rules rather than the exceptions in our conversations these days, it seems. However, I spent some tender moments with your lingering presence in the still emptiness of our home. These moments were mostly born of images, associations: memories of you smiling, or gesturing, or just being.*

     Images like these are vital because they speak to impressions that undergird but also supersede "reality." After all, reality these days more closely resembles our conversation early Sunday evening when you could barely think straight because the girls were climbing all over you, or else it reflects our talk Thursday afternoon, when you were imploring me to send the noisemaker to you in the mail so that the girls could sleep, or the talk we had before I left for the airport when I was too anxious from deadlines to think straight. If you had asked me to share my most private thoughts during any of these moments, all I probably would have done is rattle off a list of tasks: finish grading, make revisions to the book manuscript, run errands before leaving town, etc. . . .

* * *

It often takes me a long time to correlate dream and reality. When I was eighteen, I wanted to be an actor. Inspired by my mission experience, this dream evolved into a desire to be a literature professor, and eventually it came true. I felt blessed, to be sure, but the "reality" version of this dream is complicated. My professional life has taken some good turns, but it is also laced with disappointments. Initially, these disappointments seemed like bad luck, but the passing years increasingly revealed them to be extensions of my own shortcomings—failings of intelligence or wisdom or discipline or skill. Strangely, then, over time, my growing consciousness of these failings turned my reality into something of a dream, into something that felt like it should only have happened to a better version of myself, a version whose shadow I was, am, forever chasing. I began to see how I had been given more than I had earned. And so, at some point along my career path, I began trying to live my dream differently, to live it as the person I wish I had been when I was younger. That younger version of myself made promises to God. The older version, it turns out, mostly kept them. This book, for example, which indicates the priority I vowed to accord to spiritual things, is a product of those old promises.

A similar scenario has played out in my marriage. I have always felt blessed by Kerry: meeting her was, in unthinkably vivid ways, a dream come true. But the dream is complicated. I was living through a long period of anger and disillusionment when we met, and those feelings took years to dissipate. They took a toll on my mood, attitude, spirit. Add to it that Kerry and I have complementary but different personalities, and I have wondered, sometimes, whether our partnership might have been easier had we been wired more similarly. We were blessed to have children when it seemed we might not enjoy that privilege, and they are beautiful people. But parenting has driven me repeatedly to my knees, especially as our daughters have grown older and their lives have grown more complicated. My dream of family, such as it is, is therefore not exactly what I imagined in my child's eye. Over time, though, I have discerned more clearly how some of the complexities of my family life have resulted from my shortcomings. I've always been a loyal spouse, but I understand now how I could have been a more present one; I've been a dependable and loving parent, but I see now how I might have been a more attentive one; and so on.

In my marriage, as in my professional life, dream eventually yielded to reality, and reality slowly began to look like a dream, like something that should have happened to a better version of myself. At this stage of my life, years later, this has led me to new dreams and new—renewed—questions: Could I become, now, the person I wish I had been when I was younger? Given my life's experience, what do I think it means for a dream to come true—for God to keep his promises to us and for us to keep ours to God? And what is the relationship between these promises, our dreams, and our spiritual lives?

✻ ✻ ✻

After that phone call from Catherine on an early October morning of 1989, my first day at BYU, I would not have another girlfriend until I met Kerry six years later. I went on lots of dates, I met lots of amazing people, I developed one particularly intense crush (let me cut to the chase: it went nowhere), I enjoyed the company of wonderful friends, and I lived in amazing places, like New York City and Los Angeles. As I mentioned in chapter 8, I found myself in lots of betwixt-and-between, neither-this-nor-that relationships. But nothing conventionally romantic. I never forgot the electrifying dream that had enraptured me just two months off my mission; without fixating on it, I watched for its fulfillment, waiting for life to imitate art. But as my twenties dragged on, I believed a little less that that was how life worked, and I grew ever less certain about the provenance of the dream's inspiration. "That's her! She's different than I remember her, but it's her!" What was that? Was it an answer to prayer? Was it malevolent, like the enemy who sows tares among the wheat (see Matt. 13:24–30), with the effect of destroying my relationship with Catherine, my best friend? Or, most likely, was it simply a product of my complicated psyche, a residue of old attachments and new anxieties? Had I sublimated those feelings into a beautiful image, a beautiful story? Had I illegitimately accorded it spiritual meaning? Was it poetry—and nothing but?

R. S. Thomas was particularly adept at posing agonizing spiritual and psychological questions about whether our hopes and attachments, our deepest beliefs, are more than merely poetry, are actually *real*. "In a Country Church," published in 1955, conjures them with acute poignancy:

> To one kneeling down no word came,
> Only the wind's song, saddening the lips
> Of the grave saints, rigid in glass;
> Or the dry whisper of unseen wings,
> Bats, not angels, in the high roof.
>
> Was he balked by silence? He kneeled long,
> And saw love in a dark crown
> Of thorns blazing, and a winter tree
> Golden with the fruit of a man's body.[4]

Similar to "Kneeling," which we discussed in chapter 7, this poem is set in a church. Also like "Kneeling," this poem is evocative and atmospheric, "the grave saints, rigid in glass," situating us in place and mood. Movingly, the poem explores a gentle tension between its first and second stanzas. The vision of "love in a dark crown," of Christ on the cross, seems to be the ultimate answer to the supplicant's prayer inasmuch as Christ's atonement amounts to a promise of redemption— our crises, injustices, and unanswered questions resolved in a higher key. Except here, such spiritual resolution may be illusory. We do not know what has driven the supplicant to his knees, only that, in the first stanza, "no word came," only metaphors, poetic images as a kind of cheerful supplement: "the wind's song" and the "whisper" of bats' wings converting desolation into beauty. The poet takes his petition to God, and at least at first, poetry comes in the place of direct answers.

In the next stanza, however, the relationship between poetry and prayer seems more ambiguous still. "He kneeled long, / And saw. . . ." Saw what? Did he *see* at all? The poet resorts to figures of speech, specifically metonymy (a connection to something through an attribute we associate with it—here, Christ through an emblem of his sacrifice: "love in a dark crown / Of thorns") and metaphor (a tacit comparison, in this case of the effects of Christ's atonement with a bountiful harvest: "a winter tree / Golden with . . . fruit"). Hence, the poet's mode of vision is poetic language: poetry. But that begs the question of the source of that vision. Is poetry its oracle or its origin? Is poetry the poet's medium for describing what he has experienced independently of the poem, or is poetry the engine that generates that experience in the first place? Does poetry express what is real, or does poetry create it? Is it the *vehicle* for an answer to prayer, or is it *the answer itself*—that is, what is given in place of the concrete answers we seek?

By the time I was in my mid-twenties, these were the kinds of questions I routinely asked myself. For instance, what was I to do with the dream I'd had just two months off my mission? Did it portend fulfillment or reveal anything essential about my state of mind? Or was it just. . . poetry? Just a beautiful image offset from the cares and questions with which I felt burdened? Was it just a shadow flickering on the cave wall of young adult unrest?

But the dream had felt *so* real, *so* urgent, that it raised deeper questions still. Was *any* feeling of inspiration, particularly those that felt religious or spiritual, anything other than "poetry"? What did it mean for *anything* to be spiritually true? Because, during those long years that had followed—years of study and questioning and loneliness and creeping doubt, years of gaps and Holy Saturdays and gentle irony—so many tenets of my religion struck me as both true *and* false. The scriptures were true, except where they weren't; prophets spoke God's word, except when they didn't; keeping the commandments makes us happy, except when it doesn't. And so on, and so on. All these things so, so important in determining the course of our lives. And all of them just... poetry?

* * *

Dear Kerry,   *addendum to Christmas 2012*

I seem always to write my Christmas letter to you on December 24th, often late in the night. Every year, I swear to take some pressure off myself by finishing it earlier. This year, I achieved that goal, completing your letter on the afternoon of December 23rd. However, had I actually written your letter on the 24th, it would have been very different. Last night, the 23rd, you had your episode with a racing, arrhythmic heart that took us to the emergency room and kept us up until 2:30 in the morning. More medical procedures will follow, doubtlessly. But this whole experience puts everything in a different perspective.

I find it poetic that the problem that took us to the hospital was heart-related. The heart is an essential organ of which we are usually unaware. We can accelerate or lower its rate of activity by some choices (Am I exercising or sleeping? Working or at rest?), but we cannot raise or drop it beyond certain thresholds. It acts of its own accord, prompted by impulses that have nothing to do with our will. It is, as it were, a kind of bodily unconscious. When it functions, we have life, and with life, we build worlds through a complex weave of determination and circumstance, desire and opportunity. But when the heart ceases working properly, it exposes the lives we lead—the worlds we build—as unrealities, fictions. Illusions. The Christmas letter I wrote yesterday was, effectively, rooted in illusion. It reflects on what for me were persistent thoughts during an especially intense year for us individually and for our family; commenting on accomplishments and prospects, it is swept up in world-building and assumes, complacently, the durability of those worlds, those lives. But then an incident like last night comes up, and it tears away the fabric of all my seemingly durable hopes and plans, all my "worlds" and "lives."

You are my life, Kerry. Without you, I am nothing. . . .

* * *

"Without you, I am nothing": that too is illusion. Better said, it's the stuff of love letters, of poetry, of dream rather than reality; it simplifies life's complexities into a single, overriding principle of love. But my life has always been filled with dreams, poetry—whether those that blossom into reality or that pop up again through my life's soil after a season of wintry disillusionment when old realities decay and become topsoil for new dreams.

I would eventually come to praise God for the mercy of these dreams, including those that were a little too illusory—for the relationships that might have been but weren't, for the scholarly projects that seemed so important at their moment of inception only to fade into irrelevance, and for the zeal that made my religious criticisms seem so righteous, at least for a season. As time would eventually reveal, I was blessed by these illusions, many of them. Better said, I was blessed by God's poetry—by the regular, almost metrical procession of small events, the series of elegant metaphors evoking better things ("Not this exactly, Matt, but something like it, something more beautiful, even. . ."; "You're almost there, just one more horizon. Good, now one more. . ."). I now see that if God had answered many of my prayers without any varnish of illusion, I could not have handled the truth, not at that moment.

Take the persistent prayer fueled by loneliness, the one where I wondered whether I would ever marry and, if so, whom. When I was twenty-five, the truthful answer would have been "Well, Matt, the person you will marry ended up getting hitched to a 'rebound' boyfriend, and she's presently in the process of solemnizing that rebound relationship in the temple." That was true; Kerry's young adult life was as complicated as mine, if not more so. But such an answer would have made no sense to me. Or, if it had, I'd have been overwhelmed by a feeling of loss. So I reflected later how God sent (and, in some ways, still sends) me life poems—dreams—rich in imagery, rife with symbolism, dense with mood. Things in which I can believe, and can partly understand, even when they prove only to be metaphors. T. S. Eliot's glum words apply to me, albeit, I have learned, more hopefully: "human kind / cannot bear very much reality."[5]

God's poetry is not the same thing as falsehood. Something is false when it is factually incorrect or harmful. "But behold, that which is of God inviteth and enticeth to do good continually; wherefore, every thing which inviteth and enticeth to do good, and to love God, and to serve him, is inspired of God" (Moro. 7:13). That was the effect of the divine poems that lit my paths in the wilderness. Those relationships I chased? The scholarly projects into which I poured my heart and soul (this one. . . now this one. . . now this one. . .) and that laid the groundwork for some professional success and plenty of disappointment—and whose significance always faded in time? The religious convictions that seemed to be teetering and that I replaced, temporarily, with new certainties? ("Someone may prove some point of doctrine or historical claim to be false, but no matter, for ultimate truth is found only in revelation, not in theology or history!") All these things, bound in "poetry," nevertheless enticed me in the general direction of goodness—of companionship (marriage, yes, but also meaningful friendships), of learning (about things, yes, but also about thinking), and of a belief in the reality of God above all human contingencies. And gradually, like fog beneath a summer sun, these poems began to evolve stylistically into a different, more deeply redemptive experience of the Word (John 1:1). I eventually found myself in a substantive relationship; my scholarly projects, even the obscure ones, helped me build a fulfilling intellectual and professional life that refined my mind and character; and my religious convictions proved surprisingly durable, much more so than the secular theories (all those post-Nietzschean assertions of the death of God) that once threatened to take them down.

I evoke these shimmery promises, these dreams, in terms of poetry, but perhaps it's more accurate to describe them through the metaphor of the novel. Because to some questions I asked in prayer, those that plagued me during my twenties (and others that haunt me today), I do not believe there is a single word or sentence God could have communicated that would have pacified me. There is no beautiful line he could have spoken, no rapturous image that would have synthesized everything perfectly for me. The answers I sought were, often unbeknownst to me, too intricate, composed of too many parts and too dependent on timing. They had to unfold piece by piece. In effect, they weren't poems as much as novels, and I just had to keep reading. All the way to the end.

I arrived at a new appreciation of God's literary ways, of his artistry, that night in October 1995 when Kim, the woman in my ward who designed the program for Tonja's memorial service, picked me up and drove the two of us, along with her sister, to a Thai restaurant in Santa Monica. As I sat across from them, I was struck by the familiar aura, even the look—the uncanny physical resemblance—of Kim's sister to someone I'd seen, or dreamt I'd seen, so many years earlier. The words almost formed of themselves, echoing softly in the background as we talked: *That's her. She's different than I remember her, but that's her.*

* * *

Dear Kerry,   *from Christmas 2014*
    . . . As I've thought about the blur of our past year, it's seemed to me that it's been more defined by a passage through large things, or perhaps by the thickness of the texture of our lives, than it has by individual moments. And it's probably the sign of a blessed life that this is so—that these individual moments seem to meld into something bigger and more meaningful than themselves. I do feel very blessed and this despite the ever-deepening well of personal sorrows that typically accompanies age (over friendships that have decayed, periods of life that have expired, opportunities that have disappeared or that never materialized, failures I can't undo). I feel these pangs, but mostly, I feel gratitude for the blessings God grants (involving friendships that have blossomed, periods of life I presently enjoy, opportunities that have materialized, etc.). And when I think of how the memories,

the "moments," fade into "non-moments"—when I consider how the orna-
ments of my life are increasingly lost in its texture—I find you densely
woven into its weave.

Whatever the concept of eternity means relative to "eternal marriage,"
I think it must consist, at least experientially, in something that is less a
"moment" than a non-moment. It must be a deeply burnished impression
or perhaps a set of impressions that eventually grows so massive it draws
all new experiences into itself, each of them redeemed by their absorption
into the luminous whole. And so, Kerry, my deepening sense of life, God,
and eternity is bound up in you and you in them. My moments are (also)
non-moments. And they're richer for that very reason.

I'm grateful this Christmas, this year, and at this season of life for all
our non-moments. They're truer than what we typically call memories,
those relatively shallow instances of heightened experience on which we
often fixate when we recall the past. Increasingly, Kerry, with each passing
year, you are deeper to me than any memory. You are meaning itself.

I love you.

* * *

The chapter could end there. The story, really, could end there with
all of life's uncertainties, contingencies, and pains absorbed into an
impression of blissful eternity. There is something evocatively true
about such impressions: they register differences between human and
divine existence and between degrees of understanding and happiness. Spiritual experience never fails to remind us of these differences.
To register the Spirit means welcoming God's presence, but this is
not the same thing as living in that presence or experiencing what
scriptures call "fullness of joy." Spiritual experience thus graces life
even as it attests to a greater fullness that is not yet ours. Add to it that
Latter-day Saint theology teaches that eternal life does not dissolve
into choral ecstasy of never-ending praise as much as extend into an
ever-widening circle of relationships. Eternity multiplies our associations and our empathy, and with empathy comes pain as well as joy.

With that as a backdrop, let me share two more letters, written twelve years apart:

Dear Kerry,   *from Christmas 2005*

. . . One day, I was in my basement office working feverishly on some assignment when I heard your voice call out something indistinct, followed by two singsong replies from our little girls. About thirty seconds or so later, I heard plates clanking; clearly, it was time for lunch. And it dawned on me that out of 365 days in a year, you probably make, what, 250 of those lunches? 300? That's a lot of cold cuts, babe. But what struck me, more than the daily ritual itself, was your defining role in creating an atmosphere of love, reassurance, and security for our little ones. The lilting voices and rattling dishes bespoke a home environment they will cherish in memory and, at some unspoken level, in deep-seated feelings of well-being. They will grow older and, one day, old but they will carry the associations, the aura, of their childhood home with them. And while I wear a variety of domestic hats and love our girls, it is you, Kerry, who are the chief architect of that home in formative memory. You are the poet laureate of their lives. . . .

Dear Kerry,   *from Christmas 2017*

There have been several occasions this year when you've conjured an association for me of the last three sentences of Samuel Beckett's strange and powerful, but bleak, 1953 novel The Unnamable: *"You must go on. I can't go on. I'll go on." The most recent instance was just a few nights ago. We'd been out as a family to buy stocking stuffers and had had a great time; the girls were chipper as this is one of the traditions they cherish, as you know. We returned home, turned on some Christmas music, and did our "gifts to Jesus," another nice tradition. Everyone seemed happy. At some point, when it was pushing 9:00, Elena went to her room to get ready for bed; I went upstairs to do the same. You told me you were staying downstairs for just a couple minutes to do a thing or two and perhaps chat with Hadley. But a couple minutes turned into fifteen, then thirty, then sixty. Finally, when it was much later, you came upstairs looking drained, emotionally as well as physically. I'd gone to bed, and the lights were off. You hunched over in the dusky light by the foot of your side of the bed. I asked some version of "What kept you?" And you replied with some version of "What do you think?" Sometime after a happy evening and going to her room, Elena had fallen into a darker mood and had summoned you. And in what has become something of a ritual, you lay down beside her, listened to her, cried with her, expressed love and compassion for her, and imparted some of your singular energy to her—energy that seems to be one of the things these days that gives her the will to hold on.*

On a recent night previous to this, I'd come into Elena's room when you were with her. I stood by the door in the dark as you counseled her about medications, and she cried in anguish. The mood in the room was red and raw. Agonizing. And so, a couple nights later, when you came up late, slumped in the neon-lit shadows, and told me you'd been talking with Elena, I had a better feeling for where you'd been—where you'd had to go.

∗   ∗   ∗

I write Christmas letters every year to my daughters as well as my wife. This past year, 2020, I transcribed a poem in each and reflected on how that poem captured, for me, something of who or where that person is. For Kerry, it was Christina Rossetti's "In the Bleak Mid-Winter," a carol about finding God during seasons of depression. For Hadley, our eldest and a cheerful, light-bringing soul, it was Thomas Hardy's "The Darkling Thrush," a lyric about a bird's song whose hopefulness she personifies. And for Elena, it was "Life on Earth" by Dorianne Laux, a poem about the miracle of life and persevering in honor of that miracle. ("The odds are we never should have been born," it begins.)

The odds are that neither of our children should have been born. Elena in particular was a surprise as she arrived without the infertility treatment we'd needed for Hadley. Fittingly, Elena seemed to burst precociously through life: telling elaborate stories at age two, reading at age three, star student from nursery school forward, writing novels (and winning contests) before she was a teen. Precociously spiritual too—an eloquent speaker, Young Women's class president, caregiver to the marginalized on the school playground: "an old soul," a local church leader dubbed her. But the same force of nature applied to her illnesses, which came early and with ferocity: diagnosed with fibromyalgia (usually an older person's painful ailment) when she was fourteen, accompanied with chronic migraines and fatigue, undergoing blackouts and a series of concussions at sixteen, experiencing regular seizures and ministrokes by seventeen, all devolving into mental illness by eighteen. Along the way, she fell into religious despondency, declared she was bisexual, moved in with a girlfriend, and had her name removed from the records of the Church. She'd just turned nineteen. I learned about it from the stake president for whom I had been serving as counselor for nearly six years—that is, for the duration of Elena's struggles. He called one evening after dinner, grief straining his voice. "Hey, I just received a letter from Church headquarters. . . ."

Kerry and I received our daughters as miracles; we gave Hadley the middle name of Grace as a token of her meaning to us. I've always been close with each girl. My prayers for them through their midteens were mostly of gratitude, for they were glorious children: smart, beautiful, loving, faithful. As they matured and began facing more complicated emotional landscapes, my prayers for them frequently took the form of cries for inspiration. Happily, inspiration always came readily and provided temporary remedy. Then, as complexity overtook them, particularly as pain engulfed Elena, the prayers evolved yet again, this time into fervent pleas for relief or miraculous intervention. When none arrived, my prayers descended into lament.

Answers still came, thank heaven, just as they always had; I never felt that God abandoned me or left my family alone to deal with harsh new circumstances. However, I found that these latest answers to prayer increasingly took an old, familiar form: gentle irony. A light from a corner of my darkness. A soft voice echoing through deep canyons of the ominous and unknown. I was anguished, and God was not. I mourned the prospect of lost futures for my children, and God did not. I expressed regret, and God would have none of it.

I lack a language for the strange hopefulness of these spiritual ministrations, for the joy it seemed God expressed, and expresses still, on my behalf even if I could not, cannot, feel it myself. Scripture helps me make some sense of things, for example, "whoso believeth in God might with surety hope for a better world" (Ether 12:4). But in many cases, scriptural passages are too larded with layers of cultural expectation (of missions and temple marriages and "a continuation of the seeds forever and ever" [D&C 132:19]) to capture properly the spiritual impressions that suffuse me. Instead, and with a jolt of gentle surprise, I find welcome company in memories of my years of faith crisis; I take comfort in associations of that long night of the soul when I had felt besieged with doubts, burdened with disappointment, and adrift in disillusionment. For, during that season, the world had grown so large, but God had proven to be greater still. And so, as I reflect now, I came through those years. I kept my promises to God, and he kept his to me. So why not again? Then again and again, dream wilting beneath reality and reality slowly folding into the familiar contours of a deep, most persistent, most ecstatically eternal dream?

* * *

Hadley stopped by late last week to say hello. Elena came over last night, and we ordered Thai food. These are common occurrences. So is the joy each daughter brings even when, or especially because, that joy is so layered and encompasses such a spectrum of emotions. Each is an eternity unto herself.

At one point during last night's meal, Elena banteringly quipped about none of us ever guessing a few years ago the turns her life would take. Nope, Kerry and I replied one after the other, none would have guessed. Gazing down at my plate and picking at my food, I thought about my daughter, slowly healing from all her pain. I thought about Kerry and that dream from long ago. I sat for an extended moment in the stillness of my circumstances. Then my heart turned heavenward, and I gave thanks. And I renewed, again, old promises.

TEN

Ultimate, Anomalous— Wondrous

Now there is at Jerusalem by the sheep market a pool, which is called in the Hebrew tongue Bethesda, having five porches. In these lay a great multitude of impotent folk, of blind, halt, withered, waiting for the moving of the water. For an angel went down at a certain season into the pool, and troubled the water: whosoever then first after the troubling of the water stepped in was made whole of whatsoever disease he had. And a certain man was there, which had an infirmity thirty and eight years. When Jesus saw him lie, and knew that he had been now a long time in that case, he saith unto him, Wilt thou be made whole? The impotent man answered him, Sir, I have no man, when the water is troubled, to put me into the pool: but while I am coming, another steppeth down before me. Jesus saith unto him, Rise, take up thy bed, and walk. And immediately the man was made whole, and took up his bed, and walked. (John 5:2–9)

The story about the healing of a lame man beside the pool of Bethesda speaks to Christ's divinity, compassion, and power to heal. But it also says something about the relationship between God's word and what, in the last chapter, I call poetry. Think about the man's initial reply to Jesus ("Sir, I have no man"). Though brief, it reveals his investment in a beautiful legend of an angel imbuing a particular body of water with healing properties. Many at the pool were equally invested. The history and promise associated with that event functioned as a collective answer to prayer—the only answer many of these people presumably had. This helps explain the melancholy behind the man's response to Jesus; it gives us a feeling for the compounded nature of his grief: he lacks the strength (physically) to derive whatever value is to be had (spiritually, "poetically") from the trace of the divine, the one-time presence of the angel. All he can do is hope, and even that seems to be waning after so many years.

So when Christ invites the man to "Rise, take up [his] bed, and walk," it inspires a revolution of mind and spirit. The solution Jesus proposes—that the man redirect his attention, that he put down "poetry" in favor of a different relationship to God's Word—does not persuade the man of something he already understands. This is not any answer to prayer the man might have anticipated. Rather, it opens the man to the prospect of something previously inconceivable. He is "made whole" because he is not empowered to walk *only*: he is also able to discern, understand, and act in new ways. All this takes him by surprise. And as he rises, we assume, he is filled with wonder.

* * *

Spiritual experiences frequently inspire feelings of surprise and wonder. Even when we expect such experiences, when we grow accustomed to them, we rarely manage to anticipate their effects on us and others. Whether dramatic or subtle, these effects open a window onto a world vaster than the one with which we are familiar; they carry with them the aura of "things which eye has not seen, nor ear heard, nor [have] yet entered into the heart of man" (D&C 76:10; cf. Isa. 64:4).

Recall once more Parley P. Pratt's definitive statement about the gift of the Holy Ghost—what it means to our "intellectual faculties," our "natural passions and affections," our "sympathies, joys, tastes, kindred feelings, and affections of our nature," the cultivation of such virtues as "goodness, tenderness, gentleness, and charity," the development of our "form and features," and indeed, "all the faculties of the physical and intellectual" person. The Spirit brings "life to the whole being."[1] To Church members, it probably seems fitting that such insights into the nature and promise of spiritual experience should have been articulated by an apostle of the early Restoration, especially one so instrumental in advancing the doctrines and theology of a spiritually-minded religion.

As it turns out, however, even atheists who research spirituality hold similar views. One such scholar, Wesley J. Wildman, has written compellingly about the importance of spirituality to our very humanity. He sees spirituality as a leftover from our evolutionary past, "a side-effect of capacities for intense" cognitive experiences that enabled the survival of our species across tens of thousands of years, gradually producing in our deep ancestors greater complexity of thought and feeling and eventually forming the behavioral basis for such ritualistic practices as religion.[2] For Wildman, in other words, the evolutionary leap that vaulted us to a position of superiority among other animals also made possible the kinds of experiences Pratt associates with worship and the Spirit of God, for inspiration could only happen in brains designed to receive it.

Forget for a moment the areas where Pratt and Wildman are likely to disagree (concerning questions of creation and human origin, for example), and consider the provocative areas of overlap. From the perspective of brain science, spiritual experiences are "intense" cognitive events calibrated to our survival. They consist, Wildman remarks, of "strong and broad neural activation, corresponding to existential potency and wide awareness, [and involve] strength of

feeling and interconnectedness of ideas, memories, and emotions."
This interconnectedness, corresponding with Pratt's vision of the
spiritual enhancement of our natural capacities, means that spiritual
experiences often accompany "significant personal change and social
effects" (104), merging thought and feeling, memory and sensation,
our individual selves and our relationships with others. Integrating
all facets of our being, they influence all the ways we come to feel
and act and arrive at meaning in the world and thus transform our
outlook and behavior. This is why spiritual experiences bear such
names as "*mysterium tremendum* [or tremendous mystery] . . . peak
experiences . . . pure consciousness . . . [and] absolute unitary being"
and coincide with experiences we consider "profound . . . extreme,
transcendental . . . sublime," and so on (105).

For the apostle and the atheist, spiritual experiences enhance our
native capacities, making us more ourselves by seeming to make us
more *than* ourselves. Pratt's "quicken[ing of] the intellectual faculties"
becomes scholarship's "strong and broad neural activation." For some,
like Wildman, this phenomenon is wholly natural—nothing mystical
or sacred about it—whereas for Pratt, it represents a divine satura-
tion of the natural world, a realization of our potential as children
of God. Together, Pratt and secular scholars like Wildman make up
integral parts of an important equation: Pratt puts a finger on the
supernatural origins of a natural process, while scholars explain the
natural mechanics of seemingly supernatural effects; Pratt connects
our everyday spiritual experiences to our divine natures, while scholars root our feelings of spiritual transport to our nature as embodied
beings. Pratt explains how spiritual experiences attach us to God,
while scholars grant us a larger vocabulary for describing what that
means and how it happens.

As part of that more extensive vocabulary, Wildman draws a
distinction that is especially helpful. Spiritual experiences generally
fall into two categories, he observes. We see one set, strange or out
of the ordinary experiences, in "hallucination, synesthesia, lucid
dreaming, out-of-body experiences, alien abduction, [miraculous]

healing, past-life, near-death . . . and mystical experiences." Wildman labels these "anomalous" experiences. They include "drug-induced altered states, psychiatric disorders, extreme circumstances, ecstatic states, group frenzy, snake-handling, fire-walking, possession, as well as more marginally anomalous experiences such as dramatic self-deception, uncanny insight, and spectacular creativity" (82). Such experiences "usually feel out of the control of those who have them"; they are "emotionally and cognitively potent" and, often, "have little to do with religion and spirituality" (83). By contrast, Wildman's second category, "ultimacy" experiences, "are defined by subjective judgments of [great] significance. These are experiences that a person feels are of vital importance for his or her life. They bring orientation and coping power, inspire great acts of courage and devotion, underlie key life decisions, and heavily influence social affiliation" (84). Where an anomalous spiritual experience is something one might see featured on a cable TV show dedicated to accounts of the bizarre, an ultimate spiritual experience is the kind one typically hears in a testimony meeting or a conversion narrative: somebody felt a conviction that something was true, and that conviction spurred actions that subsequently redirected that person's life.

Both kinds of experiences figure into religious traditions. Latter-day Saints may not ascribe spiritual value to fire-walking and snake-handling, but Joseph Smith's First Vision certainly qualifies as an anomalous (or extraordinary, unusual) spiritual experience. And yet, it was one that would have long-lasting, "ultimate" effects, inspiring life-orientation, devotion, courage, and sacrifice in millions of people. More typically, Church members tend to distinguish extraordinary—anomalous—spiritual events (like an act of healing through a priesthood blessing or an unusually vivid answer to prayer) from the slow burn of the companionship of the Holy Ghost, the gentle nudge toward what is *ultimately* good and true.

Where anomalous spiritual experiences are associated with strangeness, ultimate spiritual experiences inspire sanctification. Anomalous experiences are surprising, and ultimate experiences usually are not; but the effects of ultimacy over time—on individuals or, in the case of the Church, on whole communities—can be immense and sometimes wondrously strange. The two operate in tandem. Together, they capture something of the experience of the lame man lying beside the pool of Bethesda, a moment of surprise leading, presumably, to a change of life, to the wonder of being made "whole."

✳ ✳ ✳

The dialectic between anomalousness and ultimacy pervades literature. It precipitates, in the Jewish poet Hank Lazer's words, "an intensified awareness of being," an "erratic movement" between what is familiar and what we do not yet fully understand (or, in some cases, even perceive).[3] Often categorized as an effect of wonder, literature's presentation of ordinary things in new and surprising ways amounts to an "anomalous" tactic for "ultimate" purposes. It reveals the spiritual—human and divine—mystery of our lives.

As a brief illustration, consider "The Windhover" by Gerard Manley Hopkins, a sonnet that rehearses and enacts an iconic spiritual experience. The poet recounts how, one morning, he catches sight of a kestrel (or falcon) as it hovers high in the air. His mind is drawn to the wonders of creation: "My heart in hiding / Stirred for a bird,— the achieve of, the mastery of the thing!"[4] Then, as the bird suddenly dives to the ground, the poet perceives something "a billion / Times told lovelier" (ll. 10–11), a vision of Christ in his descent to earth for the purpose of redeeming humankind from the mortal effects of the fall of Adam and Eve. The poem thus shifts from the description of the bird to a declaration of its meaning for the poet, implying that the epiphany is nothing visible to the natural eye even if the theology of Christ's redemptive promise is widely shared (such that we might see it reflected, as Hopkins does in his poem's conclusion, in such mundane aspects of life as the plowing of a field or a fire in the hearth—"plough down sillion" and "blue-bleak embers").

By the terms we discuss above, the spiritual experience the poet rehearses would fall into the category of ultimacy. There is nothing strange about witnessing the beauties of nature—certainly not a bird in flight, even one as beautiful as a kestrel. And the Christian vision the poem articulates reflects the poet's long-term discipleship, not a strange experience that comes out of nowhere. And yet, while the episode and theme are of the ultimate variety, the language of the poem is decidedly anomalous. This is true both in word choice and meter, rhythm. Take the opening lines:

> I caught this morning morning's minion, king-
>   dom of daylight's dauphin, dapple-dawn-drawn Falcon, in
>   his riding
>   Of the rolling level underneath him steady air, and striding
> High there, how he rung upon the rein of a wimpling wing
> In his ecstasy!
>
> (ll. 1–5)

This is not the stuff of everyday conversation or even high ecclesial speech. Rather, it is odd, arresting, alternately tongue-twisting and elegant—a symphony of sound and signification. The repetition of words ("morning morning's") and diverse alliterations ("m" in the first line, "d" in the second, "s" in the third, "w" in the fourth) create a lilting, musical effect accentuated by poetic meter. Note the stresses: "I *caught* this *morning* morning's *minion*, *king*dom of *daylight's dau*phin, *dapple-dawn-drawn Falcon*, in his *riding*," and so on. Dubbed "sprung rhythm," Hopkins wove alternating numbers of unstressed syllables into his lines to break up the repetitive cadences of poetic diction. The effect slows us down, decomposing words and phrases into orchestras of sound, composites of tone and rhythm as much as grammatical sense. Language in such a poem becomes a cathedral of contemplation, a place set apart from quotidian speech, rendered sacred and strange and utterly defamiliarized.

Compare Hopkins's magisterial achievement with another classic sonnet, William Wordsworth's "Composed upon Westminster Bridge, September 3, 1802":

> Earth has not any thing to show more fair:
> Dull would he be of soul who could pass by
> A sight so touching in its majesty:
> The City now doth, like a garment, wear
> The beauty of the morning: silent, bare,
> Ships, towers, domes, theatres, and temples lie
> Open unto the fields, and to the sky;
> All bright and glittering in the smokeless air.
> Never did sun more beautifully steep
> In his first splendour, valley, rock, or hill;
> Ne'er saw I, never felt, a calm so deep!
> The river glideth at his own sweet will:
> Dear God! the very houses seem asleep;
> And all that mighty heart is lying still![5]

The language is unmistakably poetic ("The City now doth, like a garment, wear / The beauty of the morning"; "Never did sun more beautifully steep / In his first splendour"), but it amounts more to an elevation of everyday speech ("Earth has not any thing to show more fair"; "All bright and glittering in the smokeless air") than to the estrangement of it one finds in the Hopkins poem. This is language rendered a little less ordinary, a little more sacred; it carries the air of ultimacy. But what the poet finds ultimate, meanwhile, seems a little unusual in its degree of rapture—unusual, that is, because it is in some ways exceedingly mundane. London is a spectacle, to be sure, with its "[s]hips, towers, domes, theatres, and temples." But the degree of splendor seems almost excessive. Where the poet in "The Windhover" is moved by nature (the pre-visionary sight of the kestrel), the spectator in Wordsworth's poem is almost beside himself at the achievements of civilization, which acquires the aura of nature, its monuments lying "[o]pen unto the fields, and to the sky." "Ne'er saw

I, never felt, a calm so deep": this is a city as seemingly nobody has seen one before, inspiring an ecstasy out of keeping even with tourist awe—a reverence not for cityscapes but for something like urban soul: "Dear God! the very houses seem asleep . . .!"

Ultimacy and anomalousness—the effects of wonder—play off each other in these two sonnets. For Hopkins, anomalous language underscores the ultimacy of the vision, whereas for Wordsworth, the ultimacy of the language heightens the wondrously strange spectacle of human accomplishment. In each case, anomalousness and ultimacy combine to create a forceful spiritual impression. Hence, where Wildman rightly distinguishes between modes of spiritual experience, Hopkins and Wordsworth reveal how literature overlays such modes, enriching and even potentially recreating the intensities they describe. Take, for example, the present-tense language of each poem. For Hopkins, such language recreates the drama of the bird's dive to earth and the sudden apparition of the poetic vision: "Brute beauty and valour and act, oh, air, pride, plume, here / Buckle!" or collapse. The breathiness of the consecutive commas gives way to an enjambed line, literal "inspiration," or breathing, giving way to exclamatory exhalation, a virtual "I see!" For Wordsworth, likewise, the scene is the ecstatic present, the poet's vision momentarily becoming our own: "all that mighty heart is lying still!" It all seems so unusual and yet so resonantly real; word becomes feeling and thought grows into experience. This is dynamic experience, fully (per Pratt and Wildman) *spiritual* experience, the "human spirit fully in act."[6]

* * *

Most of my spiritual experiences are subtle: impressions of unusual depth or illuminations of uncommon clarity. They're nothing outwardly remarkable, and people of greater spiritual capacities would probably deem my intense experiences humdrum. For me, they possess ultimate value as they turn my mind to a greater power, and the fact that I enjoy them at all always strikes me as an anomaly: they always take me at least a little by surprise. Their collective effect is one of wonder. Such experiences channel how I think and feel and believe; they shape who I am.

Every now and then, however, something happens that breaches the limits of what I deem normal, ratcheting up degrees of anomalousness and ultimacy and thus recasting my sense of the possible. With that as a backdrop, the timing of the story I am going to share is important: March 2012. We were home in Salt Lake City, though for how long we weren't sure. I had worked out an arrangement with my half-time Scottish employer that I would return to the States for somewhere between twelve and eighteen months before coming back to work full-time at the University of Aberdeen. The truth was, I still was not sure what to do. I felt unsettled about (if deeply enticed by) the prospect of permanently moving the family overseas, and nothing had yet occurred to persuade me that life was better for us, or for me, in Utah. In so many ways, it was a quintessential midlife decision: it affected me and those closest to me, it would impact us into the future, and it would partly determine how I interpreted the meaning of the past, the course my life had taken. Sensing that this was a decision of unusual consequence for me and my family, I prayed daily for direction, but rather than receiving a clear answer—for, it turns out, the door through which I would eventually walk had not yet opened—I felt impressed to reflect on the reasons why I might choose one path or the other, examining less what I should do than the person I would be in choosing one or the other. Instead of a roadmap, then, I found something like a rest station, a place for waiting. And for self-reflection. And lots of divine silence.

I was not particularly happy about it or about the Spirit's counterintuitive methods of illumination. One morning, anxious about the thought of permanently leaving my life in Scotland, I prayed and expressed, in anguish, "I can't go back there!"—that is, back to my life at BYU the way it had been prior to my experience in Aberdeen. The spiritual impression that gathered immediately was disconcerting not for anything it communicated by way of affirmation or rebuke but for having all the energy of an almighty yawn: *You can, you know you can, and you know that I know that you can.* And that beguiled me because this was one of the most dramatic decisions of my life, I was putting my plea before my Maker, and the divine response seemed like a version of something I knew only too well from my years as a missionary: *Non, monsieur, ça ne m'intéresse pas.* And so, I brooded over the matter, day after day, week after week—more time in my rest station of divine silence but no further enlightenment, not yet.

I was at this place in life on the second-to-last Sunday of March 2012 when my ward's priesthood quorum leader made a special announcement. The following week, he said, a man from our neighborhood, a lifelong member of the Church now in his eighties, would be attending our services for the first time in more than fifty years. When you see him, he encouraged us, say hello; make him feel welcome. Fair enough, I thought, though it didn't seem like anybody in our friendly group would need such instruction.

The following week, the last Sunday of March, this man, Jerry, joined us. I instantly took to him: white hair and goatee, simple but stylish clothing, unassuming demeanor—a pleasant presence. He stood and introduced himself in a soft, plainspoken voice. When the meeting adjourned, I stepped into the hallway for a couple minutes. Sunday School, our next meeting, was held in that same room. When I returned, there was an open seat next to Jerry, so I took it and extended my hand.

I forget the topic of our Sunday School class that day. I remember, though, that it was based on the Book of Mormon, and all Jerry had was an old Bible that looked as if it had not been cracked open in a long, long time. So as the teacher moved through the lesson and as the discussion ensued, I opened my scriptures so that Jerry could follow along.

When the class ended, people began filing to the chapel for sacrament meeting. But Jerry remained slumped in his chair, staring at the floor. I stayed there with him.

"Everything all right?"

He blinked a couple times, formulating a thought. What he finally emitted was remarkably complete. And dour. "That discussion went over my head. Everyone here knows so much about the gospel, and I know so little. I feel like I've wasted my life. I should never have come back."

His words landed like a gut punch. Out of nowhere, I found myself in a crisis moment not of my own life narrative but someone else's, and I was completely unqualified to assess it. I did not know this man and was roughly half his age; my aim in sitting beside him had simply been to convey the welcoming spirit of our ward community. If he said he didn't like the lesson, I might have commiserated; if he said he didn't understand a particular gospel principle, I might have filled in some gaps; if he asked whether ward members socialized much outside church, I might have invited him over for dinner. What I was not equipped to deliver was judgment on the meaning of his life. Or on much of anything else.

But the occasion called for an earnest, substantive reply and for an understanding of this man and his circumstances that I simply did not possess. So I sat still: one second, two seconds... three... praying silently to know what to say. And then, like a lightning flash, a thought burst into my mind.

I tapped his Bible. "When you get home today, I want you to open to Matthew 20. There's a parable there about laborers in a vineyard. The Lord calls some workers early, some a little later, some later and then later still, and some at the last hour of the day. But if they go to work for him, he pays them all the same wage. The message is that it's never too late for us to respond to God. In his eyes, we're never too late."

His brow softened a little. "I like the sound of that."

"I like it too, and I believe it's true. So today, after you get home, read that parable. And then, the next time we're here at church, I want you to tell me what your impressions were as you read it."

"Yeah, okay. I can do that. Matthew 20?"

"Matthew 20."

The following week, the first Sunday of April, we didn't hold meetings at our ward as it was general conference, televised globally for the entire Church. One of the talks that weekend struck me with particular force. It was Jeffrey R. Holland's, and it was titled "The Laborers in the Vineyard." He expounded on that parable from Matthew 20 and then expressed one of the beautiful thoughts for which he is best known:

> I do not know who in this vast audience today may need to hear the message of forgiveness inherent in this parable, but however late you think you are, however many chances you think you have missed, however many mistakes you feel you have made or talents you think you don't have, or however far from home and family and God you feel you have traveled, I testify that you have *not* traveled beyond the reach of divine love. It is not possible for you to sink lower than the infinite light of Christ's Atonement shines.[7]

The Sunday after general conference, back at our ward building, Jerry found me. "Hey, did you hear Elder Holland's talk? He spoke about that parable!" That talk deeply resonated with Jerry; it was a message delivered to the entire Church, though to him, given his circumstances, it felt very personal. Jerry became a vital member of the ward—beloved of the regulars, a minister to those on the margins, and a pilgrim to temples in several western states. Meanwhile, some three years later, I accepted a calling requiring me to pay regular visits to wards across our stake. As it happened, one of these wards was Elder Holland's, and I would sometimes find myself seated beside him on the stand. One day, a couple years into my assignment, I told him the story about Jerry. He smiled, thanked me for sharing it, and invoked a theatrical metaphor. You seek inspiration to know what to say, he replied. But you don't always see heaven working in the wings.

* * *

"Brute beauty and valour and act, oh, air, pride, plume, here / Buckle!" In "The Windhover," the poet has been contemplating the majesty of creation when, gazing at a kestrel diving ("Buckl[ing]") toward the ground, he is struck by a new epiphany, this one about Christ's condescension. One vision of God (the creation) thus opens onto another (the incarnation and atonement); inspiration prepares the poet for more of the same.

I did not doubt that I had been inspired in my brief conversation with Jerry after Sunday School: "When you get home today, I want you to open to Matthew 20." In fact, it boggled the mind to think of how many people had to be inspired to give my flash of insight durable meaning: the bishop, stake president, and priesthood quorum leader, who had been working with Jerry prior to his return to church; Elder Holland, who was inspired to give an especially powerful talk at an especially vulnerable moment in Jerry's life; ward members (so many!) who befriended Jerry in the coming weeks and months, helping him see what a vital contributor he might be to our community; ward leaders who gave Jerry just the right callings at just the right times; and, especially, Jerry himself over countless moments during the long process of his return. As a denouement, the Lord even put me in a position where, several years later, I might tell Elder Holland about one of the fruits of his labor. "You don't always see heaven working in the wings": I recognized, instantly as well as over time, how little I understood about the divine machinery that orchestrated that outcome, that helped a long-absent man discern the gentle beckoning of the Lord to come labor in his vineyard.

Might Jerry have heard that call in some other way, from some other circumstance or set of people? Sure, probably. But God is a poet—sometimes an elegant novelist—and there was something beautiful, something delicate and true, about letting the story unfold the way it did.

But back to the Hopkins poem. The climactic vision there was prepared by what preceded it, the poet's meditative wonder at the "dapple-dawn-drawn Falcon." My burst of inspiration in responding to

Jerry, by contrast, had had no such incubation. None that I could see at least. Yes, I knew the scriptures sufficiently to direct Jerry to a particular parable. Yes, I was attending my church meetings, was mindful of the Christian injunction to care for one's neighbor, and was given to seeking inspiration. But I had been seeking it, vainly, for months. "Should we come back full-time to BYU or—please—leave for Scotland?" Day after day, week after week. My prayers, I'm sure, sounded like caricatures of Wordsworth's sonnet, with me repeatedly rehearsing for the Lord the virtues of the place I wished to call home: "Earth has not any thing to show more fair . . . Ne'er saw I, never felt, a calm so deep. . . ." And all I kept receiving was a space for prayerful reflection, that rest station of mind and heart, and deep canyons of divine silence.

As I would eventually understand, I was looking too intently, waiting too earnestly, at my personal pool of Bethesda. For, when tangible inspiration came, no angel troubled the water and revealed the direction I was to take with my life. Instead, the inspiration involved something altogether different—a kind and earnest older man's regrets over lost time. Regarding my own question, it would become clear to me later why I had needed to wait for an answer: there was still a missing piece of the puzzle I could not have foreseen, and I also needed time to reflect on my priorities so that when I had to make a difficult decision, I could do so with greater self-understanding. And as the story with Jerry illustrates, the Lord had his own ways of making sure that I understood he was still there.

A familiar principle reimpressed itself on my mind. It surprised me again, as it always does. We can't always see heaven working on our behalf, but any experience with the Spirit, no matter how small, is evidence that God is doing just that. Forget for a moment receiving some great answer to prayer. Do we feel the Spirit, even a little, as we *seek* the Lord in prayer? Have we felt the Spirit convey that God loves us, or that he understands us, or that he has great hopes for us, or that he sorrows with us, or rejoices with us, or that he appreciates our gratitude to him or our kind deed for someone else? Have we felt the Spirit open our mind to help us learn something new, or turn us to something good, or inspire us to perceive something beautiful, or reassure us that things will be okay, that we aren't lost, that God knows exactly where we are? If we've ever had any of these experiences or myriad others like them, we've effectively experienced our Father's plan of salvation in a grain of sand. That is, and as I discuss in chapter 1, we've been shown that God is real, that our life has a purpose—that there's a reason God reached out to us through the Spirit—and that Christ's atonement is making it possible for us to feel God's presence a little more fully.

Ultimate, anomalous—wondrous. Spiritual experiences help us see everything differently. Marion G. Romney is reported to have remarked, "I always know when I am speaking under the inspiration of the Holy Ghost, because I always learn something from what I've said."[8] The Spirit, that is, always seems to take us at least a little by surprise; it changes not only how we speak but also where, how, and sometimes to whom we look. And so while I have learned that there is much we can do to prepare for the Spirit's inspiration, it still catches us off guard. For, it seems, we habitually find ourselves in the crabbed posture of the man lying beside the pool of Bethesda. We know what we want, we think we know how to get it, and we also know, alas, why it eludes us: we "have no man, when the water is troubled, to put [us] into the pool." We lack what we think is most needful. So we offer our earnest prayers over and over; we cling to answers the Lord gives, even when we know they are incomplete, when we know, or at least suspect, that they are just "poetry." What we never manage to anticipate, not fully, is the experience of being beckoned to rise, take up our bed, and walk.

ELEVEN

Spiritual Transformations, Quick and Slow

Transformation is one of the hallmarks of spiritual experience. Its effects can be dramatic or subtle. Either way, they reveal how the Spirit pushes us beyond our present horizons. Provocatively, experience alone suggests as much, as its word root means to pass through peril (*ex-periri*), rendering us different than we were before. Philip Sheldrake, a widely published scholar on spirituality, underscores this quality by associating our spiritual journeys with "ultimate values," we learn to set against "an instrumentalized or purely materialistic approach to life."[1] Spiritual experience changes how we perceive the world and our place in it, thus revealing to us an alternative life story, a different and better way to be. Sandra M. Schneiders, a peer of Sheldrake's, elaborates that spirituality is a "conscious and deliberate way of living" that "orients the subject beyond purely private satisfaction toward the ultimate good, the highest value, that the person recognizes."[2] This "ultimate good" "lur[es us] toward growth" (17), driving us toward new and better versions of ourselves. Spirituality is the discipline of the disciple.

There is something inherently compelling about such a discipline, about the prospects of those who venture to and beyond the limits of who they are or once were. This is what I began to realize once I returned to BYU and began studying and teaching about spiritual experience. Mary Frohlich, a friend and Catholic theologian, writes that "we are fascinated" by the thought of "being persons who live and act according to our most radical potential," fascinated by individuals who possess and harness "this charisma, either for ourselves or others."[3] Such lives reveal "the human spirit fully in act." "Affectively experienced as 'presence' or 'communion'" with God, spiritual experience "is manifested in such forms as human love, intuitive knowing, or a sense of group solidarity. It is as important to extroverted forms of spirituality such as commitment to social justice or involvement in a Christian community as it is to traditional forms of . . . prayer" (74). Hence, for Frohlich, spirituality entails adopting a new manner in how we engage God and the world. It means becoming people who seek a certain quality of experience, who are transformed by the Spirit in how we learn and live.

This resonates with the expansive version of the promise we find at the conclusion of the Book of Mormon. Readers often take Moroni's declaration that we may know for ourselves the truthfulness of the book to conclude with the confident avowal that "by the power of the Holy Ghost [we] may know the truth of all things" (Moro. 10:5). But what follows are two important extensions of that promise. The first is an assertion that all good things testify of Christ: "Nothing that is good denieth the Christ, but acknowledgeth that he is. And ye may know that he is, by the power of the Holy Ghost" (Moro. 10:6–7). And this knowledge, this testimony, comes to us most vibrantly through the exercise of our spiritual gifts: To know God is to know him not only in word but in action, by participation. The gifts Moroni mentions include wisdom, knowledge, faith, healing, and prophecy, but his list seems more indicative than exhaustive. There are scores of gifts, thousands of them, more. The Book of Mormon is filled with them: the gift of discerning God's presence across the particularities of our experience (as Nephi does in claiming to have been "highly favored of the Lord in all [his] days" despite his "many afflictions" [1 Ne. 1:1]); the gift of empathy (in "mourn[ing] with those that mourn" [Mosiah 18:9]); the gift of knowing how and not just for what to pray, of learning how to reason with a responsive God (see, for example, Hel. 11:10–17); and myriad others.[4] In each case, the exercise of spiritual gifts implies a partnership with God, a kind of apprenticeship that brings us closer to God even as it transforms our lives, our worlds by filling them with spiritual things.

I've seen how drawing on these unique gifts can bring us closer to God, perhaps because they call on parts of ourselves that are closer to God already. One day, a friend reached out to me wanting to know whether I thought she should speak out about something that had been bothering her. As it happened, she contacted me as I was writing a talk on spiritual thriving for a BYU devotional, so I asked her whether she'd sought the Spirit to know what to do. She said she'd tried but that she sometimes felt confused as to whether her inspiration came from God or herself. I wondered whether my friend and God might work more seamlessly together rather than in opposition, so I asked her instead about her spiritual gifts. What are they? And might they serve as conduits for her to receive inspiration? She shared three of her gifts: discernment, love, and forgiveness. I replied that perhaps these beautiful gifts directed her not to the question of whether she should speak but how, that perhaps addressing the situation that was bothering her in a discerning, loving, and forgiving way would allow the Spirit to communicate with and also through her. This small suggestion that she trust her own spiritual gifts seemed to open in her a channel of inspiration and increase her spiritual confidence.

Spiritual gifts are precious because they are traces in us of our divine natures, aspects of ourselves in which we more fully reflect our Heavenly Parents. Many years ago, I taught a prep course for English majors thinking about pursuing PhDs. One exceptionally gifted student, smart and diversely talented, completed the class requirements but seemed more interested in pursuing other opportunities. Several years later, she contacted me and asked if we could talk. I invited her to my home and learned that she had gotten married, found herself living in places she hadn't anticipated, and no longer felt as assured about following a lifelong career dream. She'd explored other options, and nothing seemed right, so she was revisiting her original decision not to pursue a PhD. We began talking again about some of the items we'd discussed in our prep class years before: the parts of a grad school application, what kind of writing sample to use, what to emphasize in a letter of intent, and so forth. She diligently took a few notes, but I could sense feelings of uncertainty and unhappiness. Then the Spirit impressed me with a new thought. I told her not to worry about career tracks for a moment and reflect instead on her spiritual gifts. If she thought about pursuing a life most in keeping with those gifts, what kind of life would that be? The mood in the room instantly changed; she said she hadn't thought about approaching her future with that question in mind. Later in the week, she sent me a note relating that she was moved by the guidance to seek out her spiritual gifts: "I already feel more at peace even though my future is still undecided. . . . It is amazing how much clarity gospel principles can shed on 'worldly' topics and decisions."

If we learn to let him, the Lord through the Spirit can animate all facets of our lives. But seeking the Spirit as our guide can feel a little daunting, at least until we remember that we are co-creators with God—co-creators of our lives and the world around us. While we do confront matters of right *or* wrong and truth *or* falsehood and while it's vital to seek the Spirit's confirmation regarding such things, most inspiration is less binary and absolute in nature. Rather, it tends to be broader and more open-ended: What moves us, or what *might* move us? What might we learn, and how might we learn it? What talents, traits, and virtues might we cultivate? What in our world might be better because of our involvement? In these and so many other areas, the Spirit is a creative partner that can help us fashion better ways to live and be. For every occasion when the Spirit helps us narrow our choices, there are many others when the Spirit assists us in multiplying them.

In his famous promise about the Book of Mormon, Moroni rehearses a process in which a formative revelation opens onto an entire way of life, a fullness of life in the Spirit. Ask, receive, act: this process not only marks the conclusion of the Book of Mormon, it represents the transformative qualities of spiritual experience. To know through the Spirit is to come to live through the Spirit; it is to be born, in any of an endless diversity of ways, to a more dynamic existence.

* * *

In March of 2012, when I met Jerry in my Salt Lake ward (see chapter 10), I was jointly employed by two universities, one in Utah and the other in Scotland, and our family was contemplating the prospects of permanently leaving the US. Just two years earlier, in the winter of 2010, we'd found ourselves at the threshold of that new life—a two- or three-year window when we would be dividing time between these two very different spots on the globe. So it was that, on the first Sunday in February, we were standing at a bus stop outside a chapel on the outskirts of Aberdeen, a city on the North Sea. We'd just made it over earlier in the week, and I felt so blessed to be here. Only a few years back, I'd been so frustrated by so many things. One of them was my academic life—and there was a history there. I had come somewhat reluctantly to BYU as a transfer student in 1989; surprisingly to me, I thrived there. However, once I graduated, I never planned, or particularly desired, to be back. I saw BYU as one chapter of my life, not a volume. It was with some ambivalence, then, that I had returned in 2000 as a new member of the faculty. Once again, though, the university had been wonderful to me and had helped me grow in my career. But hey, "enter to learn, go forth to serve": BYU's motto and my attitude. Here, in Aberdeen, I was on the verge of new horizons. And it felt liberating, spiritually fulfilling.

These thoughts were running through my mind as I gazed down the street. No bus quite yet, just trees waving in the ever-present Scottish breeze. Cold but beautiful. I had one nagging concern though, and it involved the ward mission leader. When I'd been offered the job here, I'd negotiated for a half-year arrangement, hoping to wean my family off living in the US, to accustom us to different circumstances. The ward mission leader knew this; he knew we'd only be here six months at a time for the first couple years and that most church callings aren't suited to a quirky calendar like the one we'd be keeping as we went back and forth, back and forth, across the Atlantic. He was deeply invested in the university—he owned a large home on the fringes of its campus—and I'd heard him express his hopes of making the Church's presence more felt there. I feared he was going to petition the bishop to make me a ward missionary so he could get me to serve as his campus liaison. Thoughts of what that might entail made me queasy. Formal introduction of the missionaries to my new bosses and colleagues? Sitting with them at booths along the main campus drag in four-hour shifts, begging students to take a Book of Mormon or, okay, how about—pretty please—just this pamphlet?

I shuddered, this time not from the cold. "No," I was rehearsing in my head. "Sorry. I was hired to teach Scottish literature, that's a responsibility I take very seriously, I'm not going to violate university policies regarding religious neutrality," etc. Were there such policies? I hoped so; they would provide cover. For, at the prospects of a calling as ward missionary, as with so many other callings over the years, I'd grown expert at ducking. I was not resistant to the idea of church involvement—I was an eager volunteer for service projects, for example. But I'd long been drinking from wells of ecclesiastical disillusionment, and I harbored a deep reserve. I believed in God but had grown suspicious of the human capacity to channel the mind of God, to understand the will and ways of God, to speak for God. In my experience, God's silence exceeded his speech; whatever we thought we understood, there was always more we didn't. That was as true for Church leaders as for me.

As a result, I began nourishing an aesthetic relation to my religion; my attitude toward the Church evolved into one of suspended disbelief.[5] I approached it the way I would a work of art or literature. To say that the Church was true, for me, meant that it was true enough to inspire fallen mortals; it was "truthy," a workshop for our growth. But it existed at a remove from God. God was real, had delivered me, blessed me, heard me, loved me. God loved all people. But the Church was different: the Church inspired me, but it also hurt me, hurt others. And when it didn't, it sometimes bored me, depressed me. God loved the Church, sure, I could believe that: God was endlessly kind. And so, I could be kind too: I could believe in the Church, *kind of*. I could be in the Church but not of it—remain attached to it without investing too much credence or hope in it. When it was good, I could appreciate it, and when it was bad, it would give me something to talk about, like I would a novel, a poem, a film, a painting. I could analyze what was "problematic" about it; I could speculate on things that would make it better. Religion could become, for me, an object of critical engagement.

I don't want to seem too glib. I cared very much about my faith. But being in Aberdeen, working for the university there, loosened my tether to the Church. That freedom would purify my relationship with it, I hoped, make it more a matter of choice than compulsion. Who knew? It might make me more devout. Or it could render my relationship to the Church even more aesthetic, even more a matter of taste, judgment, critical distance. I might tell the ward mission leader, tell the bishop, "No, that calling's not quite right, not quite to my liking. Try again." At least, I could if I could find the nerve.

I glanced heavenward. The rain had stopped maybe thirty minutes before, and bright patches of blue radiated behind swatches of racing gray. I was a couple years past forty: still young for a scholar, many years of my career in front of me, many of them probably, hopefully, spent here. I saw the February wind tug at my wife's coat, at my daughters' hair. They were shivering, but first week in February, we all knew it was colder right now back in Utah. We'd all get used to it.

My gaze lingered, however, on my older daughter, Hadley. "Angel," I often called her, one sent from God, firstborn to parents who were not certain they could even have children. She'd been a daddy's girl since she was barely a few weeks old and, colicky, would fuss until she was in my arms. I had been less prepared for parenthood than my wife, but something happened to me in those early months, holding our baby to soothe her: With her tiny body folded against mine, I could feel a distinctive bond between us. It was wordless but visceral, rooted in layers of biological, emotional, and spiritual sediment. Its effect on me was transformative. I doted on her for years afterward. Watching her now, at the bus stop, two memories leapt to mind. The first was of three summers back when I had led a BYU study abroad group in Scotland. Late during our time in the country, I'd needed to run some errands, and my little buddy had come with me. I rewarded her at our last stop with a distinctive Scottish soda whose medicinal taste would probably seem like punishment to any but a perpetually smiling seven-year-old. She loved it. So happy, always: "Our little lark," my wife dubbed her. The second memory had occurred only a year ago when I'd come to Aberdeen alone for just a couple days and, on my last day in town, had called Kerry to tell her I'd been offered the job. She was joyful for me, though a bit distracted as she was running about getting ready for Hadley's birthday party. I got our little lark on the phone and apologized for being absent on her special day. She chirped several notes of ready forgiveness, excited at the prospect of friends and games and cake and presents. The elation I had felt only moments earlier fell by several moods; set against the joy of the approaching festivities, my professional ambitions, my own "special day," suddenly seemed so empty. Still gazing at her here at the bus stop, I thought of how we'd be holding another birthday party for her the week after next. This time, though, it would just be our little family celebrating. Her friends were all back home.

I'd told myself that this would be a wonderful opportunity for my family, for our daughters. And that would prove to be true. But deep down, I knew that my incentive in taking this job had little to do with family. Instead, it was driven by something all too human in me, something selfish and a little desperate, something confused and anxious to matter. Pained, I glanced back down the street. Still no bus.

A twentysomething male walked past: Leon. They'd introduced him during the last of our church meetings an hour ago. *A new convert. Please say hello.* So, I stopped him, engaged in small talk. He shifted a little, shyly. His accent was. . . not Scottish.

"Manchester," he replied. In England.

"Oh, really? What brings you up here?"

"I'm a student at the university."

I should have guessed as much, should have seen it coming. Still, his answer stung. I heard my response as an echo from someplace far away: "You don't say. The university. That's why we're here too."

I was suddenly having a "Waverley moment." Walter Scott's 1814 historical novel *Waverley* recounts the fortunes of a young English soldier who visits relatives in Scotland at what proves to be an auspicious moment. Scott sets his novel in 1745 as Jacobite armies, supporters of a deposed royal family, are preparing to launch an attack to restore the old regime. The uprising proceeds from the Scottish Highlands where clans have assembled into militant forces. And young Edward Waverley, who happens to be visiting a Highland chief on the cusp of battle, gets swept up in the fray, becomes intoxicated with the sentimental fervor of the cause, and begins fighting on the Jacobite side. But during a battle, he saves the life of an opponent, an English soldier who is a friend of his family's. The soldier is shocked to behold Edward in Highland military attire. And Edward is "mortified, abashed, and distressed" at his own appearance when he sees himself through the eyes of his countryman.[6]

In my case, in Aberdeen, I was hardly drawn unwittingly into battle. And there was nothing scandalous about finding myself a teacher of Scottish literature, living in Scotland, and confronting an English citizen at a bus stop. But in Leon's presence, I was startled to hear the echo of my complaints about our ward mission leader, startled to hear the excuses I was preparing to absolve myself from being a proponent of my faith. Fresh off my two-year mission, I would tell people how much I respected converts, respected anyone able to make significant life changes because of their love for God. I repeated those lines for years afterward. So, when Leon, a new convert, replied that he was in town because he was a student at the university, my university, the place where I feared identifying outwardly with my religion, I was startled, dismayed by the gap I perceived separating my actual life practices from my long-held ideals.

I gazed again at my huddling family, then back at Leon. I was at the zenith of my career. And I felt very small. A prayer welled up in my heart: *Father, forgive me. I'm still here. I'll do anything.*

Our bus turned the corner and came trundling up the street. As it did, a gust of wind wafted in that gentle irony to which I'd grown so accustomed over the years. I looked from my family to Leon to the sky overhead. It was a beautiful day, and I stood on the verge of a new life. But spiritually, I felt myself at once in a familiar place—a little desperate, anxious, and locked in old habits of mind—and yet, or for that reason, far from home.

* * *

Was there anything awful about my experience at BYU that had me so desperate to leave? No, quite the contrary. As both a student and young professor, the university had been so, so good to and for me: it had educated me, given me a platform for my work, supported me generously, and improved me through the influence of colleagues and students. However, as I discussed briefly in the introduction, BYU is different. And to embrace it means being a little different oneself. It means attaching "Yes, I *believe* that" to the academic's more comfortable "Yes, I *think* that." It means letting one's light shine (Matt. 5:16) even when one has very little of it, lost as we can be—as I have been—in doubt or depression or everyday mediocrity. It means looking to Christ, with all it may portend to follow him, when it is so much safer and more soothingly distracting just to look to books.

Complicating things, for me, there was our experience in Aberdeen, which became a good home to us. I loved the university—the students, my colleagues, the place, and the history. I loved our ward and our daughters' new school. We made new friends and learned how to navigate the city. The landscape was beautiful and afforded many small moments of joy. Sunday mornings, for example, if we sat on the upper deck of the bus on our ride to church, we could peer over the edge of a bridge and glimpse seals basking on a sand bar where a river met the sea. Academic jobs are hard to come by, and I'd worked hard to put myself in a position to get this one. It was a blessing of relief that felt a long time coming.

That said, the seeds of my full-time return to BYU were sown on our family's first Sunday in our new home. They were sown as I stood talking with Leon at the bus stop because I realized, in a flash of self-awareness, the degree of my religious devotion—the inseparability of my love of God from my love of the Church. That aesthetic relation to my faith, that reflective wedge I had inserted between my beliefs and the Church's truth claims, was exposed as a mere shadow of reality. Did I have, still, questions about the Church? Of course. Was I ambivalent about aspects of its culture and history and policies and (what I call in chapter 3) clunkiness? Absolutely. But had my experiences in the Church and with the Spirit culminated in aesthetic detachment? No, not at all. I was a believer. A would-be disciple of Christ. A defender of the Church even and someone dedicated to helping build it where I could. So, there in Aberdeen, I eventually accepted a calling to serve as a ward missionary. I assisted the full-time missionaries in meeting with all kinds of people, including, as it turned out, one of my students. And eventually, when it became clear that I could make a more meaningful contribution at BYU, I renounced my dream of living and working in Scotland.

As all these things began happening and as the direction of our future became clearer, I reflected more intently on how my life had taken shape. Decades earlier, shortly after my mission, I had felt a spiritual storm gathering around me. That storm was with me for a long time, and it took a serious toll on my faith. But now, twenty-plus years later, I looked up and saw blue sky. In Scotland, of all places.

How had this happened? It hadn't been anything dramatic. I was not living a life of sin and suddenly perceiving the error of my ways. Or rather, my sins (and manifold weaknesses) were not so grave that they threw my soul, like Saul's or Alma's, into a state of catalytic shock. Neither, during my long process of spiritual healing, did I witness a vision or perceive some great miracle. It would be truer to say that any visions and miracles I did experience had usually been subtle and sustained. They came in the example (sometimes radiant, sometimes stoic) of my God-fearing, God-loving parents, who instilled in me the disposition to believe in a benevolent deity. They came in the presence of saintly individuals in my wards and BYU workplace who, in their deep acceptance of me and the beautiful lives they led, showed me better ways to be. They came in the person of Kerry, who grew and changed with me. Above all, they came in the persistent kindness, the endless grace, of a God who would hear my pleading, smile gently on my frustrated venting, and faithfully manage (in his own time) to answer my prayers, verifying his word unto me "in every particular" (Alma 25:17). All these things and more had impressed me, had worked in me, until one day, standing at a bus stop and marshaling a habitually defensive posture toward the imagined incursions of the Church, I saw myself through the eyes of a new convert and thought, *That's not me. I'm different, and better, than that.*

∗ ∗ ∗

If the seeds of my return to BYU, and thus my scholarly attention to spiritual experience, were planted in that bus stop conversation with Leon, a new convert, then so too was the resolution of my spiritual crises already evident in the form of their emergence. My faith crisis had lasted two decades. In chapter 5, I described the onset of new spiritual complexities by way of different metaphors of spiritual feeling, one a campfire and the other a canyon breeze, one a confirmation of what is true in the gentle ways I had been taught to understand the Spirit (warm and fuzzy but more intensive than that) and the other a capacity to sit with contradiction and complexity, a recognition of my need to expand my register of spiritual impressions. The German philosopher Friedrich Nietzsche was emblematic of this latter feeling, certainly of its troubling aspects (which carried into so many corners of my life). But there was another important literary figure to whom I was drawn in my early twenties, and he promoted a very different kind of spiritual complexity, one ultimately rooted in a poetics of God-affirming, Christ-affirming, spiritual transformation. That was Fyodor Dostoevsky.

Nietzsche and Dostoevsky. In my early twenties, these writers were, for me, luminaries at polar ends of a spiritual spectrum. Nietzsche, the would-be antichrist (a title he conferred on himself), was a goading reminder of how religion was an instrument of violence that must be treated violently in turn and of how God was a projection of human need whose purported death was necessary for us to overcome ourselves. Dostoevsky, Russian and some twenty years Nietzsche's senior, pondered similar problems but arrived at very different conclusions. For him, we needed religion in part because of the saints we might encounter there. Meanwhile, to experience the divine in any way—to feel, however briefly, a spiritual presence—only proved that redemption is both necessary and real.

Dostoevsky's magisterial masterpiece, *The Brothers Karamazov*, speaks eloquently to this idea. One of the novel's main characters, Ivan, anticipates Nietzsche in advocating for a Godless society. To destroy belief in God, Ivan contends, would be to eradicate the grounds for moral behavior, for if God does not exist, then everything is permitted. But destruction is less Ivan's aim than re-creation: as he sees it, to level old beliefs is potentially to institute new grounds for morality, establish new forms of human possibility, and build a new society. It's a compelling and, in its era (the late nineteenth century), a popular idea. And while Dostoevsky's novel does not ultimately endorse Ivan's philosophy—it portrays God as the guiding force of a fulfilled life, not as the obstacle we must overcome—it nevertheless dignifies it by lending it eloquent expression. And Dostoevsky dignifies Ivan, crucially, on spiritual grounds. At one point, Ivan spins an elaborate parable about the human inability to handle the freedom (of mind, of spirit, of society—the freedom preached by Jesus) that God has given them. Titled "The Grand Inquisitor," this parable has Christ coming again to earth only to be arraigned and tried anew by the church on the grounds that freedom causes chaos when practiced by humans ill-equipped to exercise its privilege. If we look around us, we see that freedom brings war, not peace; division, not unity; hatred, not love. People need to be constrained, compelled to act properly; they cannot be left to choose for themselves. When called to answer this charge, Christ in Ivan's parable says nothing but simply kisses the priestly inquisitor, the same inquisitor who arraigns him for judgment and ultimately banishes him. It is a powerful gesture evocative of Christ's silence before Pilate. But what makes Ivan's parable even more poignant is that, earlier in the novel, Ivan has already performed this action before his own inquisitor, also a priest, who accuses him of sowing harmful ideas.[7] The novel thus lays the groundwork for a connection between Ivan and Christ: each promotes freedom.

This connection is crucial, not because the novel endorses an equivalence between Ivan and Jesus or because the existential freedom Ivan has in mind is the same as what Christ preaches but rather because it reveals the spiritual fulfillment that Ivan and secularists who think like him truly desire. For Dostoevsky, no human is beyond the purview of spiritual things; all women and men reflect the image of God. Earlier in the novel, the saintly Father Zosima observes that Christianity's truthfulness may be seen "in the spiritual emotions experienced equally by individual men and by masses of people," including "in the hearts of the very atheists," like Ivan, "who are trying to destroy everything. . . . This is so because even those who have renounced Christianity, even those who rebel against it . . . were created in the image of Christ and have remained in His image."[8] All reflect the glory of God, even those who are conflicted and confused and anguished and hurtful.

In this way, *The Brothers Karamazov* gives poignant, even rhapsodic expression to the Lord's declaration in the Doctrine and

Covenants: "All things unto me are spiritual" (29:34). Our challenge, Dostoevsky implies, is to recognize as much in the storm and stress of everyday life, when so many things militate against our discernment of God's presence—when we find ourselves beset with care, the victims of circumstance or others' malfeasance or our own misdeeds, laboring from a lack of understanding or an inability to feel the peace imparted by the Spirit, the *stillness* of the still, small voice.

It was this conviction of the divine in all things, all people, and my perception of Dostoevsky's capacity to vividly communicate that vision that drew me to his work. In the spirit of Parley P. Pratt's insights into the Holy Ghost (that it quickens our minds, purifies our feelings, cultivates our gifts, inspires our virtues—that it imparts "life to the whole being"), Dostoevsky's fiction suggested to me that we would be more ourselves as we became more *than* ourselves, as we learned more fully to reflect God's image. We would find fulfillment as we experienced God in the midst of everyday life, in good times and bad. God would render us more complete—more so, certainly, than the (merely) brilliant Ivan.

Or, for that matter, than Nietzsche. While Nietzsche was an extraordinary thinker, there was a complexity, a symphonic harmony to Dostoevsky's novels that reflected a more profound set of spiritual convictions. For this reason, Dostoevsky's work felt so much richer with possibility than Nietzsche's. As a powerful point of contrast, while Dostoevsky excelled at building characters like Ivan—fashioned from sophisticated philosophical positions—these positions were nevertheless less complex in themselves than the sprawling, more spiritually kaleidoscopic worlds these novels depicted. Ivan was a character in the novel; he was not the entire novel in himself. Nietzsche, meanwhile, attached himself fully to some of these same (limited) philosophical positions and virtually became what he described. Hence, where Dostoevsky could portray them somewhat ironically, distancing himself from them, they practically swallowed Nietzsche whole.

A famous story illustrates this contrast. In early January 1889, Nietzsche witnessed a coachman whipping his horse in a plaza.

Nietzsche rushed toward the horse and threw his arms around it, weeping. Shortly thereafter, the mental illness that had been steadily overtaking him consumed him altogether, and he was escorted to a sanitorium where he spent his last ten years in a semi-vegetative state. The story has become part of Nietzsche's legend; it captures the pathos of a great philosopher engulfed by the anguish he witnessed. But the story has a weirdly derivative quality to it. For, in Dostoevsky's classic novel *Crime and Punishment*, published more than twenty years earlier (in 1866), the protagonist Raskolnikov, a young man consumed by the prospect of evil in the world and eventually tormented by a murderous deed of his own (an act of symbolic and ultimately failed justice), falls into a feverish dream in which he witnesses the brutal beating of a horse. Distraught, Raskolnikov rushes forward to try to save the horse. Although others try to restrain him, he eventually reaches the mare, embracing and kissing it. But it is already dead.

Nietzsche's biographers acknowledge his fascination with Dostoevsky, and he appears to have identified so strongly with the episode in *Crime and Punishment* that, in his diminished mental state, he simply enacted it. Raskolnikov felt for the horse, and Nietzsche felt for Raskolnikov feeling for the horse. But the moral in Dostoevsky's novel is vastly different as the narrative does not beatify Raskolnikov's dream of suffering as much as complicate it. For starters, Dostoevsky portrays it as the projection of a feverish mind, one that moves us but of which we are cautioned to be wary. Moreover, Raskolnikov's eventual, lethal response to the violence that disturbs him—his pathetic killing of a corrupt old pawnbroker—will reveal itself to be implicated in the evil it derides. What Raskolnikov lacks, and only gains by novel's end, is a sanctified perspective born of his own suffering, a realization of the error of his ways and a greater hope in the redeemability of humankind (including himself). The novel illustrates, and thus promises, a process of spiritual transformation. Indeed, the novel exemplifies this process in the distance it puts between its larger vision and the episode of the beaten horse. Though vividly rendered, the latter is only a small part of a sweeping saga and a delerious part at that. It requires the resolution of the larger plot for us to see properly how to respond to suffering. Unlike Nietzsche, then, Dostoevsky does not fully identify with his troubled protagonist; rather, he animates his character while making him part of a much larger symphony of meaning.

When I encountered Dostoevsky's novels in my early twenties, I was taken with how they do not live crisis as much as enact and resolve it. They convey a hope of resolution, embodying the form of such resolution in their plots, bringing extant conflict to eventual closure. The inherent hopefulness of such an outcome—of a capacity to face struggle and yet emerge transformed, redeemed by the experience—thrilled me. I wanted to see myself not as Nietzsche saw himself in the suffering Raskolnikov but as Dostoevsky perceived the redemptive promise in Raskolnikov and, by extension, all people. Transformation in Dostoevsky's work was grander than suffering in Nietzsche's. If I was not yet ready to live that understanding, I would be eventually. Even if it took decades.

*　*　*

Transformation can be dramatic (think Saul on the road to Damascus [Acts 9]) or subtle (like the Lamanites who, we are told, "were baptized with fire and with the Holy Ghost, and they knew it not" [3 Ne. 9:20]). I had experienced both kinds. A dramatic episode in my bishop's office as an eighteen-year-old had made me, instantly, an eager missionary. But it was a more layered process over a long period of time that had revealed my deep conviction as a Latter-day Saint. I reflected on how God had been with me "in every time of trouble" (D&C 3:8) and had healed, gradually but assuredly, spiritual wounds I had suffered over many years. He had done it through answers to prayer great and small—through events that struck me as virtually miraculous (like how I met Kerry) and through the poetry of beautiful if temporary illusions, tender mercies, metaphors of better things. Such reflection moved me, filled me with gratitude, changed me. It is changing me still.

TWELVE

The Answer
of the Empty Tomb

One recent morning, I was reminded of a lesson I have learned over and over. I had gone to bed the previous night brooding over the faith crisis of a loved one. My brooding was inspired by the reminder of a note this person had written two years earlier expressing concern that, try as she might, she had not been able to feel the closeness to the Spirit to which she had grown accustomed. She was reaching out, asking that others fast with her, pray with and for her—that they help her try to recover her spiritual equilibrium. As it turns out, she had not been able to do so. It had been a rough two years.

The memory of this sequence of events sent to me sleep in a somber mood, something I carried into the next morning when I arose and began my routine: exercise, shower, read the scriptures. At its conclusion, I knelt to pray, proceeding directly to the questions I had carried since the previous night and, to some extent, for the previous two years. *Why? Why her? Where was God when she reached for him? How could this happen?*

As the questions unfolded one by one, I could feel the veil separating me from heaven grow coarser, heavier, turning from something like fabric into a denser and more solid substance—a kind of thick, low ceiling. My heart, which was hurting, grew cold. I began to feel my prayer as an echo rattling around in my head. I knew what this meant, this "stupor of thought" (D&C 9:9): I would have no answer to this question. Once again, no answer. Not posed in this way.

I also knew though, I had learned, that this need not be the last word. So I shifted my thoughts, adjusted—more than my attitude, almost the angle of prayer at which I approached God. Then I began again with different questions: Who was she in God's eyes? And what could I do to help? At once that thick, impenetrable substance separating me from heaven began to attenuate, grow thin, almost flutter in a breeze of inspiration, the Spirit gently rushing through me with words, images, feelings. God was not despairing; all seemed well—or, if not entirely well, then certainly better and more hopeful than how I saw things.

The incident reminded me, again, that spiritual experience is not only about asking and receiving; it is rarely a simple game of question and answer. Instead, there is usually something kinetic about it; it requires us to move, shift our minds, find new questions, and take virtual steps in God's direction. Once we are in that different place and from that new vantage point, God may provide answers. But he almost always shows us something else too, something we could not have seen if we had kept ourselves fixed in our previous place.

Spiritual experiences move us but often only after we move in their direction, move in heaven's direction. That's also how they are able to help change us, open us: to a degree, we are changing, opening already.

*   *   *

Sunset Song, first novel in the trilogy *A Scots Quair* (or "quire," a bundle of papers) by Lewis Grassic Gibbon, is one of the most beautiful works of Scottish literature. Published in 1932, it telescopes a vision of Scottish modernization—its transformative shifts from an agricultural to a commercial society and from close-knit to war-torn communities—onto the story of Chris (i.e., Christine) Guthrie. Chris grapples with change as she grows to adulthood, from the usual dramas of adolescence to more complex decisions. For example, after the death of her parents, emigration of her older brother to South America, and departure of her orphaned younger siblings to live with relatives, should she remain alone on the farm where she was raised? Or should she leave to become a schoolteacher in the city where she was educated? Ultimately choosing to stay at home, Chris witnesses change begin to happen all around her. She marries, then bears a child, then watches her husband enlist for service in the Great War (World War I). Eventually, she loses her husband, first to brutality (when he returns home on leave, greatly changed) and then to death (when, realizing the folly of the war and his treatment of Chris, he deserts the front in France and is captured and shot).

In one of the most widely cited passages in the novel, Chris reflects on the relationship between change and permanence.

> [A] queer thought came to her there in the drookèd [or deep-drenched] fields, that nothing endured at all, nothing but the land she passed across, tossed and turned and perpetually changed below the hands of the crofter [or subsistence farm] folk since the oldest of them had set the Standing Stones by the loch . . . and climbed there on their holy days and saw their terraced crops ride brave in the wind and sun. Sea and sky and folk who wrote and fought and were learned, teaching and saying and praying, they lasted but as a breath, a mist of fog in the hills, but the land was forever, it moved and changed below you, but was forever, you were close to it and it to you, not at a bleak remove it held you and hurted you.[1]

What seems important about this passage is not only its train of association—from the durability of the land to the virtual ghosts of the people who once dwelled on it (those who raised the Standing Stones and then the crofters who arrived much later)—but also the conjunctive rhythm of the language: the land "tossed *and* turned *and* perpetually changed"; farmers "climbed there on their holy days *and* saw their terraced crops"; "sea *and* sky *and* folk who wrote *and* fought *and* were learned . . . lasted but as a breath. . . ." The rhetorical linkages ("and . . . and . . . and . . .") evoke a sense of coherence. All is transient, all but the land, and yet, everything is deeply connected. The passage implicitly evokes a phenomenon that the neurophysicists Andrew Newberg and Eugene D'Aquili, studying the brain science of spirituality, call "Absolute Unitary Being," a feeling of oneness with all things in the universe, of bliss, "of peace and happiness, as well as reduced fear of death."[2] Chris, for example, suddenly feels connected to her ancestors, both named and anonymous, those "crofter folk" who subsisted off the soil, enriched by atmosphere of "sea and sky."

While Gibbon's novel presents the flow of history, it is also taken with the spiritual currents that inform Chris's experience and influence her decisions—her feelings of attachment to family and place that cause her to mature in her thinking. We thus see her undergo a process of transformation even as she remains in place, at home, on the farm. In fact, this capacity to change also enables Chris to transcend her circumstances, to endure even as things (including entire ways of life) pass away around her. She learns, she grows—she is moved. This is spiritual understanding, and it is Chris's saving grace.

I love and often teach *Sunset Song*. I did so most recently in my course on literature and spiritual experience. I find its tale about spiritual awakening all the more compelling given the disdain its author expressed elsewhere toward religion. "[A] corpus of archaic science," Gibbon called religion; a tool only for primitive members of our species. In the modern world, with science allegedly displacing superstition, religion is little more than "a cortical abortion," a misfiring of the mind.[3] But the currents of Gibbon's novel suggest a more nuanced view. While *Sunset Song* is largely about history, Gibbon also demonstrates, through Chris, processes of spiritual if not religious rebirth. Chris is more than the accident of her surroundings, more than the material conditions that influence her attitudes, opinions, dreams, and beliefs. What is it,

Gibbon implicitly asks, that renders us capable of weaving together the diverse elements of our lives, that makes us able to connect so profoundly to places and people and create meaning between aspects of our experience ("sea and sky and folk . . . teaching and saying and praying")?

These are spiritual questions. There is something in us—earthy and historical creatures that we are—that transcends the world into which we are born. As creatures who create meaning, we also fashion the worlds we inhabit. It's like an equation $n + 1$, where n = the world: we are more than ("$+ 1$") the factor ("n") that supposedly defines us. If Gibbon is ultimately a religious as well as a spiritual writer—if he bore religious impulses despite his expressed hostility toward religion—it is because he poses large, meaningful questions (Who are we? Of what are we made?) that his novel illustrates but cannot answer.

I call these religious impulses because religion is the foundation of a spiritual life; it is the set of practices through which we pose— repeatedly, ritualistically—those questions that are too big to answer. I speak of my own experience here and not only of *Sunset Song*. Religion is the part of my life that has always reminded me that what I most value is larger than anything I presently am or comprehend, even as it reassures me that I also belong to that greater, vaster thing ("the kingdom of God"; "the plan of salvation"; "God's covenants with the house of Israel"). Religion is the medium, therefore, through which I explore who I am and what I am becoming, what all people and things are becoming. It is the institution that reminds me, paradoxically, that what I most care about is less what I know than what I cannot fully grasp—that what I know most deeply about the people and things I love is that I actually only "know in part" who and what they ultimately are (1 Cor. 13:12). And yet, despite this dim understanding, religion asks me to move, to act. *Fast*, it tells me. *Pray. Serve. Find your answers in the perpetual motion machine that is religious activity.*

Religion asks so much of us, and yet, in some ways, we ask so little of religion. Yes, we sometimes demand that it account for its own history (e.g., the Church's practice of polygamy or its racist attitudes) and exclusions (say, of women from positions of authority); we occasionally plead for it to provide us with the direction to help us fulfill our dreams (of relationships, education, jobs) or guide us through life's quagmires (of grief, injustice, addiction, and more). All these concerns are of real import. And, in some instances, this makes religion an object of disappointment: it seems too mired in its own humanity, its own fallenness, to help us transcend our own. But we're probably wrong to expect religion to address our concerns in a wholly satisfying way. In a sense, Gibbon was right: when it comes to dealing with complex matters of history and psychology and politics (and race relations and human sexuality and so many other areas of modern life), religion is an "archaic science"—its answers aren't really adequate of themselves. And in some circumstances, like when we hear a particularly insensitive remark (or worse) from a fellow churchgoer or when our tangled lives meet with little more than moral platitudes from an ecclesiastical leader, leaving us feeling more desolate than before, religion may even seem to be a "cortical abortion." All this can be painful, confusing, and (as I have lived it) deeply disillusioning. We categorize such things as faith crises.

But religion is not truly itself until we ask it to do the impossible— until, fasting, praying, and serving, we petition it to help bring us, mere mortals, into the presence of what is most sacred. To know we ask for the impossible (*Is God really there?* or *Can Christ really heal one as broken as I?*) but to ask for it anyway and to ask in a way that we believe we will be heard, even answered, by a loving and compassionate and electrifyingly real God—to believe and even *know* that our religious devotion to God will be met by his devotion to us: *that* is faith. Faith doesn't solve all problems or answer all questions. Of itself, detached from knowledge about the world and a deep and sometimes hard-won understanding of ourselves, it answers relatively few. But faith, "the *moving* cause of all action,"[4] connects us to God, and God dispels crisis, whether by answering our questions or calming our hearts. Religion helps us build faith, in large measure by making us move and thus shifting our thinking. Religion makes the world bigger: $n + 1 + \text{One}$.

* * *

Religion helps us build faith by making us move—that is ultimately one of the overarching themes of this book. Many of the chapters have come at this theme through a side door by describing the struggle religion has often represented for me. It has compelled me to do things I did not initially wish to do (like serve a mission); it has forced me to immerse myself in a culture, even practices, I describe as clunky; the truths it reveals have also exposed or opened gaps, large and small, in my understanding; and the terminology it has given me through which to communicate the things of God ("Restoration," "the fulness of times," "covenants and ordinances") has constrained me by that same measure ("*Non, monsieur, ça ne m'intéresse pas*": the response to my use of it). All this has turned me to literature as a way to understand life's paradoxes and provide a more expansive language. But I have returned, chapter after chapter, to the blessing the Church has also been to me. My experience as a missionary changed the course of my life; members of my religious community (from all across the spectrum: apostles on one end, people I met in homeless shelters on the other) have served as messengers of divine words that struck me to my core; Church doctrines (that God lives, answers prayers, and keeps promises; that Jesus Christ heals us, redeems us) and priesthood covenants have carried me across wastes of disappointment and incomprehension, leading me to my richest relationships and greatest sense of fulfillment as a husband and father, friend and minister, teacher and scholar, seeker and dreamer, and more.

This might have been, then, a very different book—one discussing not just *that* religion helps us build faith but more specifically *how* the Church does so, how spiritual and religious experiences enrich each other, how Church teachings and practices open minds and change hearts, and so much more. So, so much more.[5] And this book addresses some of these things. But its message is simpler: *The Spirit brings life to our whole being; we thus need to enhance our capacity to perceive and receive it across the breadth of its manifestations in all seasons of life, in good times and in bad.* The Church plays a vital role here, for it is a uniquely powerful vehicle for God to reach us, to move us. I have seen this in my own life and the lives of so many others. So, so many.

Indeed, I see it week after week, God gracing the lives of Church members with whom I interact. I witness it, for example, as I sit across from them in temple recommend interviews.[6]

The convert as a late teen, now in her sixties, declaring her love for the gospel and its continually transformative role in her life. She calls it her favorite topic, which I know to be true from previous conversations. She feels so endlessly blessed, she says, and she proceeds, again, to count the ways.

The divorcée back on her feet emotionally after several rough years—decades. I ask the second question in the temple recommend interview: "Do you have a testimony of Jesus Christ as your Savior and Redeemer?" She opens her mouth to answer, then closes it. Tears fill her eyes. She smiles a little bashfully as the seconds pass, still unable to speak.

The longtime Church leader, a man of holiness. Deep conviction carries through his response to every question; I feel awed by the gentle power behind a succession of simple answers, yes and no.

The eastern European woman sitting beside her mother to help translate. Question, translation, answer, translation. The woman smiles at my questions before rehearsing them to her mother in their native tongue, then smiles more deeply at her mother's animated replies. Even before I hear them in English, the answers are obvious.

The recovering addict shifting in his seat. It's been many years since he attended the temple; he's suffered so many losses since then—relationships, jobs, homes. And now, being here, he feels so grateful, just so grateful. So grateful, he keeps repeating, so grateful.

The elderly widow smiling tranquilly, radiantly. She lives as closely to heaven as anyone I know. "May I ask? How often do you attend the temple?" She pauses for a moment, thinking. Her reply is so matter-of-fact: "Oh, I don't know, four or five times a week."

The young mother from India, excited to renew her recommend. When the Church announced plans to build a temple in her native country, she wept. She shouted with joy. She texted, called, videoed with family back home. Then, she says, she wept again.

The man who has accepted so many callings, filled so many roles, done so much good, served with such energy. He's also made mistakes. I ask the second to last question in the interview, the one about whether there are serious sins that still need to be resolved. He smiles and replies no, his baritone voice almost carrying a note of song. He's already been through that in the past, I know. The Spirit fills the room; this is a man with a deep understanding of repentance.

The single woman, now past forty, a blessing in her ward and a leader in her workplace. It's so strange, she remarks. She never expected to find herself at this place in life, in these circumstances. But God has been so good to her; he brings her so many bright days. And brighter days ahead, she says with a confidence born of grace.

The young father who takes his turn after his wife. He answers calmly, simply. It hadn't been this way two years ago; we'd spent a lot of time talking about his crisis of faith, his dissatisfaction with churchy answers to his questions. But a little time has passed; he understands things differently now. He radiates peace.

There are so many others, each unique, spiritually resplendent. Each bears witness, verbally but also viscerally, through the eloquence of their acts, their countenances, to the rhythms of God at work in their lives. At work by way of the Church. I write above that this might be a different book, that I might discuss how the Church helps build faith. But the truth is, aside from my grasp of a few foundational principles, that book is beyond me. Yes, I know what the Church teaches; I know what it demands; I know how individuals respond, how I respond, to the Lord's call, to the Spirit. I understand how the Spirit prompts us to move. At doctrinal and experiential levels, I "get it." But when I step back and consider all this in aggregate, when I try to take in all the spiritual harmonies in all these lives, it blows my mind. It is at once too large and too subtle. Yet another gap in my understanding: the sublime wonder of $n + 1 +$ One in life after life after life.

* * *

I reflect often on a poem by R. S. Thomas. It's my favorite poem about spiritual things. This is less because of its language or formal sophistication—its features are understated; it doesn't dazzle us like a poem by, say, Gerard Manley Hopkins—than because of a brilliant paradox it articulates that goes to the heart of faith:

> Not darkness but twilight
> in which even the best
> of minds must make its way
> now. And slowly the questions
> occur, vague but formidable
> for all that. We pass our hands
> over their surface like blind
> men, feeling for the mechanism
> that will swing them aside. They
> yield, but only to re-form
> as new problems; and one
> does not even do that
> but towers immovable
> before us.
>   Is there no way
> other than thought of answering
> its challenge? There is an anticipation
> of it to the point of
> dying. There have been times
> when, after long on my knees
> in a cold chancel, a stone has rolled
> from my mind, and I have looked
> in and seen the old questions lie
> folded and in a place
> by themselves, like the piled
> graveclothes of love's risen body.[7]

Titled "The Answer," Thomas's poem is really more about questions. Those to which he refers are never named, though they evoke any we might pose, "vague but formidable": questions of theological quandary, of Church history, of the failings of Church leaders, of tensions between religion and science or religion and politics or religion and identity, and more; also questions pertaining to our personal disappointments, tragedies, punctured dreams, and bruised spirits. All important; all, in their way, potentially faith-eroding. "They / yield," do these questions; answers are always available. For Latter-day Saints, they seem ever more so in an age of greater transparency. The gospel topics essays on the Church's website (on the historical authenticity of scripture, race, plural marriage, Heavenly Mother, and more) provide some answers; dedicated scholarship on these and other subjects offers still more. And for our personal griefs, nurturing in ward communities sometimes works wonders. But because many of these answers draw on domains of experience (e.g., history, psychology, sociology, etc.) where facts beg further facts and ideas demand elaboration through further ideas, our questions "re-form / as new problems." Scholarly and personal inquiry are by their nature insatiable. There is always more to explore, always more to question, always more we do not know. More, more, more.

Fortunately, one question "towers immovable / before us" and towers so massively that Thomas concludes his first stanza on that note. This is the question of whether God exists at all, of whether there is purpose behind our creation, meaning to life, or ultimate direction to our existence. I call it fortunate that this question looms over us because it is the quintessentially religious question, an impossible question for anything other than a religious idiom. (What besides religion could even pretend to answer that question or answer it well?) And, fittingly, that answer—"The Answer"—comes in the form of nothing at all: no word or doctrine, no explanation as to what or why or how. It comes, rather, in the experience of emptiness—specifically, of an empty tomb: "There have been times / when, after long on my knees / in a cold chancel, a stone has rolled / from my mind." The poet finds himself in the position of the disciple John, outrunning Peter to the sepulcher, and "stooping down, and looking in, saw the linen clothes lying. . . . And he saw, and believed" (John 20:5, 8). Christ's body should have been there, but it had disappeared. Thus emerges the great paradox: God was absent; therefore, God lived.

In Thomas's poem, that enigmatic presence through absence, that fulsome vacuity—the empty tomb as the sign of Christ's resurrection—becomes the greatest of all possible answers to any conceivable question. For nothing is as unthinkable, as impossible, as the prospect of the resurrected Jesus. Nothing so radically revolutionizes our conception of life. We are only ourselves because we are not ourselves *only*: before we draw our first breath, arrive at our first thought, perform our first act, we are already Christ's. And his singular life means that our lives become multiple, raised to more glorious and ultimately resurrected versions of themselves. In the light of Christ's redemption, our lives acquire motion, they change, whether instantly or through a slow, gradual process: what was sick is made well, what was wounded is healed, what was wrong is made right, what was confused becomes clear. "I have looked / in and seen the old questions lie / folded and in a place / by themselves."

My conviction of Christ's resurrection and all it promises is inseparable from my experience of the Church. In the terms given by Thomas's poem, the Church is not God; it's more like the tomb where I come to pay my devotions (most literally in taking the sacrament in memory of Christ's sacrifice). So often, I have experienced the emptiness of that tomb as a source of frustration, not yielding exactly what I seek. But when Christ calls to me through the Spirit, he usually does so from there. Why is this? Why does Christ speak from within the shadow of the Church? Partly, I imagine, it's a matter of context. For just as the tomb's emptiness provided meaning to others regarding the risen Lord, so Church doctrines, ritual practices, and covenants lend shape, meaning, and purpose to our pulsations of spiritual experience. They move belief in the direction of understanding.

Think again of the characteristics of spiritual experience: feelings of connectedness, transcendence, vitality, ultimacy—all intensely personal. It's that personal quality that evokes, for me, the presence of a distinctive being: the Spirit of God. So my religion teaches me to label such experiences. And that teaching rings true; it enlightens my understanding. For, to feel the Spirit to any degree, whether intensely or subtly, is to enjoy the presence of a member of the Godhead; it is to be brought at least partly into God's presence. And this, in turn, is where I most fully discern the presence of Christ. For it is Christ's sacrifice that reconciles me to God. Without Christ, there would be no spiritual experience. To have *any* spiritual experience—whether directly religious or simply in feeling a sense of greater connectedness, radiant vitality, transcendent purpose, sacred presence, or ultimate meaning—is already to be the beneficiary of Christ's atonement. No one "cometh unto the Father" but by Christ (John 14:6). Before we move or act in accordance with a spiritual prompting, whatever that prompting may be, our mere awareness of the Spirit's subtle impulsions is already a witness of Christ. To feel the Spirit is thus to experience conversion, even if we cannot yet conceptualize it as such.

Who Christ is and why he is necessary—these are doctrines the Church teaches, doctrines the Lord reveals through the Church. Does the Church answer all my questions? No. But my experience there, the Spirit there, the way the Lord communes with me there, *moves* me there, has a way of suspending many of these questions because it helps me understand something more fundamental: What does it mean to have a spiritual experience? That is, to feel the Spirit? That is, to know vividly that Christ is risen?

So, to return to Thomas's poem and, from there, to the myriad questions that find in Christ the ultimate "Answer": Is there a God? Is there a purpose to existence? Can things be better for humankind? For the planet? Their corollaries, the gut-wrenching personal questions I have asked (and continue to ask) myself—What if God leaves me alone to deal with this problem? What if I or others I love have been damaged beyond human repair? What if my prayers for people or things go unanswered?—suddenly seem like those outworn, "piled / graveclothes" once draped over the now-risen Jesus. This is not to say that the questions are not valid or important, sometimes desperately so. But when I consider Christ as the "Answer" of answers, when I internalize his import and recognize his suspension above every circumstance and instance of suffering, then my questions no longer seem so encompassing or provoke the same anxiety. Instead, and almost strangely, these questions too are reborn and carry an aura of promise. Where I mourned—and where I thus questioned—I sense, I believe, I understand I will be comforted (Matt. 5:4). Where I hungered and thirsted (whether after righteousness or justice)—and where I was thus moved to question—I sense, believe, and understand I will be filled (Matt. 5:6). And so much more. This is the promise of the empty tomb, a promise made more real to me because of my experience with the Spirit and my experience of and in the Church.

* * *

Ultimately, spiritual experience is about our connection to God. And prayer is perhaps the most intimate form of that connection. As I have thought about prayer over the years, and particularly about answers I have received through prayer, it has seemed to me that they take two principal forms. There are prayers I utter in the moment and answers that come in the moment (including a later moment)—whether confirmations that something is true, impressions that something is right, promptings to act, epiphanies in which something suddenly becomes clear, or a sense of peace that all is (or will be) well. When we speak about answers to prayer in church lessons, we usually speak of these prayers and answers "in the moment." This is true even of silent, wordless prayers—prayers in which nothing is said but much is felt. Communication still happens. But then there is another category of prayer and another kind of answer. These only coalesce over time and are the product of habits, of rhythms—prayers less uttered than lived as a function of the circumstances we face, the choices we make, the things we desire. It takes time to learn how to recognize let alone articulate them. Likewise, answers to these prayers also tend to coalesce slowly, a function of a gradual increase in understanding, and of the persistent shaping of our lives, and of transformation over time.

The first kind of prayer is, call it, verbal: we speak to the Lord or perhaps communicate silently, and one way or another, he speaks back. The second kind of prayer is kinetic: we move and so does the Lord. "Draw near unto me and I will draw near unto you; seek me diligently and ye shall find me; ask, and ye shall receive; knock, and it shall be opened unto you" (D&C 88:63).

I have learned that, for the most part, if answers to prayer do not come in "verbal" form, they probably will "kinetically," as I move and as things move around me. They will come in the course of living. This is probably because I do not yet know how to pose a sufficiently refined question; I have not yet passed sufficiently through a refiner's fire; I am not yet the person I need to be to understand the answers God provides. I have posed so many of these questions over the years, questions whose answers could only be had at a later time. "Who will I marry?" Good question but a better one would have been "Who will I need to become such that I can sustain a relationship with the person I will marry?" That answer only came kinetically over time. Then there's the prayer I frequently preached as a missionary—"Is the Church true?" Again, good (verbal) question but a better (kinetic) one proved to be "In what ways will the Church bring me to Christ?"[8] There are so many others: Why this pain? Why (not) now? Why so much mess of things? When I began posing or simply ruminating over these and other questions, God began answering them. But the answers were as long in coming as my speed or slowness in developing, in moving. When God speaks, when he communicates with us through the Spirit, he communes not only with who we are but with who we are becoming. So, these days, when I receive a spiritual impression that feels a little incomplete—when I formulate a question whose answer, effectively, is an empty tomb—I take it as a promise of

redemption. Of transformation through Christ once I have been sufficiently moved. He will call, and I will turn, as did Mary at the tomb
(John 20:14–16): God will answer this prayer as he has all the others.

Sometimes these prayers converge; sometimes God communicates something to us in what feels like a moment but that takes us
a long time to understand—a long time and much movement, much
growth and change. Such experiences change how we think and how
we pray, both verbally and kinetically. It is with such an experience
that I conclude this book.

* * *

It was mid-May and absolutely glorious outside: bright, temperate, and
fragrant. This was true even within the narrow, cobblestoned streets of
the ancient French city where I was serving as a missionary, fruit and
flowers lading the small markets. It was lunchtime, and my companion
and I were just getting back to our apartment for the customary hour
or two of pause when all of France slowed down. Though loving the
spring, my mood did not match the lustrous atmosphere outdoors. I
had less than a week left of my mission—four, five days, something like
that—and I felt heavy. Burdened. Grateful, to be sure (see the story I
tell at the end of chapter 4), but a little melancholy.

I grabbed some food from the kitchen and walked to the bedroom
where I gazed down on the street and shops below, then over and up
at the clock tower, then across at the building on the other side of the
street. It was a mirror of ours; they all were: several hundred years
old, a few stories high, and horizontally attached, residence by residence, to every other building along the circuitous streets. The town
was a labyrinth of weathered, musty stone.

Back down on the street, a couple residents caught my eye, the
strolling riddles of everyday missionary life: French and yet children of God; children of God and yet. . . French. (Right, got it: *Non,
monsieur, ça ne m'intéresse pas.*) I watched them saunter slowly down
the sun-splashed cobblestone, eventually disappearing from view,

consumed in mundane mystery along with most everything else I'd seen during my two years.

I don't understand anything, I felt myself conclude.

My companion came into the room, looking weary—wanting, as I, a little quiet time. So, I got up, not knowing where to move. Almost not knowing how. The feeling prompted an overwhelming desire to pray, to express to the Lord my sense of heaviness and deep, almost existential confusion. I walked into the bathroom, closed the door, knelt by the sink, and paused. I wasn't sure how to begin. *I don't understand anything*: that was the mood, but it wasn't the mode. *Help me; help all of us*: that was closer.

I waited, trying to muster the capacity to articulate a question that felt beyond me. What I finally managed was hopelessly vague: *What does it all mean?*

The question was impossibly open-ended and inexact—at once pretentious and naïve. I was seeking for a way to frame, summarize my experience as a missionary: What lessons might I take from the past two years? How might I begin to work through the rush of impressions, the miracles and disappointments, the convictions and disillusionment, the gratitude and frustration, the blessings and— sometimes—the blankness? Those questions, though still too large, at least might have provided clearer avenues for personal reflection and hence for inspiration. But instead, *What does it all mean?* How nebulous! I may as well have asked, "What is the relationship between string theory and the soul?" or "What is the highest prime number of thy numberless creations?" or, a childhood favorite, "Why is the sky?" *What does it all mean?* As in, the meaning of life? As if I could ever be entitled to know! Only a God could answer such a question, not because the question was so big but because the person asking it was so unformed.

But answer it God did. And it was unlike any other answer to prayer I've ever had. From out of the dullness and grayness and crampedness of my befogged soul, I felt a light begin to well and surge within me. It burst from my heart and flooded my body and then deluged my mind. Its effect was extraordinary: in place of "peace" or "understanding," I felt overtaken by an irrepressible urge to laugh. It burst from my lips, audibly. And not a single chuckle—a sustained impulse to belly laugh. Unaccustomed to such boisterousness in my devotion, I tried clamping the laughter inside, but it only bounced more forcefully off the narrow bathroom walls. I then tried opening my mouth and releasing it voicelessly into the air, but I was unable to control the contraction in my throat that kept converting it to sound.

On and on it went; I was shaking uncontrollably. I wasn't laughing *at* anything; nothing funny had leapt to mind. And given how private I tended to be about opening my heart to God, I was also anxious at the thought of my companion hearing me from the adjacent room. A gentle-hearted farm kid, he already believed I was a little loco, victim as he was to too many philosophical rants fueled by the "big ideas" I was poaching from Cocteau and Camus and translating into missionary idiom. (My mission president shared similar concerns as, for that matter, did my parents: I'd converted too many of these rants into weekly letters.) I knew, also, that the laughter was partly attributable to the glee I felt at the rapidly approaching end of my mission, the terminus to the *peine forte et dure* ("hard and forceful punishment") of knocking on doors and street contacting and sixty-plus-hour work weeks with no vacation and no movies and no music and no girl-friends and no. . . No. . . *Non, monsieur, ça ne m'intéresse pas.* I was almost home, and I was elated.

But there was more to the laughter than that. It wasn't humor, madness, or the prospects of family and friends and leisure in the suburbs of San Diego that had me splitting my sides in the bathroom of a rundown apartment in a six-hundred-year-old building in an antique French city. The feeling wasn't an exhalation of relief but an eruption of joy. *What does it all mean?* What a bad (ambiguous, imprecise, impossibly open-ended) question. But also, how perfect! I had spent two years talking with strangers in a foreign language about the meaning of life. And now, communing with God, I had extracted from those lessons something of a root essence phrased in my own tongue, a way of asking *Is this good?* And the Lord, in turn, had responded in his. I felt awash in a flood tide of opalescent radiance; overcome, I could not suppress my bliss. And like the child I was and am, I laughed.

The episode lasted only a couple minutes. The laughter subsided and left in its wake a residue of low heat, a gentle sunburn of the soul. I sat on the bathroom floor recovering my bearings, finding myself again in the immediacy of my surroundings as I ran the experience through my head, my body. I had spent two years proclaiming the Lord's gospel to others; was this how it felt to have the Lord proclaim it to me? "Whether by mine own voice or by the voice of my servants, it is the same" (D&C 1:38). In priesthood authority, perhaps. But in visceral force? In the unleashing of unrestrainable ecstasy? In the ability to induce spine-tingling, nerve-untangling, mind-rearranging rapture? In the power to animate, even electrify, such classically Christian doctrines as the joy of the saints and the coming of the kingdom? Not even close.

I don't know that I had put it this way to myself, but a conviction had gradually settled on me that my mission experience, and perhaps life itself, was a story of tragedy, of noble but futile struggle against adverse forces (and not so much evil as indifference, a generalized desensitization to spiritual things). It turns out I was wrong. Life is a rollicking comedy, and my darker moods are merely the setup to a climactic punchline, the grandest of all glorious disclosures. The tomb is empty. Christ lives. And ultimately, because of that. . . everything.

I cannot count the times I have lost this feeling over the years, obscured as it has been by periods of sorrow, or by the gravity of certain questions, or by my own occasional desensitization to spiritual things. But memory of this experience endures on my line of sight, emanating as a warm glow just beneath the horizon of everyday life. It bestows not laughter now but brightness of hope. It captures, for me, the promise intrinsic to spiritual experience. No matter how small, every such experience carries with it a testimony of the reality of God, his plan of salvation, and the redemptive power of Jesus Christ— that is, of a being who moves us, a purpose for his intervention, and the means by which we are brought at least partly into his presence. Whatever my concerns may be or whatever the circumstance, this reality accompanies every experience with the Spirit. Whether intense or subtle, such experiences always transport me in the direction of that place of ultimate joy. Like golden waves, they carry me across the deep of struggles great and small and of questions answered or still open.

Notes

Preface

1. Matthew Wickman, "Thriving Spiritually," BYU devotional, December 1, 2020. https://speeches.byu.edu/talks/matthew-wickman/thriving-spiritually/. Accessed December 26, 2020.

Introduction

1. "*L'enfer, c'est les autres*," the bitter, summative statement of Sartre's 1944 play *No Exit*.

2. Patriarchal blessings are one-time blessings, usually administered to youth, that give individuals specific counsel and direction.

    See https://www.churchofjesuschrist.org/study/manual/gospel-topics/patriarchal-blessings. Accessed January 1, 2021.

Chapter 1

1. Parley P. Pratt, *Key to the Science of Theology*, 10th ed. (Salt Lake City, UT: Deseret Book Company, 1973), 101.

2. Ibid., 101.

3. Blake's poem "Auguries of Innocence" opens this way: "To see the World in a Grain of Sand / And a Heaven in a Wild Flower / Hold Infinity in the palm of your hand / And Eternity in an hour. . ." His point is that we potentially behold heaven in human things.

4. "If you could see humanity spread out in time, as God sees it, it would not look like a lot of separate things dotted about. It would look like one single growing thing—rather like a very complicated tree. Every individual would appear connected with every other." C. S. Lewis, *Mere Christianity* (New York: HarperOne, 1952), 180.

5. Marvin J. Ashton, "There Are Many Gifts," October 1987 general conference of The Church of Jesus Christ of Latter-day Saints, https://www.churchofjesuschrist.org/study/general-conference/1987/10/there-are-many-gifts. Accessed October 26, 2019.

6. I take this idea about literature's fusion of music and philosophy from *The Philosophy of Fine Art* by the early nineteenth-century German philosopher G. W. F. Hegel.

7. "The saintly character is the character for which spiritual emotions are the habitual centre of the personal energy. . . ." William James, *The Varieties of Religious Experience: A Study in Human Nature* (1902; New York: The Modern Library, 2002), 298.

8. Marx wrote this in 1843 in *A Contribution to the Critique of Hegel's* Philosophy of Right.

9. I generally resort to the male pronoun in referring to God throughout the manuscript. It should be said, however, that Latter-day Saint theology concerning the existence of a Heavenly Mother as well as a Heavenly Father might legitimate the plural pronoun "their." (Fiona and Terryl Givens opt for that pronoun in *All Things New: Rethinking Sin, Salvation, and Everything in Between* [Meridian, ID: Faith Matters, 2020], 27 and passim.)

Chapter 2

1. I draw here from James, *Varieties of Religious Experience*, 528–29; Philip Sheldrake, *Spirituality: A Brief History* (Malden, MA: Wiley-Blackwell, 2013), 3–4; and Wesley J. Wildman, *Religious and Spiritual Experiences* (New York: Cambridge University Press, 2011), 104. I distill the paragraph's concluding sentence from scripture and several faith traditions.

2. David Perrin, *Studying Christian Spirituality* (New York: Routledge, 2007), 22.

3. Elisabeth Hense, Frans Jespers, and Peter Nissen, eds. *Present-Day Spiritualities: Contrasts and Overlaps* (Leiden: Brill, 2014), 5. In *A Secular Age*, Charles Taylor also famously invokes spirituality as "fullness of life."

See *A Secular Age* (Cambridge, MA: Belknap Press of Harvard University Press, 2007), 5–16 and 600–07.

4. Kees Waaijman, *Spirituality: Forms, Foundations, Methods* (Leuven, Belgium: Peeters, 2002), 6.

5. Andrew Prevot, *Thinking Prayer: Theology and Spirituality Amid the Crises of Modernity* (South Bend, IN: Notre Dame University Press, 2015), 17.

6. On the "self-implicating" status of spirituality as an academic discipline, see Mary Frohlich, "Spiritual Discipline, Discipline of Spirituality: Revisiting Questions of Definition and Method," *Spiritus* 1.1 (2001), 65–78 (68–69).

7. Denise Levertov, "Poetics of Faith," in *Denise Levertov: Collected Poems*, 963–64, ll. 1–7. Subsequent references are cited in the text.

Chapter 3

1. Pratt, *Key to the Science of Theology*, 101.

2. "Verily I say, men should be anxiously engaged in a good cause, and do many things of their own free will, and bring to pass much righteousness" (D&C 58:27).

3. Louise Erdrich, *The Last Report on the Miracles at Little No Horse* (New York: HarperCollins, 2001), 42. Subsequent references are cited in the text.

4. For those unfamiliar with organizational units in the Church of Jesus Christ of Latter-day Saints, most local units are called wards. These wards are then grouped into stakes. Bishops are leaders of wards, stake presidents of stakes. A branch, to which I refer below, is smaller than a ward and is led by a branch president.

Chapter 4

1. This was not the last usurpation of its kind. Literature itself is often said to have been displaced by film, which in turn has had its place upset by TV, the internet, and video games.

2. I may condemn myself for my inadequacies, but I never feel condemnation, as such, from God. When the Spirit is present, I never feel anything but God's intense love for me and those around me. But its effect is subtle, nuanced; I liken it to what Moses expresses in the wake of a vision: "Now, for this cause I know that man is nothing, which thing I never had supposed" (Moses 1:10). The Spirit makes me, makes all of us, stronger, which is precisely why it also reveals my—our—weakness (see Ether 12:27).

3. Daniel Defoe, *Robinson Crusoe*, ed. Michael Shinagel (New York: Norton, 1994), 4.
4. "Ode: Intimations of Immortality from Recollections of Early Childhood," in Wordsworth, *The Poems*, 2 vols., ed. John O. Hayden (London: Penguin, 1990), 1:523–29, l. 204.
5. Denise Levertov, "Caedmon," in *The Collected Poems of Denise Levertov*, ed. Paul A. Lacey and Anne Dewey (New York: New Directions, 2013), 766–67, lines 1–14. Subsequent passages are cited in the text.
6. As my friend and colleague Miranda Wilcox, a scholar of medieval literature, reminds me, *clodhopper* is a compound noun, which is a distinctive feature of Old English poetry. So, while it may sound inelegant to modern ears, it represents an attempt of Levertov's to capture the flavor of Caedmon's writing.
7. Levertov echoes the influential, eighth-century account of Caedmon given by Bede. See *The Ecclesiastical History of the English People*, trans. Bertram Colgrave, ed. Judith McClure and Roger Collins (New York: Oxford University Press, 2008), 215–18. I am grateful to Miranda Wilcox for this reference.
8. From John Milton's *Paradise Lost*, Book 1, line 26.
9. YSAS: young single adults—a Church demographic of unmarried 18- to 30-year-olds.
10. *Rien*: "nothing" in French.
11. The word *poet* comes from a Greek word meaning "maker" or "creator."

Chapter 5

1. Gerard Manley Hopkins, "God's Grandeur," in *The Major Works*, ed. Catherine Phillips (Oxford: Oxford University Press, 1986), 128.
2. Friedrich Nietzsche, *Thus Spoke Zarathustra*, trans. Walter Kaufmann (New York: Penguin, 1978), 9.
3. Ibid., 10–12.

Chapter 6

1. Anya Krugovoy Silver, "Pedals," in *Second Bloom* (Eugene, OR: Cascade Books, 2017), 44.
2. Larry R. Lawrence, "What Lack I Yet?," October 2015 general conference of The Church of Jesus Christ of Latter-day Saints, https://www.churchofjesuschrist.org/study/general-conference/2015/10/what-lack-i-yet. Accessed June 18, 2019.

3. "I will pray the Father, and he shall give you another Comforter, that he may abide with you for ever; even the Spirit of truth.... I will not leave you comfortless: I will come to you" (John 14:16–18).

4. T. S. Eliot, "Little Gidding," in *Four Quartets* (San Diego: Harcourt Brace Jovanovich, 1943), 59, ll. 241–42.

5. Rowan Williams, *The Edge of Words: God and the Habits of Language* (London: Bloomsbury, 2014), 22.

6. Ibid., 88.

7. "Spirit," https://www.churchofjesuschrist.org/study/scriptures/bd/spirit. Accessed January 22, 2020.

8. Richard G. Scott, "To Acquire Spiritual Guidance," October 2009 general conference of The Church of Jesus Christ of Latter-day Saints, https://www.churchofjesuschrist.org/study/general-conference/2009/10/to-acquire-spiritual-guidance. Accessed January 22, 2020.

9. Lawrence, "What Lack I Yet?."

10. Marion G. Romney, "Guidance of the Holy Spirit," BYU devotional, March 20, 1979. https://speeches.byu.edu/talks/marion-g-romney/guidance-holy-spirit/. Accessed January 22, 2020.

11. Douglas D. Holmes, "What Every Aaronic Priesthood Holder Needs to Understand," April 2018 general conference of The Church of Jesus Christ of Latter-day Saints, https://www.churchofjesuschrist.org/study/general-conference/2018/04/what-every-aaronic-priesthood-holder-needs-to-understand. Accessed January 22, 2020. Holmes is citing Bruce R. McConkie and Wilford Woodruff.

12. E. E. Cummings, "O sweet spontaneous," in *Complete Poems: 1904–1962*, ed. George J. Firmage (New York: Liveright, 1991), 58.

13. Mary Frohlich, *Breathed into Wholeness: Catholicity and Life in the Spirit* (Maryknoll, NY: Orbis, 2019), 138.

14. Anonymous, *The Cloud of Unknowing and The Book of Privy Counseling*, trans. and ed. William Johnston (New York: Image, 1973), 40–41. Subsequent references are cited in the text.

15. Frohlich, *Breathed into Wholeness*, 140.

16. Lawrence, "What Lack I Yet?."

17. Boyd K. Packer later served as president of the Quorum of the Twelve Apostles, so his correct title is President Packer. But I will refer to him as Elder Packer because that was his title at the time of this story.

Chapter 7

1. Iconic phrase from Walt Whitman's classic long poem *Song of Myself*.
2. Richard McLauchlan, "R. S. Thomas: Poet of Holy Saturday," *The Heythrop Journal* 52 (2011): 976–985 (976, 977).
3. R. S. Thomas, "Kneeling," in *Collected Poems, 1945–1990* (London: Phoenix, 2000), 199.
4. Institute is a Church organization for Latter-day Saints usually located on or near college campuses—a meeting place for instruction and social interaction.
5. Christian Wiman, *My Bright Abyss: Meditation of a Modern Believer* (New York: Farrar, Straus and Giroux, 2013), 155.
6. Christian Wiman, *He Held Radical Light: The Art of Faith, the Faith of Art* (New York: Farrar, Straus and Giroux, 2018), 68–69.
7. Christian Wiman, *Once in the West: Poems* (New York: Farrar, Straus and Giroux, 2014), 22.
8. Wiman, *My Bright Abyss*, 169.

Chapter 8

1. Virginia Woolf, *To the Lighthouse* (San Diego: Harcourt Brace Jovanovich, 1927), 128. Subsequent references are cited in the text.
2. Judith Wilt, "Steamboat Surfacing: Scott and the English Novelists," *Nineteenth-Century Fiction* 35 (1981): 459–86 (477).
3. See chapter 2's discussion of the qualities associated with spirituality.
4. Matthew Mutter, *Restless Secularism: Modernism and the Religious Inheritance* (New Haven: Yale University Press, 2017), 2.

Chapter 9

1. Bonnie D. Parkin, "Celebrating Covenants," April 1995 general conference of The Church of Jesus Christ of Latter-day Saints, https://www.churchofjesuschrist.org/study/general-conference/1995/04/celebrating-covenants. Accessed January 12, 2021.
2. Barbara Thompson, "Cleave unto the Covenants," October 2011 general conference of The Church of Jesus Christ of Latter-day Saints, https://www.churchofjesuschrist.org/study/general-conference/2011/10/cleave-unto-the-covenants. Accessed January 12, 2021.

3. I allude here to the famous, two-line 1913 poem "In a Station of the Metro" by Ezra Pound: "The apparition of these faces in the crowd: / Petals on a wet, black bough."

4. R. S. Thomas, "In a Country Church," in *Collected Poems*, 67.

5. T. S. Eliot, "Burnt Norton," in *Four Quartets* (Harvest, 1943), 14, ll. 42–43.

Chapter 10

1. Pratt, *Key to the Science of Theology*, 101.

2. Wildman, *Religious and Spiritual Experiences*, 217. Subsequent references are cited in the text.

3. "Grace, & the Spiritual Reach of Representation," *Religion and Literature* 49.2 (2017): 287–339 (303, 308).

4. Gerard Manley Hopkins, "The Windhover," in *The Major Works*, ed. Catherine Phillips (Oxford: Oxford University Press, 2002), 132, ll. 7–8. Subsequent references are cited in the text.

5. William Wordsworth, "Composed upon Westminster Bridge, September 3, 1802," in *The Poems*, 2 vols., ed. Christopher Ricks (London: Penguin, 1977), 1:574–75.

6. Frohlich, "Spiritual Discipline," 65–78 (71).

7. Jeffrey R. Holland, "The Laborers in the Vineyard," April 2012 general conference of The Church of Jesus Christ of Latter-day Saints, https://www.churchofjesuschrist.org/study/general-conference/2012/04/the-laborers-in-the-vineyard. Accessed December 29, 2019.

8. Quoted in Neal A. Maxwell, "Teaching by the Spirit—'The Language of Inspiration,'" https://www.churchofjesuschrist.org/study/manual/teaching-seminary-preservice-readings-religion-370-471-and-475/teaching-by-the-spirit-the-language-of-inspiration. Accessed December 30, 2019.

Chapter 11

1. Sheldrake, *Spirituality*, 4.

2. Sandra M. Schneiders, "Approaches to the Study of Christian Spirituality," in *The Blackwell Companion to Christian Spirituality*, ed. Arthur Holder (Malden, MA: Wiley-Blackwell, 2011), 16. Subsequent references are cited in the text.

3. Frohlich, "Spiritual Discipline," 65–78 (72). Subsequent references are cited in the text.

4. My friend and former student, Zachary M. Hutchins, now an accomplished scholar, discusses several such gifts, among them "Lehi and the Gift of Gratitude"; "Abish and the Gift of Gathering"; "Teancum and the Gift of Being Anxiously Engaged." See *The Best Gifts: Seeking Earnestly for Spiritual Power* (American Fork, UT: Covenant, 2019), chapters 5–7.

5. The "willing suspension of disbelief" is how the Romantic poet Samuel Taylor Coleridge claims we nourish "poetic faith"—a belief in literary constructs we know to be fictitious. On this subject, see Michael Tomko, *Beyond the Willing Suspension of Disbelief: Poetic Faith from Coleridge to Tolkien* (London: Bloomsbury, 2016).

6. Walter Scott, *Waverley; or, 'Tis Sixty Years Since*, ed. Claire Lamont (Oxford: Oxford University Press, 1986), 236.

7. See Fyodor Dostoevsky, *The Brothers Karamazov*, trans. Andrew H. MacAndrew (Toronto: Bantam, 1981), 80–81.

8. Ibid., 204–05.

Chapter 12

1. Lewis Grassic Gibbon, *Sunset Song*, ed. William K. Malcolm (London: Penguin, 2007), 126.

2. Frohlich, *Breathed into Wholeness*, 119.

3. Lewis Grassic Gibbon, "Religion," in Lewis Grassic Gibbon and Hugh MacDiarmid, *Scottish Scene; or, The Intelligent Man's Guide to Albyn* (London: Jarrolds, 1934), 313, 325.

4. Joseph Smith, Jr., *Lectures on Faith* (Springville, UT: Cedar Fort, 2010), 11–12, emphasis added.

5. Other books in the Living Faith series do this beautifully and much more completely. For a short (alphabetical) list, see Sam Brown, *First Principles and Ordinances*; George Handley, *If Truth Were a Child*; Melissa Inouye, *Crossings*; Patrick Mason, *Planted*; and Adam Miller, *Letters to a Young Mormon*.

6. These are interviews members hold with ecclesiastical leaders in preparation for entering the temple to perform sacred ordinances.

7. R. S. Thomas, "The Answer," in *Collected Poems*, 359.

8. My friend Morgan Davis adds a question here that reminds me of the responsibility of any who wish to be Christ's disciples: "What am I doing, or what should I be doing, to make the Church truer for myself and others?"

Literary Texts Index

Scripture Index

BOOK OF MORMON

DOCTRINE AND COVENANTS

PEARL OF GREAT PRICE

Index

MATTHEW WICKMAN is a professor of English at Brigham Young University and the founding director of the BYU Humanities Center. He has published two scholarly books, one edited volume, and dozens of articles on subjects ranging across literary history and theory, often bringing literature into conversation with disciplines such as philosophy, law, mathematics, and the sciences. Scottish literature, to which he has devoted much of his professional life, bears a special place in his heart. His current work explores spiritual experience, religion, theology, and postsecular theory and criticism, and he presently serves on the international board of the Society for the Study of Christian Spirituality. He and his wife Kerry are the grateful parents of two daughters and live in Salt Lake City.